D1616738

Tidal Waves of School Reform

Tidal Waves of School Reform

Types of Reforms, Government Controls, and Community Advocates

Samuel Mitchell

PRAEGER

Westport, Connecticut
London

Library of Congress Cataloging-in-Publication Data

Mitchell, Samuel, 1936–
    Tidal waves of school reform : types of reforms, government
controls, and community advocates / Samuel Mitchell.
        p.   cm.
    Includes bibliographical references and index.
    ISBN 0–275–95644–X (alk. paper)
    1. Education and state—Case studies.   2. Educational change—
Illinois—Chicago.   3. Educational change—Kentucky.
4. Educational change—Alberta.   5. Industry and education—Case
studies.   6. Community and school—Case studies.   I. Title.
LC71.M58   1996   96–16281
379—dc20

British Library Cataloguing in Publication Data is available.

Library of Congress Catalog Card Number: 96–16281
ISBN: 0–275–95644–X

First published in 1996

Praeger Publishers, 88 Post Road West, Westport, CT 06881
An imprint of Greenwood Publishing Group, Inc.

Printed in the United States of America

The paper used in this book complies with the
Permanent Paper Standard issued by the National
Information Standards Organization (Z39.48–1984).

10 9 8 7 6 5 4 3 2 1

Contents

Charts

Acknowledgments

Many supporters and helpers have made this work possible. There have been contributors who were research assistants, readers, and a general editor. Voluntary research assistants included Sheryl Krill, Michelle Batiuk, and Marie Farrell; Mrs. Farrell's own work on combining the theories of Boudon and Foucault was helpful in developing the interpretation of ideology that is used in Chapters 5 and 6. Three colleagues were particularly helpful in reading the various drafts: Joyce Bellous, Cathy Littlejohn, and Diana Lauber. My daughter, Heloise, has criticized chapters as well as assisted me, a too mature student, in my introduction to the computer. My wife, Helen, has been insightful and understanding of a very neglectful husband. Several students have read and criticized the various chapters in both Regina and Calgary, particularly Carol Suddards. The major contributor has been my chief assistant and editor, who prefers to remain anonymous.

Assistance for this study has come from three sources, who have each given permission to reproduce material. The Consortium on Chicago School Research has given permission to reproduce items 1, 2, 13–16, 24–26 and 66 in its 1994 Survey of Grade 8 Students, *The Student Speaks*. *New Expression*, which is produced by Youth Communications, has given permission to reproduce items 1–6 in its art survey from the Art Supplement of April 1994. United Parcel Service has kindly consented to the reproduction of any material from *Thematic Lesson Plan* from which the flow pattern, Chart 6.1 is taken. Our appreciation for these contributions as well as the time given by many individuals cannot be adequately expressed.

Chapter 1

Choices Within the Reform Movement

> The metaphor used here is "a third wave," but I am not sure that
> is correct. We need an earthquake that causes a tidal wave
> before we are going to get the type of educational reform that is
> necessary. (Conference Board, 1989, p. 64)

From 1983 to the present, the reform movement has moved from an initial campaign for higher academic achievement to a debate about progressive processes. The change in educational aims and approaches has been referred to as two waves of reform (Kirst, 1990, p.25). However, the reform movement in education can also be distinguished in terms of the intensity with which individuals have been attracted to it and the scope of the issues that have been raised by the large and extensive reforms. More revolutionary movements have led to changes in education which are far greater than the people involved have expected. The current revolutionary efforts include mandated changes for an entire system that are very different from more evolutionary and more limited innovations in the past which were stagemanaged by a few leaders within education. Large numbers of people are involved with the current, more explosive reforms which originate from business, community organizations, and government in response to a variety of problems.

The larger, more drastic changes are usually those that have been supported by new governmental legislation. For example, a single change, such as school-based management, may be supported by a single school superintendent. However, when school-based management is supported by government, it is frequently a part of a larger program for changing the entire educational system. Such drastic reform is the case in Chicago, Kentucky, and the Canadian province of Alberta. Though differing fundamentally from each other, each of these cases is expected, by those involved in them, to transform education. The study of different directions for reform has only just begun. There may, indeed, be many other cases that should be examined. California is an obvious additional candidate because it has been both the source of so many innovations and the subject of extreme financial constraints. In Canadian adult education, the community or Antigonish movement in Nova Scotia is another option. It is important to realize that education is not a single process, even in waves, which is replacing the equally unitary factory model of education (Fiske, 1992). The single conception does not help explain how Kentucky's program of new assessments, the school councils for governing education democratically, or, the Key School, with its varied program based on seven different forms of intelligence, are all a part of the same movement.

CHARTING CHANGE

The three case studies are developed from the perspective of those involved in these changes; the greatest consequence of studying the three cases is that alternatives for educational reform are formulated. While Chicago developed a local movement of resistance to the school bureaucracy, Kentucky's changes played to a national scene of educational experts and business leaders. Alberta is a part of an international demonstration of how government can be reinvented in order to make education a matter of consumer choice which would also benefit the economy. Each of these three types of reform would seem very strange to a being from another world: Chicago's system is more political than any that can be imagined; Alberta's government is more concerned with the bottom line than any business; and Kentucky's partnership elite is much too occupied with getting support for an expert-inspired approach.

The strategy for choosing these three extreme cases is suggested by Chart 1.1. The reforms of more moderate governments can be visualized in terms of how close they are to the alternative aims of expert guidance, social activism, and an instrumental evaluation of education. These approaches involve changing relationships between reform and educational relationships and different political alliances, particularly with the religious right. The three extreme cases should show the different aims which can be the dimensions for other more moderate reform efforts. Particularly if the diagram is molded more like a globe will choices be seen to involve various mixes of educational, social, or financial purposes.

However, it is also important to realize how people in each of these extreme situations see other changes and situations. A locally reactive movement in Chicago seems unable to integrate itself; it offers a variety of reforms with the help of business and foundations while trying to retain its original emphasis of support by social activists. While Kentucky sought national recognition, it has, initially, involved lawyers or governmental leaders within the state and has more recently sought national leaders drawn

Chart 1.1
Three Systems of Innovations and Common Elements

	United States			Canada	
	Kentucky South Carolina	Chicago	Minnesota Texas	Alberta Ontario	
	National Goals Business Influences Conservative Politics	Social activism		Provincial Aims Business Organizations Conservatives and Religious Groups	
	Expert dependency			Instrumental view	
	Professionals establish models	Political efforts are to change what has been		Business is the model for schools	
	Right wing is in opposition to reforms	Right wing is on fringe with proposals if main line reforms are unsuccessful		Right wing is a part of the government	

from business, education, and government. Kentucky and Chicago are not linked in any meaningful way. Leaders from Kentucky have visited Chicago and adopted, for their own purposes, one of Chicago's innovations, a program of lawyers assisting school councils (Robert Sexton, interview, May 4, 1995). Even more definitively separate has been the so-called slash and burn program of Alberta, which has cut financing for early childhood education in half, reduced special education, and brought in private options for the public system. Still, specific innovations in Alberta, particularly in Edmonton, have been studied because more education expenditures are controlled by the school councils than they are elsewhere (Diana Lauber, October 11, 1993). When Chicago leaders visit Alberta, they are aware that the involvement of citizens is missing from the decentralization which is practiced there.

Each reform system develops specific innovations in different ways. Kentucky copies the use of lawyers as volunteers for school councils from Chicago. However, in Chicago, the lawyers are one of several professional groups who are assisting a variety of competing groups which attempt to train council members. In Kentucky, council members' requests are referred to the central organization for reform and professional judgments are made about what advice the council members should have.

In Alberta, there is, as yet, no need felt for separate legal services for council members, and plans for training council members are just being developed. In Chicago, a series of unrelated local and citywide efforts are made to integrate education with social and health programs. In Kentucky, a unified statewide program of family and youth centers is offered in most schools. The newer program in Alberta features four experimental centers of integrated services. In Alberta, in contrast to Chicago and Kentucky, business and community groups are seen as contributing directly to education and even providing courses in the future (Alberta Education, n.d.). Chicago has developed separate advocacy groups of businesspeople, while Kentucky has woven business partners together with a host of other supporters for progressive educational reform.

Similar reforms are adopted in each case together with parallel procedures. The three types include school-based management, school councils, integration of health and social services with education, and statistical controls to establish accountability. The reforms in each situation were established by legislation, while advocacy groups were involved in both initiating and implementing the legislation. The reforms in every case required the support of those groups who are thought to be responsible for education, but the support of students for whom the service is directed was not sought anywhere. These similarities simply make the differences among reforms that much more striking.

The specific innovations and political processes are modified in each case by their context. For example, school councils have been promoted in Chicago together with educational programs to council members which have been provided by a variety of groups, whereas in Kentucky and Alberta, less promotion of school councils has been done and the training which is available is planned in a centralized way. Chicago and Kentucky have developed an association of councils in order to develop a body larger than the individual school while Alberta has not considered coordinating its new councils.

The distinctive character of reforms in Chicago, Kentucky, or Alberta is not explained by their national or regional context. The major contexts of the three extreme versions of the types of reform are largely similar. Chicago is part of a state that adjoins Kentucky, while Alberta and Kentucky have similar religious and business backgrounds including oil and farming. However, background differences are insignificant when considered from the standpoint of both the extreme types and total distribution of cases. Size and rural urban characteristics could hardly explain why Minnesota and Chicago share grass-root organization for education and Texas, Alberta, and Ontario increasingly have adopted a business conception of schooling.

Internal crises, rather than environmental differences, led to reforms in each of the three cases. Kentucky turned to experts because of its dismal educational performance; the courts held that this state was failing to provide a reasonable education. Chicago reacted to the continuing series of teacher strikes and financial problems by forming a movement that changed the formal educational system. Before reform, the schools in Chicago tried to be so isolated that they did not make their phone numbers available to parents; after reform, in some cases, schools were trying to meet the needs of parents by equipping new parent rooms with phones (Bonita Street, interview, May 11, 1995). Alberta was confident of its high level of educational achievement while attempting to reduce expenditures and reduce the scope of government at all levels (Dempster & Bicknell, 1994, March, p. B3).

A number of other states or provinces have reacted somewhat similarly to three extreme types, as Chart 1.1 tries to suggest. Texas has had a highly instrumental view of reform that is similar to Alberta's, but, in Texas, reform was a mixture of efforts by business leaders, such as Ross Perot, and social activists, such as Ernesto Cortes (Toch, 1991). Minnesota has a tradition of progressive reform that appears to underlie its alternative education approaches. Minnesota has almost the same variety of groups that Chicago produces. Finally, Kentucky is representative of southern states that have perceived their inadequacies in education. South Carolina is very active and the former governor became secretary of education although the state does not have as extensive an organization as does Kentucky.

SEQUENCE OF CHAPTERS

The development of the trilogy is more than just a constant reiteration of their differences. The activism of Chicago should be viewed in relation to the city's traditions of community organizing as well as its current concerns with declining educational achievements, increasing financial problems, and the presence of gangs. The problems of Chicago are also increasingly the problems of most educational systems. Activism in the community is a solution that Chicago offers to other school reformers. However, the advocacy groups of Chicago are shown, in the next chapter, to be strikingly different from those in Canada or even the national efforts by organizations in the United States. The more inclusive organization for reform in Kentucky tries to prevent the conflict and competition among reformers that occurs in Chicago; Kentucky's case is discussed in Chapter 4.

Kentucky is the leading example of reform by committee and the related committees are composed of national business and professional experts as well as those in the state. Neither vouchers nor private education for profit has been the dominant focus of the models for education in any of the three regions. However, business involvement, traced in Chapter 5, has provided models for schools, while Chapter 6 follows the development of broader alliances for reform in which business can play an important role. The broader development, followed in Chapter 7, involves integrated services which, unfortunately, is often planned by experts without being accountable to students, parents, or the broader community. The lack of political constituencies for integrated services is manifested in different ways in the three cases.

In the final chapter, students' concerns are more directly considered in order to reveal the problems of each type of reform. Each of the reforms attempts to capture students with differing measures of success. In Kentucky, the most dutiful students can even be seen studying the problems of statistics involved in the new measures of their own evaluations (Toadvine, 1993, p. 13). Chicago provides opportunities for students to express themselves and organize their own writing and art while students in Kentucky can do these things as a part of a statewide program. The Kentucky educational program features realistic problems or demonstrations as a part of its more authentic testing; Alberta provides opportunities for students, parents, and employers to rate the school's performance though with using orthodox testing.

The limited sense of local decision making, which is confined by central or superagency supervision of results, is another common problem for the three reform approaches that has even greater potential consequences than testing. Such limits can threaten democratic control of education. Business can, like political agencies, press against school democracy. In Alberta, business can direct education into vocational areas, while, in Chicago and Kentucky, business works with community allies to improve the academic thrust of education. The spell that business has over educational politics and all social institutions is a common threat to all attempts at building a broader sense of reform. Such problems or dilemmas replace the division of types as a focus for this study.

PERSONAL CONCERNS

This work neither began with charts or outlines nor was expected to end with the statement of dilemmas. The next chapter began as a letter to a colleague, Joyce Bellous, about what I had learned during a study in Chicago while on leave. The political nature of reform in Chicago made an overwhelming impression on me, particularly when I was told that "the fix was in for reform in Chicago" (Dan Lewis, interview, October 1993). Chapter 3 began as a part of a conference at DePaul University, Education in Three World Cities, which involved comparisons of educational reforms in a number of countries. The emphasis on the difference between advocacy groups in the United States and Canada was also part of a reflection on the educational reform bill that had been introduced by the Conservative party in Alberta. My concern was that, without the tradition of local advocacy groups in Chicago, Alberta would be herded into a program with many new restraints and few local resources.

A more hopeful view of these changes was developed when I began to communicate with the Prichard Committee in Kentucky. The early experience of this committee was, indeed, high drama. The sacrifice of the hero, Ed Prichard, in order to start educational reform suggested parallels to early years of reform in Chicago when the first Black mayor, Harold Washington, called a business-education conference as a prelude to reform in that city, but died before reform could be realized. The convening of selected parties in Alberta for reform by a very popular premier, Ralph Klein, was similar to the roundtable conferences, a common public relations device, in Kentucky (Alberta Education, 1993). My contacts with Kentucky led to the development of the threefold comparison of what seem to be increasingly different paths for reform in Chapter 4.

The development of the typology seems to accentuate only the difference among the three cases. The cases were similar in that they each yielded a story of how business was, increasingly, involved in education through organizations of businesspeople. The influence of business on education, in the case of Kentucky, involved the links to national efforts by the Business Roundtable. Business produced an advocacy group to support reform in Chicago, but was also the source of options for private competitors or voucher options in the same city. Business was a part of the governing coalition in Alberta which was so close that business leaders could recount tales of being asked to travel with the minister of education (John Ballheim, interview, May 17, 1994). Chapter 5 attempts to draw the anatomy of the business and education context in order to set the stage for the three reform plays.

Business strategies differed in each case but these strategies always included the development of a broad network of organizations that attempted to affect the outcome of reform. In Chicago, the elite business groups had sponsored an advocacy group for education which, in the early stages of reform, made common cause with social activists, but which, later, focused on measures needed to ensure accountability; the change threatened the links to other advocacy and community groups. In Kentucky, business has been among the most important helpers for teachers and for the dominant reform organization. My impressions of what business could do for education changed substantially after seeing reform efforts in Kentucky. Horror stories which are reported in the educational press, such as a representative of Eli Oliver distributing Prozac while visiting schools, are still enough to call for guidelines and limitations, probably by law, for the involvement of business in education (Lawton, 1995, February, p.10).

Unlike in the relationships with business, education has been involved with social and health agencies for most of this century, including efforts by such reformers as Jane Adams. New efforts at integrated services have been endorsed by business organizations with the assistance of educational experts. However, the integration of services has not been universally accepted by teachers or businesspeople. The integration of services described in different situations in Chapter 7 has remained a marginal effort. There are fascinating problems involved. In Chicago, for example, one high school with its feeder elementary schools is linked with over twenty different organizations that contribute to the educational program of that school (Bank of America, 1995). Schools can be linked to art galleries, universities, and the higher professions; this is the new meaning of integrated services. Since the issues involved in integrated services were both interesting and confusing, I made special trips to Chicago and Kentucky in order to study the sites of such services. On returning to Canada I discovered that similar trial programs were being run by some of my former students!

Integrated services touch the diverse needs of families and students; these reforms across different institutions should be more meaningful than educational reforms alone. However, neither parents nor students are actively involved in establishing policies for integrated services. For a limited number of students, their involvement with writing new independent papers as well as criticism of reform reveals the separation of student views from those of the educational reformers. Writing is only one part of the progressive curriculum in Kentucky, one of the new national efforts which are being offered in Chicago, and a function of a network that spread to Alberta from the United States. As is documented in Chapter 8, student newspapers directed by administrators were particularly striking in showing the school control that is still exercised in Alberta. Student writing has nowhere developed the active interest of large numbers of students in reform and none of the three cases has developed strong advocates for students.

THEORETICAL IDEAS

The distance between students and reformers can be viewed as a conflict between different types of knowledge of the social world. For students, knowledge is often interactive and centered on the people involved; student knowledge is more expressive; for reformers, knowledge is mainly impersonal and instrumental (Everhart, 1983). Effective school research is the basic emphasis of reformers for the first wave of reform in most situations (Moore, 1991). The view of different types of knowledge is one of the theoretical concerns in the final chapter, Chapter 8.

Chapter 7 discusses the barriers that separate professions and organizations, together with questions about the aims of integrative services. Similarly, theoretical concerns emerge together with the study of cases in each of the other chapters. Chapters 5 and 6 involve the study of ideology and coalitions which may or may not be dominated by a hegemonic business position. Chapters 3 and 4 present contrasts between groups which act on the basis of narrow interests and organizations which represent a broad consensus. Organizations of special interests fight for power while integrative organizations seek the acceptance of their ideas. Ideas can and have become a part of the power struggle as the ideas themselves, such as accountability measures, have become coercive (Foucault, 1979).

In social movements, ideas can develop from interaction in the situation of people's lives or through the abstractions of experts. Knowledge can tell the story of the people involved (Freire & Macedo, 1987). Such knowledge can be poetic, expressive, and still very structured. Reform can be a model for education though those with roles in formal education can never be very active participants in the reform activities themselves (Chapter 2). Reform has not yet sought ways to be based on the expectations and commitments of students to improve their education, but it can be more relevant to those it is designed to serve. The interpretations in this book are meant to be grounded on the experience of students, parents, advocates, and educators; they are not meant to be limitations of any of these groups, whose views are respected by the author.

VOLUNTARY ORGANIZATIONS: THE
FURTHER EVOLUTION OF THE STUDY

Our approach becomes more complicated when the description of local groups in Chicago is shown to lead to more widespread organization of activists. Saul Alinsky, who influenced most of the local organizers of reform in Chicago, also founded the Industrial Areas Foundation. The foundation has developed local affiliates in Texas, Los Angeles, New York, England, and other places; this organization is now returning to Chicago after an absence of over twenty years. The Chicago reformers, themselves, have expanded beyond Chicago to form a league with Seattle, Denver, Philadelphia, New York City, and, possibly, Toronto.

Voluntary organizations cross the boundaries of our three sites and this leads to a discussion of the differences among advocacy groups. The networks of reformers, such as the Coalition of Essential Schools, are somewhat similar to the coalitions which are supported by the federal government in Canada, such as Canadian Parents for French. Both Canadian and American examples stand in contrast to more locally based organizations in Chicago or elsewhere which appeal to the self-interest of those who are organized. Since there is a sense of separate interest as a nation, Canadians have tended not to join the national American networks, particularly when they are linked to government, as is the case of the Coalition of Essential Schools. The educational networks are also financed by foundations in the United States, while the federal government has been the major source of financing in Canada. Foundations in Canada are also smaller and more conservative; they will have difficulty providing additional support when government withdraws.

The legislation of government is influenced by voluntary organizations. In Kentucky, the Business Roundtable has supported the reforms, while right-wing groups, such as the Eagle Forum, have led the opposition. However, there are other voluntary organizations among government officials that have also been involved. The National Governors Association has certainly publicized the Kentucky case (David, 1993). Kentucky and Illinois are both Re-Learning states, where selected schools receive extra financial aid from state governments and are given additional consultation from the Educational Commission of the States and the Coalition of Essential Schools. The Educational Commission of the States is a voluntary research and consulting agency which all states other than Montana support. In Canada, there is only the Council of Ministers, though the Americans have a number of organizations for state legislators and officials as well as the governors. Also in Canada, there is no support for one set of schools similar to that provided by the Coalition of Essential Schools and the Educational Commission of the States to create a Re-Learning network of schools.

While voluntary organizations which involve government may not cross international boundaries, business organizations most definitely do so. The Conference Board and the Chamber of Commerce have been important players in Canada as well as in the United States. The parallel of the Business Roundtable (BRT) in Canada, the Business Council on National Issues, has not made anything like the ten-year commitment to education that the American group has proclaimed. In Chicago, a local group with a long history, the Civic Committee, has more influence on educational reform than does the BRT. American business associations have expanded into Canada as well as other countries. The large number of business groups and their typical interests are described in Chapter 5, while the variations among the three sites as well as coalitions which they have helped organize are detailed in Chapter 6.

The last two chapters discuss the influence of voluntary organizations on the three prime patterns insofar as the integration of services and student activities is concerned. Cities in Schools, a private organization which was founded by social activists, has been deeply involved with integrated services in Chicago and Kentucky; it has recently begun developing a program in Canada. In order to improve student expression of their ideas, the National Writing Project have been one of the most significant opportunities that has resulted from opening a previously closed system in Chicago; the writing process ideas have been incorporated by Kentucky into its general set of reforms. At least five Canadian cities in Canada, including one in Alberta, have affiliates of this American program. The writing program has spread to five other Commonwealth countries.

In Chicago, students who have been influenced by the writing program have developed a publication, *New Expression*, which has led to similar publications in five other cities. A rival group of students in Chicago has founded the Student Alliance in order to represent students across the nation as well as in Chicago who serve on school boards, school councils, and even advisory committees for integrated services. In Kentucky, students have become speakers for reform as well as scholars of reform; one of them even founded a newspaper. As suggested earlier, students play a more limited role in Alberta. Youth groups parallel the adult organizations in each case study.

All of the voluntary organizations act as advocates for change, and this complicates our analysis, but these organizations are also the most interesting part of the story. Though I had met Saul Alinsky and some of his friends while living in Chicago thirty years before, I never imagined that he would have so much influence on community organizations and educational change. For another point, the difference between Canadian and American organizations revealed that Canadians maintain their separateness, generally, by not joining the American organizations, though they adopt many of the American ideas. More generally, the function of organizations became a nagging question since it is clear that the distinction between interest groups and integrative organizations is a very crude categorization. In order to start reforms, organizations that promote conflict or develop publicity, such as those in Chicago or Kentucky, may be very effective. Organizations that have relationships with government, such as the Coalition of Essential Schools, may enhance the number of schools involved in the reforms or ensure their continuance. Autonomous and selective organizations, similar to the National Writing Project, may help spread innovations to other countries as well as provide resourceful people when other changes in the system are introduced. In general, voluntary and autonomous organizations provide the alternative to government control of educational reform, which has become extremely important since educational change is now legislated, publicized, and promoted as never before.

REFERENCES

Alberta Education (n.d.). *Three-year business plan for education 1995/96–1997/98.* Edmonton: Alberta Education.

Alberta Education (1993). *Meeting the challenge: What we heard.* Edmonton: Alberta Education.

Bank of America (1995). *The Orr school network: A community-based educational partnership 1989–1995.* Chicago: Bank of America.

The Conference Board (1989). *Business leadership: The third wave of education reform.* New York: The Conference Board.

David, J. (1993). *Redesigning an education system.* Washington, D. C.: National Governors' Association.

Dempster, L. & Bicknell, D. (1994, March 20). Charting a new course. *Calgary Herald*, B3.

Everhart, R. (1983). *Reading, writing and resistance.* Boston: Routledge & Kegan Paul.

Fiske, E. (1991). *Smart schools, smart kids.* New York: Touchstone.

Foucault, M. (1979). *Discipline and punish.* New York: Vintage Books, Random House.

Freire, P. & Macedo, D. (1987). *Literacy.* New York: Bergin & Garvey.

Kirst, M.(1990). The crash of the first wave. In Bacharach, S.B. (Ed.), *Education Reform.* Boston: Allyn & Bacon.

Kyle, C. & Kantowicz, E. (1992). *Kids first-primero los niños.* Springfield: Illinois Issues.

Lawton, M. (1995, February 8). Drug firm's visit to school prompts inquiry by F.D.A. *Education Week*, 14(20), 10.

Moore, K. (1991). *Chicago school reform.* Chicago: Designs for Change.

Toadvine, S. (1993, August). Real-life learning and assessment: One success story. *Kentucky Teacher*, 13.

Toch, T. (1991). *In the name of excellence.* New York: Oxford.

Chapter 2

Transforming the Institutions

'We are really talking about rebuilding entire communities with schools at the center.' —Leonard Dominguez, deputy mayor for education, Chicago (Selinker and Weissman, 1993)

It has long been argued that education can either reinforce the status quo or develop new ideas that change society. Traditional public schooling in small towns often prepares students to follow the lives of their parents; this is the first view. The role of science from its base in higher education has changed the occupations and expectations of students away from traditions: the second perspective. A third alternative has, more recently, been developed that schools and society can be transformed by developing the capacity of communities and schools so that individuals will integrate the past traditions with future hopes while they confront major contradictions and challenges in our current world (Giroux, 1987). The newer alternative calls for a reorganization of institutions as well as individual lives. According to this third approach, links can develop among schools, business, parents, and higher education in order that schools can become a place where parents and students organize and protest so that social and political skills are learned together with the traditional three focuses of schooling, namely reading, writing, and arithmetic.

This transformation has appeared most clearly in large urban schools that have had to deal with major problems including the destruction caused by conflicts resulting from their large size. The traditional bureaucratic schools have been confronted by crises in cities such as Chicago. The problem of gangs and gang fights in schools now has spread to once-isolated rural areas. Financial crises have become common even in places that once were affluent and which originally attracted parents to move from other problem-plagued schools. Educational achievements have not seemed to increase with greater expenditures for education (Corporate-Higher Education Forum, 1991). The problems of gangs and discipline, financial retrenchment, and educational standards have not been solved by the current educational establishment. Integrative approaches across institutions and professions have been called for in order to respond in new ways to these problems, which are associated with growth when society is transformed.

Transformations occur through social movements that mobilize isolated individuals and relate separate institutions. Movements that have led to a conjunction of business, parents, and community activists are most significant. Business partnerships and the revolution whereby parents govern schools in one of the most problem-plagued urban cities, Chicago, are considered in more detail in later chapters. Chicago exemplifies the active involvement of voluntary organizations in school reform; such involvement appears to be the best hope of preventing authoritarian governments from taking control of educational change. Active social movements are considered along with impersonal private foundations. Foundations bring more than gifts for new change efforts and have been transformed, in part, by the changes they try to bring to others.

The omission of religion from the mix of groups attempting change is particularly related to the current type of activism that focuses on immediate problems while ignoring the traditions in a community. Community organizing can be further transformed by organizations with a religious base. The spread of the change from society to schools requires connections between education and other institutions including religious organizations. However, the integration of changes among cities shows how far these innovations can spread beyond both city limits and school walls.

The links between education and other institutions can lead to a drastically different type of leader. For traditional, hierarchical, and isolated educational systems, experts usually work together with administrative officials. Such experts try to be scientific and to gain acceptance from the established sciences and professions (Mitchell, 1992, p.7). Transformative changes seem to suggest the people most influential will be those who work across turfs of either organizations or knowledge. Transformative intellectuals grasp a vision of the way all of the forces in a community can act together; they can also relate present struggles to past conflicts. Leaders who move back and forth between institutions and foundations and who create new groups are particularly close to such ideal intellectuals. Because of uprooting from past movements, Chicago's intellectuals only occasionally have such ties to their traditions, including religion. The connections of education to the other institutions of society can be grasped by intellectuals with roots in traditions and with links to the people. Organic leaders who link the past and the future are like the social movements on behalf of which they speak and cannot be planned. New leaders act together in order to complement each other. Organic leaders can attempt to direct and nourish the changes in which they are involved and for which they act as catalysts.

CHANGE AS A SOCIAL MOVEMENT

The public education system spread as a common experience for citizenship. Most innovations since then have been more limited. Some innovations, such as computers, are technological. Other, more managerial innovations are site-based and allow individual schools to decide on their own budget and policy management. Periodically, trumpet calls for reform are based on emotional appeals and moral concerns that are very different from these technological or managerial approaches.

The claim by *A Nation at Risk* that if a foreign power took over the United States it could do nothing worse than impose the current system is typical of the shock to which the educational system is exposed (National Commission on Excellence in Education, 1983). Often experts develop their rational solutions for crises such as *A Nation at Risk* claimed to find (Mitchell, 1992). The experts' position is frequently incorporated into symbolic changes such as attempts to reorganize the system. An effective change, if that is what is desired, can occur when the school as a whole is reorganized, rather than merely adding specific programs or general slogans (Goodlad, 1984).

When either grass-roots movements or government from on high acts, reform of the educational establishment can become more than an in-house celebration. It is possible for parents, community leaders, and business executives to get involved in the restructuring of education (Timpane & McNeill, 1991). When frustrated by the school system's stonewalling of their attempts to reform, new and unplanned alliances have developed between these external players (O'Connell, 1991). When successful reforms never seem to spread and when the academic achievements of the system are interpreted as steadily declining, then hopes and dreams become more a basis for action than a calculation that focuses on exact methods while ignoring ultimate aims (Kyle & Kantowicz, 1992).

The development of a common cause through interaction and new symbols, rather than debate and traditional beliefs, has long been seen to be the character of social movements (Blumer, 1951). Movements and their charismatic leaders are similar to the entrepreneurs who, unlike managers, can see a new way of utilizing existing people and resources rather than only a way of distributing existing goods (Schumpeter, 1942). Past traditions are reworked to overcome tensions and develop new codes, as exemplified by revitalization movements in current educational groupings as well as underdeveloped countries (Moncey & McQuillan, 1990). Politicians and community leaders as well as educators cannot be taught to have such personal influence or grace that they can influence changes in education. Creative leaders of citywide movements have changed innovations, such as effective schools or site-based management. When parents, through local councils, become the major force for selecting principals, setting budgets, and improving school appearances, local transformations have truly begun.

A number of American cities have involved parents and community leaders in educational changes. New York pioneered in both community representation and schools within schools that provide parents and students with influence and options (Hess, 1991). The New York plan has been dominated by teachers in boards that are based on very large districts. The options, such as schools within schools, have been slow to spread within even the New York metropolitan area. Boston developed compacts between business and schools to provide students with jobs and to improve school performance. After six years, business leaders in Boston refused to renew the agreement since they found only marginal improvements in the school performance and the dropout rate had increased (Timpane & McNeill, 1991, p.17). In a number of large cities, schools have developed joint programs with the teachers' union, which have led to teacher development schemes, as in Pittsburgh and in the Miami area (Rosow & Zager, 1989).

Regardless of content or sponsor, most of the large cities have turned, increasingly, to site-based management. Such localized management may be no more than a system established by the superintendent, as in Edmonton (Hill & Bonan, 1991 and Wohlstetter & Buffett, 1992). The result of a more managerial approach to site-based management can be that a larger percentage of the budget decisions are made at the local level; the other two components, curriculum planning and personnel decisions, can also be made more consistently with administrative direction. Task forces can develop that are even written into the collective bargaining contract, as in Denver (Center for Quality Schools, 1992). However, where business or community groups are involved, school-based management can become a basis for mutual interaction and new ideas even if developed more unevenly.

The conditions for a social movement built around site-based management have occurred only in Chicago. Only there were experts so driven to distraction as to declare the schools the worst in the nation. Only in Chicago were large-scale efforts by business, such as reports by Chicago United, openly rejected by school administrators (O'Connell, 1991). More positively, Chicago had been the base from which Saul Alinsky developed a large number of community organizations and trained their leaders (Kyle & Kantowicz, 1992, p.343). Alinsky was a criminologist who, initially, developed community councils near the packing houses. He believed that getting people organized was even more important than promoting literacy since they would have to learn how to read in order to run the organization. The community activism became, as a result of Alinsky's teaching even years later, a potent force in reform!

When, in 1988, business people in Chicago discovered that they needed the community organizations, the fire of a social movement had begun to spread. An organizer who had worked for the Industrial Areas Foundation, the organization founded by Alinsky, states that four elements contributed to the reform movement in Chicago: the existence of tough organizations since the 1940s which were started by Alinsky: the development of collaborative efforts among these and other organizations by the 1970s: the dissatisfaction of the business community with the school system because of the low skills of students in the 1980s; and several professional educators who also worked with advocacy organizations to reform education in the late 1980s (Peter Martinez, interview, October 29, 1993). This man's view supplemented a woman's perspective that reform in action is continued by a very large number of talented women who run the related business, civic, community, and educational organizations (Diana Lauber, interview, October 26, 1993). Men such as Alinsky and Harold Washington, the first Black mayor of Chicago who initiated the reform summit meeting on education, are continuing symbols of reform (Lens, interview, October 5, 1993). The women in the community organizations, however, were the directly inspirational leaders who lay their hands on those involved (Kyle & Kantowicz, 1992, pp. 239–244). Men and women provide different forms of organic leadership in the mysterious mix of reforms in Chicago.

The miracle of reform in Chicago is founded more on faith that schools must be changed than on evidence that significant changes have occurred. Standardized exam results have actually declined (Lenz, 1993, April). Reformers explain away these results in terms of the time that change requires. They ignore the process whereby they continue to change the rhetoric of reform from effective school practices in the early years to more open processes such as the National Writing Project today (Hess, 1992 and John Ayers, interview, October 5, 1993). You cannot evaluate a moving object of educational ideas, or at least you cannot do so very easily! Some very recent evidence suggests reforms are having measurable effects (Bradley, 1993, November, p. 3). This new evidence was immediately criticized by those outside the reform movement, but no advocate for reform did so.

The Chicago reformers, uncritically, accept the evidence of change. Studies of the Chicago changes show that democratic school councils are the basis of implementing reform, in general, and school-based management, in particular (Consortium on Chicago School Research, 1993). The evidence for such democratic councils and its relation to restructuring attempts by the councils is very closely linked to the ethnic and racial background of those who serve on the councils. Latinos, rather than Blacks, account for most of the open and democratic councils. It appears that all that has been shown is that Latinos are similar to the Irish in that they excel in political skills more than most other immigrant groups. The status of a committee from all universities in the area is, perhaps, the reason that an alternative explanation for this research is not proposed. Explanations are sought when there are no achievement results favorable for reform. Alternative explanations are not considered when exam results are favorable. A professor associated with

the one major university not represented in the consortium of universities
has said that "the fix is in for reform in Chicago" (Dan Lewis, interview,
October 25, 1993). Research may correspond to Chicago's well-known
tendency to settle problems informally or illegally, but the researchers have
taken the role of making changes acceptable to a wider audience; this role
was played by the church in earlier times.

Without researchers or other authority figures, more questions might be
asked about the limitations of educational reform. The limits on the reform
movement can lead to the exclusion of individuals and groups who were not
involved in the movements' most celebrated actions. One individual, Jan
Hively, was particularly critical, complaining of her exclusion from the
movement (interview, November 15, 1993). She was rejected by leaders in
the movement such as Ann Hallett because of her boss, Martin Koldyke,
and the superior air of Mr.Koldyke even though she ran an organization, the
Golden Apple, that mainly gave awards to successful teachers (William
Ayers, interview, April 25, 1994). Koldyke is a successful businessman who
started the Golden Apple and who at the time headed the superagency for
financial control of Chicago schools. Koldyke is also the person who began
the cluster initiative of major Chicago institutions that will be discussed
later.

Organizations as well as individuals can be partially excluded from the
reform movement. A small difference, such as charging small sums for their
services, can be grounds for rejecting a new organization (Diana Lauber,
interview, April 11, 1994). The Association of Community Organizations for
Reform Now (ACORN) charged fees and was finally accepted by some of
the more established reformers, but its executive director, Madeline Talbot,
does not yet feel she can openly express some of her opinions in meetings
of reformers (Madeline Talbot, interview, April 28, 1994). Researchers with
different perspectives may, similarly, choose not to get involved with the
research consortium that supports reform in Chicago. Whether by choice
or exclusion, movements lose the critical eyes that can contribute to their
future course. Democratic movements require an articulate opposition that
both asks questions and gets answers even from researchers.

For the believers, research that supports the faith and legitimacy of the
reform movement is needed to keep a fix on the infallibility of the reform
movement. For the Chicago reform law, the emphasis is on governance
primarily by parents and community leaders in Chicago or teachers in other
places. Curriculum change is expected to follow a change in control. The
curriculum can, however, be more easily controlled by experts and
administrators (Hess, 1991). The separation of governance from curriculum
can further segregate parents from educational experts. Some parents
report that their role on school councils is trivial (Dan Lewis, interview,
October 25, 1993).

Other aspects of reform can further divide its supporters. Reform, in
providing for decentralization, may be a substitute for additional funding

insofar as the attention of parents, teachers, or reformers is fixed on the division and use of existing resources rather than the need for new funds. Business is likely to follow its own agenda. In spite of extensive cooperation between community activist and business leaders over six years, in Chicago, suspicions still linger that business is still primarily interested in low corporate taxes (Diane Lauber, interview, April 11, 1994).   Until perspectives are shared more fully, the representativeness of groups must always be considered. National goals for education are set by leaders of business organizations, government, and teacher unions (National Education Goals Panel, 1992). Religious leaders and leaders of other lay movements are conspicuously missing from the current discussions.

Until the movement develops a more representative and integrated policy, there is always the possibility that current failure will yield to new faiths; the emerging new faith is vouchers. Voucher systems allow parents to choose between public or private schools.   Both leading newspapers and very conservative businessmen have campaigned for such a system of choice in Chicago, California, and Canada (Allen, 1993, October and Kyle & Kantowicz, 1992, pp. 193, 328). Vouchers mean that the traditions of public schooling are left behind and integration with a broader, more humane purpose is that much more difficult.

THE RELIGIOUS TIE THAT IS LOOSE

The dynamic nature of the reform movement is revealed not only by its current emphasis on governing the schools or deciding to opt away from them. There is also a progressive or "hands-on" effort in curriculum, and this approach is combined with efforts to restructure the schools by the use of awards. Efforts are made by a number of award programs for teachers, students, and local councils to maintain these current positions. The current posture is also restricted by the structure of community and business interests. Business support is particularly solicited to supplement efforts by parents and teachers, with the aim of improving schools rather than choosing between schools. Awards of up to $10,000 were given for over three years for school councils and individual teachers. Award programs included the use of the Socratic method in teaching, holding meetings in neighborhoods from which students are bused, and requiring school uniforms in order to prevent students from displaying gang symbols in school (Illinois Bell, 1991 and Jan Hively, interview, November 15, 1993). Awards emphasize the results of the current achievement rather than future directions. Limited training of council members in progressive education so they consider such principles in selecting principals also shows how only one progressive faith is being taught.

The current coalition in Chicago seems to be justified by faith, but the faith is not specifically religious. Religious leaders were involved in the early stages in Chicago and remain behind the stage now. The Reverend

Kenneth Smith was a cochairman of the Summit on Education in Chicago that the mayor convened as a prelude to reform. While Mayor Harold Washington has become a martyr for the current reform group, the Reverend Smith believes that a rump section of his summit got the reform legislation passed, but that there is no vehicle to provide a link between religious leaders and the reform movement now (interview, October 21, 1993). In the schools, religious leaders can only become involved in the local councils since they do not control civic organizations, as do businesspeople, that can enable them to influence the movement indirectly.

There are several members of the clergy on the Chicago school board and there is one Methodist organization, Child-Save, that is a member of the oldest Chicago organization for reform, the Citizens Schools Committee. Though Smith is still an adviser to the same committee, no religious images and few moral aims are included in the program of the Chicago reform groups. Smith notes, tellingly, that the City Missionary Society changed its name to the Community Renewal Society. The religious leaders are divided by their support for parochial schools, though the United Church of Christ remains a sponsor of important organizations (Fred Hess, interview, November 15, 1993). Individual churches are even recruiting grounds for accountants who want to be involved in reform. In other research in the Midwest, educational reform is led by true believers who are similar to the moral and religious educators in the nineteenth century (Smith et al. 1986).

However, it is not necessary to look into the souls of reformers to find links with religion. The original development of social organizations in Chicago by Alinsky was often in partnership with churches. Furthermore, the Catholic Latinos are the most stable supporters of the reform movement. The cost of Catholic education has apparently kept the Spanish-speaking group attending public schools in the United States, while they would be placed in separate schools in Canada. One of the advocacy groups in Chicago most closely linked with Alinsky, United Neighborhood Organization, leaves open the possibility of parish organizations joining their clustering of schools and community organizations (Juan Rangel, interview, October 29, 1993). One of the leaders of this organization would support a limited experiment with vouchers, which appeal to Catholics who must support two systems of education (Dan Solis, interview, November 24, 1993).

Alinsky's death led to a separation between the Chicago organizations influenced by him and the Alinsky-founded organization (Ken Rolling, interview, October 23, 1993). The position of executive director of the Industrial Areas Foundation was assumed by Edward Chambers, who moved the organization to New York. Though the New York organization has developed close ties to some schools, particularly in the South Bronx, it has been the Texas organization that has developed the largest alliance with over thirty schools (Ann Hallett, interview, October 25, 1993). The Texas organization has also formed the most extensive ties with religious groups, including conservative Protestant ones as well as liberationist Catholic parishes. The Industrial Areas Foundation (IAF) also has organizations in California, Arizona, Maryland, Tennessee, and the United Kingdom as part of its quest for social justice that corresponds to Jewish and Christian ideas. In the past, while Alinsky was alive, the IAF was active in organizing native communities in Canada. Alinsky went to native reserves himself and his ideas were carried to other reserves by adult educators with Frontier College (Joy Nielsen, personal communication, November 26, 1994). The IAF is helping with organizations in over a dozen other areas and claims to provide leadership training for over thirty organizations which represent nearly one thousand institutions and over 1 million families (Texas Industrial Areas Foundation, 1990 and Cortes, n.d.).

In spite of its many achievements, the IAF became isolated from its original base in Chicago. The Reverend Smith reported being invited to a meeting three weeks before our interview in which he was asked, together with other religious leaders, to consider IAF's return to Chicago. Two other former community organizers reported these meetings are occurring, but both added that the Catholic church in Chicago has promised IAF over a million dollars and that the organization was seeking a quarter of a million dollars from Jewish organizations and Protestant churches (Ken Rolling, interview, October 19, 1993 and Peter Martinez, interview, October 29, 1993). Recently, the Industrial Areas Foundation has moved its national office back to Chicago and established a local organization for the northern Illinois area that includes Chicago (Ken Rolling, interview, May 11, 1995). IAF has reportedly received $2.3 million from churches. Even the Moslems provided the IAF with moral support.

The return of IAF could provide the link between religion and school reform that has been missing in Chicago in recent years. Religious leaders had been involved in most social movements there for the past century (Hogan, 1985, p.74). Other movements have derived a vision from socialism and have sought to improve the lot of poor people. None of these past alternatives is any more involved in Chicago reform than are the churches. The community organizers believe that IAF will provide organizers superior to those now available and will focus on leadership training. The religiously related organization is clearly viewed in instrumental and political terms.

Even the Alinsky-trained organizers may not accept guidance from IAF. Because of its more political position, foundation and reform executives have been willing to talk with IAF officials, but they have not linked with them in cross-city efforts at organization (Hallett, interview, October 25, 1993). Foundations that stress community development, such as the Woods, expect to support IAF once their basic campaign is established with the funds they have already raised (Ken Rolling, interview, May 11, 1995). The ability of community organizations to work together may be tested in Chicago by the addition of the more radical and religiously related IAF. The one leader Alinsky trained, who most wants IAF to return, also supports an experiment with voucher plans that current reform leaders have wanted to avoid (Dan Solis, interview, November 24, 1993). A leader who was trained in Alinsky methods, but who is religious, says she had to "deprogram herself" (Coretta McFerren, interview, April, 1994). Ironically, the local development of the Alinsky tradition as the basis for Chicago reform may not mix with the reality of IAF's return to Chicago (Kyle & Kantowicz, 1992). Neither the recent feminist movement nor the older labor unions have had any serious connection with Chicago reforms; Chapter 5 will show business has had a far greater impact on all major recent educational changes.

ACTIVE FOUNDATIONS

Foundations which exist for improvements in society may reflect private purposes, usually business aims. After Alinsky's death, foundations, particularly the Woods and Wieboldt foundations, supported community development in Chicago (McKersie, 1993). The foundations supported the direction of reform toward community and parental involvement proposals (McKersie, 1993, p. 118). The executive with the Joyce Foundation, William McKersie, said he would fight his own board to get support for school reform. As a group, the foundations considered but would not endorse legislative proposals for changing school governance because of the possible loss of their nonprofit tax status if they were seen to be lobbying (William McKersie, interview, November 2, 1993). Still, twenty-one funders signed a letter urging adoption of reform principles, principles that corresponded closely to the legislation that was adopted.

The foundations had, however, become organized under the name of the Donors Forum Education Group as a means of supporting reform in Chicago. Other cities have developed even more central structures for gift giving in the United States. In Chicago, several specific projects required cooperation among foundations. In order to found a journal and newsletter of the highest quality, *Catalyst*, four foundations came together: AT&T, the Chicago Community Trust, Joyce Foundation, and MacArthur Foundation. As movement toward reform developed, several foundations supported a public meeting in order to gauge the success of reform (McKersie, 1993).

Other programs that have required joint efforts include a current emphasis on cross-city programs and integrated services in the community. In the cross-city work, the executive director of the Wieboldt Foundation became the agent for organizing information and establishing the agenda for the work between cities. Within the city, the executive director of the MacArthur Foundation has been involved in heading youth agencies and in providing space for and supporting the clustering of schools and the cities' other major agencies: parks, police, and so on. (Selinker & Weissmann, 1993). In order to support small grants to individual schools, the major foundations support a smaller and more central agency, the Fund for Educational Reform (*Catalyst*, 1994, May). In others, including those much smaller ones in Canada, a general small foundation is established by business, such as the Calgary Educational Partnership Foundation or a local trust, such as the Muttart.

Reform efforts to change governance, curriculum, or procedures for schools have become increasingly dependent on foundations. In order to train thousands of new parent and community leaders, funds have been needed in Chicago. To develop staff training for teachers and administrators, support at the local level was required. Unfortunately, the foundations appear to provide less than half the Chicago schools with funds for reform. In order to keep reform groups going, more money was required than fund raising could provide, particularly, since, unlike in Canada, no government funds are provided for advocacy groups, the continuation of reform is widely acknowledged to need continuing foundation supports (Coretta McFerren, interview, Oct. 26, 1993). From 1989 to 1995 over $100 million has been given or promised by foundations for school reform. The MacArthur Foundation alone has committed $40 million over ten years (Smart Schools/Smart Kids, p. 17). The Chicago school system was unable, because of financial pressures, to provide as much money for staff development as it had even before the reform legislation passed in December 1988. The reformers have charged that the school system wanted reform to fail so they deliberately limited their support for the training program (Hess, 1991, pp.184-191). According to the historian Michael Katz, the Chicago movement, including the training programs, is one of the largest adult education enterprises ever undertaken (Katz et al., 1991).

The foundations in Chicago have changed, and so have the groups that are involved in reform. As noted earlier, the foundations have hired community activists and supported reform principles. The individual Chicago foundations, furthermore, have started to talk of themselves as agents for social change. Particularly after reform legislation was enacted, the foundations increased their support to community groups nearly threefold (McKersie, 1993, p. 115). The foundation personnel were "likeminded" people whose progressive tendencies were particularly activated by the arrival of Peter Martinez with the largest foundation in Chicago, the MacArthur Foundation (William McKersie, interview, November 2, 1993). In Chicago, as well as in other cities, a core group of foundation executives had begun working together as students in the National Coalition of Advocates for Students, and were still involved as foundation executives in the National Coalition of Education Activists (Ann Hallett, interview, October 25, 1993). The five or six executives for foundations in this group were on the brink of becoming political radicals. The very elite organization, the Pew Forum, which is supported by the Pew Charitable Trust, has urged California foundations to be far more active in educational reform (Miller, 1993, December). In Chapter 5 the Panasonic Foundation is shown to have transformed itself into a consulting firm for individual schools and departments of education who have attempted many reforms.

These active foundation executives are different from the radical theorists outside foundations. The radical writers have argued that foundations are a way of disguising the conservative power of large corporations (Knowles, 1973). In relation to education, historical analyses of foundations have shown that conservative positions have been promoted by educational reports which foundations supported in the United States and abroad, including, in the recent past, racial segregation (Berman, 1989). More conservative interpreters of foundations stress the separation of foundations from corporations and indicate that the political knowledge which foundations support involves setting the agenda for policy and encouraging participation (Lagemann, 1989). Foundations are involved in redrawing the line between public and private support. For this reason they fund advocacy groups in the United States which would probably be governmentally supported in Canada. More radical educators report, unlike governments, foundations are very conservative in Canada (Aimee Horton, interview, October 5, 1993). In Chicago foundations are more active than elsewhere; the large MacArthur group is expected to support the IAF in the future and has given the leader of the Texas IAF, Ernesto Cortes, a "genius" grant in the past (Ken Rolling, interview, May 11, 1995).

The foundations, even in Chicago, are limited by their need to show results in education, no matter how radical their executives are. The foundations shifted their funds to public schooling only because the movement in Chicago has had legislative success and wide-scale publicity (McKersie, 1993). The lack of clear achievement increases by Chicago's students causes pressure on the foundation executives to justify their investment. The MacArthur Foundation has responded to the pressure by emphasizing more conventional projects, such as standard setting and staff training (Peter Martinez, interview, April 25, 1994). MacArthur has come to work with central school administration and is not now supporting unsolicited community organizing grants. Insofar as foundations focus on results, they are similar to governments; the policies of governments are discussed in later chapters.

The increasing involvement of activist leaders with foundations brought, ironically, a group of more conservative players into the reform camp. Before reform and before foundations increased their funding for reform, in general, and community groups, in particular, universities were hardly involved in Chicago's reform activities. One professor, Dan Lewis, made a study of school decentralization which became the basis for a citywide conference (McKerzie, 1993, p. 113). There were few other research studies or regular academic groups involved in reform, though themes from the mass media appear in reform much as they always have during school board elections (Kerr, 1964 and Hess, 1992). Since the reforms were introduced and increased foundation activity came to support the reformers' efforts, a host of more academic groups have started providing their services as well as providing research in the consortium that is seen to support reform by the reformers. By 1990, in addition to the universities, major grants began to be made to the Coalition of Essential Schools, Paideia Institute, Teachers' Task Force and, most interestingly, the Chicago Teachers' Union.

The union, in the eyes of businesspeople and reformers, has seldom supported the movement toward local management by parent councils in Chicago. During its last negotiations, attempts were made to take decisions on school expenditures away from the school councils as well as maintain a number of work rules that would hinder the ability of school councils to make decisions (Pearson, 1993, November). Recently, legislation has denied the union the right to strike for eighteen months (Harp, 1995, June, p. 11). The union has worked toward a site-based management in which teachers were the more important decision makers; though fighting for its right, the union is prepared to accept any system of governance (Bradley, 1995, June, p. 11). The program of the Chicago Teachers' Union for the education of teachers is very much like the programs of other reform groups (Deborah Walsh, interview, November 11, 1993). The teachers' union has, however, developed plans to offer an M.Ed. degree to teachers in reform education.

COOPERATIVE NETWORKS

Though some organizations such as the Chicago Teachers' Union may promote parallel reform activities rather than unified efforts, an increasing number of agencies are cooperating. Between cities and between national organizations and local ones this cooperation widens the perspective and the expertise that can be shared (Ann Hallett, interview, October 25, 1993). There are similar benefits to cooperation among very different organizations within a city, such as parks, schools, housing projects, and police—the cluster project (Greg Darnieder, interview, October 17, 1993). This cluster project developed a grand plan beyond their immediate situation for which foundation support could not be found.

However, more limited programs have coordinated specific services around specific instructional aims. Even these more limited projects are substantially affected by change in key staff. The most modest programs at the local level are changed by rotation of principals (Selinker & Weissman, 1993, p. 6 and Martin, 1993, p. 11). Cooperative projects of all sorts are exercises of compatible individuals as executives as they try to go beyond the frontiers of their separate institutions. Top executives of different city organizations and lifelong associations among foundation executives are only two ways in which executives are being involved in top-down coordination. The former American president, Jimmy Carter, has attracted twenty cluster communities into the Atlanta project. Programs in Atlanta as well as Baltimore are admired by the first director of the Chicago cluster project (Greg Darnieder, interview, October 17, 1993).

When the scale of the program is very large and when the initiative is in its beginning stages, a congenial group is most critical to the development of a project. With respect to foundations, we have already argued that such a friendship group was essential. A friendship group brought together the executives of the police, parks, public housing, schools, and school finance authority in Chicago; unfortunately, when key leaders changed, so did their interest in the cluster project. The group appears to be necessary to overcome the desire to protect one's turf, but a common purpose is necessary to prevent a recurrence of turf wars. Changes in the institutional leaders have disrupted the Chicago cluster initiative. The changes have led to meetings of middle-level managers that cross the institutional boundaries; such meetings were more difficult even to arrange. For any permanent activity to occur, the middle level must be brought in by grass-roots activity if the top level participants cannot be counted on; the middle-level executives are, apparently, more prone to isolation and competition.

At the grass-roots levels, more gradual integration can occur so that common activities and common publicity of those activities mitigate against competition between levels of the organizations involved. The step by step integration of up to twenty-five individual projects has occurred over time with one integration project in Chicago; the Bank of America has become the center of such an integration. Elementary schools are linked with the high school to which they feed students. The students are linked through busing so the health programs, social services, and academic work are coordinated when necessary. The services have programs which bring together both unwed mothers and their children. Organizations have developed their contributions so that hands-on science activities are linked, for example, with art enrichment approaches for the same schools. The provision of programs must include avoiding turf boundaries of gangs as well as among professionals as school and community merge (Nancy Brandt, interview, October 18, 1993 and Continental Bank, 1993).

THE ALIENATED STUDENT AND CREATIVE LEADERS

Student life is probably most affected by the disruption and new relationships that reformers create. In the cluster plan to public housing, education, and city parks, students working with landscape architects have developed striking plans for a new school in the heart of one of the worst areas of Chicago (Greg Darnieder, interview, October 17, 1993). A plan for open space between an elementary school and a high school was developed by students, together with the architects; the proposed outdoor learning center would include tennis and basketball courts, an outdoor theater, a community garden and a "walk of fame" to be completed by each of the graduating classes of the school for the next twelve years. This is the clearest example of professionals working together with the schools, a subject that Chapter 7 will develop.

Individual students have been affected by involvement in a variety of other ways that include demonstrating and lobbying. Some students have participated with their parents; others have been paid to write about their educational experiences. Student organizations provide a significant voice; they will be described in Chapter 8. Gang members in Chicago have become involved in school elections by demonstrating as 21st Century Votes and running candidates for school council (Weissman, 1993, November, p. 7). Council members now include 21st Century spokesmen, but the gang members who ran so openly were generally rejected. However, students are indirectly seeing opportunities develop for them as the school system opens. No longer will they be buried in the bureaucracy. Programs with cross-institutional boundaries guarantee that new opportunities are emerging. These new opportunities are dependent on the visions of transformative leaders. One such leader, Sokoni Karanja, says: "The real problem is that the gangs have a product, and we don't: They are selling safety, camaraderie, employment, a group that shares a set of values—all the things that teenagers look for" (Weissman, 1993, November, p.6). Karanja has organized a center that provides preemployment counseling, school tutoring, parent counseling, and recreational activities. He has worked with a cooperative attempt to develop the area, encourage Black industry, stress cultural resources, and develop group pride. He is attempting to provide all the benefits that teenagers seek from gangs. At an earlier period when teachers were on strike, he told the parents to pitch tents outside the school board offices until the teachers were back in the classrooms (Steinberg, 1993). Karanja believes that middleclass housing is needed before shops and industry, in areas that have been almost completely abandoned, will return. Understandably, Karanja emerged as one of the leaders of Chicago's reform, though he constantly defers to his partner, Ben Kendrick, who runs a series of social agencies in another part of the city (Sokoni Karanja, interview, April 4, 1994).

However, a more typical combination of leaders are women who are providing the ideas and energy to complement the political dominance of men. Danny Solis and Lourdi Monteagudo are one such combination. Danny was a student activist who joined an organization whose founders followed Saul Alinsky. Danny now serves as the executive director for that organization, the United Neighborhood Organization. Lourdi is a Cuban who was picked as a symbolic new elementary principal because she was young, female, and Spanish. Together they developed many new reform initiatives. Grass-root organizing turned out the largely Mexican vote in local school elections. The Spanish became the strongest supporters of Chicago reform. Creative use was made of the Spanish radio and television stations to empower the Spanish parents who might prefer separate Catholic education but could only afford public schools. Social and educational clusters of organizations other than schools would result from Lourdi's political perception, though she, in turn, relies on men whose ideas she adopts (interview, April 14, 1994 and interview, November 29, 1993).

Both Lourdi Monteagudo and Dan Solis would become increasingly important players in the reform drama. She was often the only principal actively working with parents and business leaders for reform. He became an important leader who had to be won over by coalition groups seeking reform. She became the deputy mayor for education. He would be the mayor's representative on the committee to nominate school board members and the mayor's appointee to the top-down cluster effort between schools and other institutions. She would attempt to link city school boards, the state department of education, and the mayor to new efforts including the national program led by Ted Sizer. He would try to register Latinos and unify the Spanish vote, keep the Black vote split, and ensure Mayor Daley's reelection. She has recently become the director of a program of science education begun at the Illinois Institute of Technology, which had become a major problem even though it was sponsored by the federal government. He is now a candidate for alderman (interview, November 24, 1993). He views her as an expressive "technician" and she views him as an "astute politician." They met when she was the new principal and he was a concerned parent.

These combinations are not unique. There is a husband and wife team in one parent organization. Male founders and women executives have worked together in other community or parent groups; the organization Danny leads was founded by such a team. However, there are other effective combinations of women that are typical of creative movements. When the reformers met to plan their lobbying, only a handful of men were present. In actual lobbying against changes in the Illinois legislation for 1993, Joan Jeter Slay was the director who coordinated the lobbying of principals and other organizations like a chess game. Coretta McFerren articulated the feelings of those present and tried to get everyone, including me, involved in the political process. As well, both reflected their relationship to a professional man and a business leader, respectively. Coretta said that Joan had been trained by Alinsky, while she learned from Alinsky students in the organization now headed by Danny. Joan says very little about herself (Coretta McFerren, interview, October 26, 1993). It is through such teams that organic leaders cross organizations in the city.

THE CROSS CITY CAMPAIGN

A new project is emerging that promises to further develop the Chicago reforms and those involved with them. The City Campaign for Urban School Reform is based in Chicago and is staffed by two key figures from the movement in that city. The initial staff consisted of Ann Hallett, who is the executive director, and Diana Lauber, who is the senior consultant. The aim of the campaign is to exchange information, support local autonomous schools, and create a national policy for reform in local communities. Reformers, community activists, and union leaders from Denver, Philadelphia, New York, and Seattle have held organizing meetings and formed working groups. Participants from Milwaukee, Oakland, San Francisco, Toronto, Los Angeles, Cleveland, and Cincinnati have also attended meetings.

Among those involved there appear to be the interest and confidence in doing the impossible that characterize reformers; the same people may, alternately, show great anxiety regarding their success. Both positive and negative concerns are submerged by the constant activity that characterizes these reformers as it does others. Ann Hallett and Diana Lauber have already lived two lives in reform as they prepare for a third reincarnation. Ann was the first executive director for the Chicago Panel on School Policy, one of two most important advocacy groups that brought reform to Chicago. Ann became the executive director for the Wieboldt Foundation during the key period when, influenced by her, foundations became politically as active for reform legislation as the law allows. Ann Hallett has constantly been one of the three most influential people in the Chicago reform coalitions; she denied one newcomer acceptance to reform groups though she is herself an outsider from Seattle (William Ayers, interview, April 25, 1994). In the Cross City campaign she is the person who systematizes the reports of other people and suggests direction when it is needed in meetings. She seems to be a planner as well as a tactician and social director (interview, October, 25, 1993).

Diana Lauber is neither an analytical planner nor a director of people and events as is Ann; she is an intuitive person with the courage to stand against any authority when she thinks it is wrong (interview, April 11, 1994). She was originally a special education teacher who became a specialist on school finance with the Chicago Panel on School Policy after Ann had left that organization. Diana Lauber helped write key sections of the Chicago reform act (Kyle & Kantowicz, 1992, p. 287). In order to work for the implementation of the school reform act, she joined the advocacy group which the elite businesses in Chicago have sponsored, Leadership for Quality Education (LQE). With LQE, she organized reform groups, lobbied, and continued to criticize school board financial practices until the organization adopted a more conservative stance. She has been able to act as a financial critic with other cities as she had anticipated joining the new organization. A black reformer who is very critical of all the white leaders has grudging admiration for her (James Dean, interview, April 8, 1994). Diana Lauber had represented LQE on the Cross City Campaign before joining the latter organization. She appears to complement Ann Hallett and both show how the reform movement is a revolving door of people and programs.

The staff and working groups with Cross City Campaign have written, met, and lobbied for a variety of schools and communities in the few years since they became organized (Cross City Campaign, 1994, May). One group spent six months trying to win improvements in the U.S. federal program for poor children, Chapter 1. A paper on community resources was developed and meetings on small schools and charter alternatives were held. Initial efforts to develop assessments have been made that would be useful at the school level, but their greatest concentration of efforts has been on sharing approaches to decentralization. They have also developed a plan for urban schools with the Educational Commission of the States, whose work will be discussed in the next chapter. The aim of these various threads appears to be to use educational and organizational expertise to develop a democratic approach to schools in cities other than Chicago.

Cross City has been the basis for integrating the Chicago experiment with the change in governance as a model for school councils in other cities: New York provides a model for school community linkages, Philadelphia has its successful small schools, Seattle has promising peer review efforts, and Denver has made clear efforts toward site-based management. All of the cities are reviewed by the Cross City report under the rubrics of curriculum and instruction, personnel, budgets, accountability, facilities and services, and governance. Interestingly, only Chicago has its area of excellence, which is governance, recognized as a general planning category (Cross City Campaign, 1994, pp. 4, 5). The democratic alternative of Chicago is the golden mean between "bloated inequitable bureaucracies on the one hand and vouchers private management on the other" (p. 5). A recent revision of the Cross City plan gives less prominence to Chicago (Cross City Campaign for Urban School Reform, 1995).

THE LAZY SUSAN OF POLICIES

As far as Chicago is concerned, the Cross City Campaign has increased the options that are available while making it still more difficult to organize these options into a consistent program. In a draft for a paper on central office, Cross City is still reacting to the old bureaucracy; a principal is quoted: "The tendency for policy makers is to want to extract more quantitative results (from highly dysfunctional, bureaucratic systems) through tighter curricula, higher certification standards for teachers and more testing of everyone" (Cross City Campaign, 1994, p. 3). The same general policy paper calls for school councils to enter into collective bargaining, the elimination of monopolies in training teachers, quotas for teachers of color, and many other matters (Cross City Campaign, 1994, pp. 14–16). However, concrete opposition to existing policies is usually coupled with vague remedies. How collective bargaining with teachers will be changed by including councils or how alternative routes for teacher certification and hiring are to be established is never stated. Rhetoric appears to replace strategy.

The creation of new opportunities for teachers is not particularly stressed in the Cross City policy paper, but, when a proposal for the Annenberg

Foundation was primarily developed by the leader of the Cross City Campaign, teachers received a great deal of attention. However, the teacher proposals are still cloaked in rhetoric; in a mythical school, Old Lincoln, which will be developed from the Annenberg gift, there will be a sense of "belonging and identity" and teachers will be "bold and creative" (Smart Schools/Smart Kids, n. d., p. 31). The Chicago proposal was developed primarily by Ann Hallett, the executive director of Cross City, when she read in the newspaper about the plans of the philanthropist Walter Annenberg to give the public schools $500 million (Diana Lauber, interview, December 6, 1994). To help write the proposal, Mrs. Hallett recruited Bill Ayers, an associate professor at the University of Illinois (William Ayers, interview, April 25, 1994). Mr. Ayers had earlier served as chairman of the coalition of reform groups in Chicago. Even earlier, he had been a civil rights protester and a radical student activist; he and his wife were the models for the story of the movie *Traveling on Empty*.

Bill Ayers transformed the Annenberg proposal in light of his current interests in teacher empowerment and innovations in New York City. Though leaving school councils as a focus of reforms in Chicago, the Annenberg proposal calls for the development of a teacher corps, alternative forms of certification for new teachers, and continuing training for new teachers. Only changes in teacher certification were discussed in the Cross City report on central school functions. The teacher proposals as well as proposals for small schools and school reviews are from New York City and the New York City proposal to the Annenberg Foundation, which preceded the Chicago one. Even the main title of the Chicago proposal is from a book by the former education editor of the *New York Times*, Edward Fiske.

Aside from New York City, the Annenberg proposal reflects the influence of reforms in Los Angeles. Los Angeles was the third city to receive Annenberg grants of $50 million (Olson & Summerfeld, 1994, June, p. 1). Ann Hallett had earlier been interested in Los Angeles because that city devotes its entire budget to local schools while Chicago only has a part of its budget subject to local decisions. For the Annenberg grant Chicago says it will follow Los Angeles and develop extensive networks for cooperation with business. Unless the example from other cities is very clear the proposal for Chicago is very vague; for example, the evils of the current system of teacher evaluation are clearly shown, but proposals to change them are very general.

Changes that are introduced from other cities or are designed to meet the expectations of the Annenberg Foundation have proved to be mild, compared to the earthquakes caused by the Illinois legislature, which removed control of the school system from the school board and placed it with the mayor. There have been several cases of local councils charged by inspectors from the central office and the central office has been charged with not promoting participation in council elections (Bradley, 1996, April). Though local school councils survived, all reformers have been reminded that any power they have derives from the legislature. In addition to losing the right to strike, the teachers' union must accept that the scope of any collective bargaining agreement has been severely restricted. The leader of the teachers' union, Jackie Gallagher, said, "It was our time to be drawn and quartered" (Bradley, 1995, June, p. 11). However, the success of the new regime may threaten all independent organizations. The reliance on unchecked authority may grow if the mayor is able to deliver on his promise of labor peace for four years and no large tax increases for the same period (Diana Lauber, interview, August 16, 1995).

For everyone, the new legislation means that a corporate and political style of governance will replace the amateurs and educators at the top of the Chicago schools. The mayor named his former chief of staff as president of the new five-member superboard, and his former budget officer as chief executive officer (Bradley, 1995, July, p. 3). Three educators were named to more specialized and supportive positions. The choice of the educators seemed to please the reformers and business leaders, who commented more on the quality of the people than the change in the system. Two businesspeople and two executives from city government and a health center completed the very unrepresentative superboard.

Ironically, the corporate board came a year after an individual private school, which was based on the principle that corporate specialists should replace amateur school boards, found that its only option was to join the public school board (see Chapter 5). Perhaps individual schools and the school system will continue to operate on different policies. It seems more likely that whatever one's taste in reform, all you have to do is wait for it to come around on the server for the second or third time. Centralization, school-based decision making, teacher empowerment, greater equality of opportunity for minorities and their teachers, reform based on Chicago experience, or reforms from other national or city groups all come around from time to time. The process of reform has empowered many people who were not involved with education before the reform act. Ideally, the new activists will not join the teachers in their cynicism (John Kotsakis, interview, November 18, 1993).

Concern for the problems should not negate our new awareness of the opportunities for democratic involvement in schools. Many conventional views of education have begun to be challenged. Schools can rework conventional views as social movements emerge. We will not always teach in schools like those we attended. The measure of success is the commitment of students to reform and the extent to which reform goals are made relevant to students. As will be discussed in Chapter 4, Kentucky co-opts students while Alberta denies their protests any legitimacy. In each of the reform patterns there are opportunities for integrating institutions. All community institutions can become involved with education just as, in the past, the whole community trained children in small traditional societies where many people other than parents were involved in molding them.

Schools can be influenced by dynamic community organizers. Schools will not always be classrooms separated from political realities. Experts can be shoved aside as new charismatic leaders arise. Teachers can remain with the bureaucracy or they can, like Lourdi, join the movement. The full culture, including religion, can be mobilized as visions for education become more than slogans. Schools can be seen as involved in the political process as Danny has joined the other reformers in changing school governance. Other so-called neutral institutions such as foundations, become, together with schools, the base on which the future develops. We can begin to think of schools as one of the institutions that can work for students and parents. The other institutions and specific organizations, it is hoped, will not dominate the more democratic schools.

Because of the crises that education is now confronting, large-scale innovations between education and other social institutions are probably more typical than the smaller incremental changes within schools that are more familiar to educators who worked in isolation from other agencies in the past (Mitchell, 1992). The crises of financial deficits, lower student standards, and gangs beyond the control of adults are not going to be solved by school improvement plans alone. The answers to the new problems are fundamentally different from the issues that led to innovations, such as team teaching, computer-aided instruction, or addition of specialists to the educational team. Such reforms have been successful when they were school-based in the past because the school system was a fragmented activity and the school was the largest unit in which change could be successfully implemented. Clustering between schools and between schools and community action groups means that a much larger and more complicated activity becomes the basis for change. The Cross City project shows that reforms between cities are spreading and intermingling.

It is true that reforms have only touched student issues, including the problem of school gangs, and even that was through the involvement of parents. Limited success has been achieved in raising student achievement, though the problems related to achievement have been placed at the top of the agenda. Chicago has ignored the financial problems until very recently, wheras we shall later see that movements in Kentucky and one province in Canada have, in opposite ways, placed financial accountability at the center of reform.

More generally, the reform movers differ from the model of organic intellectuals and movements we initially drew in that they never seem to integrate the past with their view of the future and to learn from their own history. The past involvement of religious and union organizations in Chicago is ignored even if, for tactical reasons, there is some movement toward religious based organizations (Wrigley, 1982). The reformers and business leaders criticize the current teachers' unions and school board administrators as being very limited. There is no awareness that the predecessors of the current reformers and businesspeople in some of the same organizations eliminated the more creative union leaders and educational administrators, such as Margaret Haley, Lilian Herstein, or Ella Flag Young, names from Chicago's past. The reform movement, even as it expands to many cities, remains reactive (Mitchell, 1984). The movement reacts against scientific and efficiency views without integrating its own broader tradition and heritage. The role of women in the movement and the tradition is seldom focused on, for example. The teams of organic leaders spin their ideas about changing the system while cross-fertilizing the reform plans of different organizations and different cities.

The process of continuing to modify reform is limited by an increasing tendency to seek mechanical measures of educational success and reliance on experts to provide a measure of social and political change that is well beyond their specialties. The search for results that are measurable is one that foundations and governments can be expected to pursue insofar as they must justify reform. Those involved in reform should base their judgments on their faith in evaluating people as human beings. The search by the current Grand Inquisitor for conventional measures of success may destroy the fragile achievement of democratic schools. The reform movement will realize its potential when students become involved for the sake of their future and directions are taken from the lessons of our past so that we get beyond reacting to the current problems of a failing school system.

One way to avoid the pattern of reacting repeatedly is to develop broader relationships. Specific programs such as the Chicago cluster initiative have looked to other cities including Atlanta. Executives with foundations were already a part of a network that stretched across America. The Cross City focused on the Chicago effort as a model for other cities. The Annenberg gift appears to lead Chicago to New York and Los Angeles. The broader scene focuses attention away from past problems, but it does not guarantee authentic initiatives that reflect the concerns of people for the democratic reform of schools.

REFERENCES

Allen, C. (1993, October 25). The hidden costs of tuition vouchers, *Chicago Tribune*, Sec. 1, 13.

Applebome, P. (1995, April 30). Annenberg school grants raise hopes and questions on extent of change. *New York Times*, 15.

Berman, E.H. (1989). The state's stake in educational reform. In Shea, C.M., Kahane, E., & Sola, P. (Eds.), *The new servants of power* (pp. 57-66). New York: Greenwood Press.

Blumer, H. (1951). Collective behavior. In Lee, A.M. (Ed.), *New outline of the principles of sociology* (pp. 167–222). New York: Barnes & Noble.

Bradley, A. (1993, November 24). Student performance in Chicago up, study finds. *Education Week*, 13(12), 3.

Bradley, A. (1994, January 26). Role of the central office in aiding schools studied. *Education Week*, 13(18), 5.

Bradley, A. (1995, June 21). Chicago mayor poised to take district's reins. *Education Week*, 14(39), 5, 11.

Bradley, A. (1996, April 10). LSC elections in Chicago test local control. *Education Week*, 15(29), 1, 16.

Catalyst (1994, May). Grants. *Catalyst*, 5(8), 20.

Center for Quality Schools (1992). *The power of collaborative decision making.* Denver: The Center for Quality Schools.

Consortium on Chicago School Research (1993). *A view from the elementary schools: The state of reform in Chicago.* Chicago: A Report of the Steering Committee Consortium on Chicago School Research.

Continental Bank (1993). *The Orr school network.* Chicago: Continental Bank.

Corporate-Higher Education Forum (1991). *To be our best.* Montreal: Corporate Higher Education Forum.

Cortes, E. (n.d.). Reweaving the fabric: The iron rule and the IAF strategy for dealing with poverty and politics. Austin: Texas Industrial Areas Foundation Network.

Cross City Campaign (1994, May). *Cross City report.* Chicago: Cross City Campaign.

Cross City Campaign (1994, September). *Reinventing central office: Toward a system of successful urban schools.* Chicago: Cross City Campaign.

Cross City Campaign for Urban School Reform (1995, May). *Reinventing central office: A primer for successful schools.* Chicago: Cross City Campaign.

Giroux, H. (1987). Literacy and the pedagogy of political empowerment. In Freire, P. & Macedo, D. (Eds.), *Literacy.* New York: Bergin & Garvey.

Goodlad, J. (1984). *A place called school.* New York: McGraw Hill.

Harp, L. (1995, April 19). Proposals to reshape Chicago schools follow shift in Ill. legislature. *Education Week*, 14(30), 13.

Hess, G.A. (1991). *School restructuring, Chicago style.* Newbury Park, California: Corwin.

Hess, G.A. (1992). *Empowering teachers and parents.* New York: Bergin & Garvey.

Hill, P.T. & Bonan, J. (1991). *Decentralization and accountability in public education.* Santa Monica: Rand.

Hogan, D.J. (1985). *Class and reform.* Philadelphia: University of Pennsylvania Press.

Illinois Bell (1991). *Local school councils ideas and successes.* Chicago: Illinois Bell.

Katz, M.B., Fine, M., & Simon, E. (1991, March 7). School reform: A view from outside. *Chicago Tribune*, Sect. 1, 27.

Kerr, N.D. (1964). The School Board as an agency of legitimation. *Sociology of Education*, 38, 34-59.

Knowles, J. (1973). *The Rockefeller financial group.* Andover, Massachusetts: Warner Modular.

Kyle, C.L. & Kantowicz, E.R. (1992). *Kids first-primero los niños.* Springfield: Illinois Issues.

Lagemann, E.C. (1989). *The politics of knowledge: The Carnegie Corporation, philanthropy and public policy.* Chicago: University of Chicago Press.

Lenz, L. (1993, April). Meager gains on tests: Cause for alarm. *Catalyst*, 5(7), 1–3.

Martin, M. (1993, September). Orr network keeps expanding while Orr turns inward. *Catalyst*, 5(1), 9–11.

McKersie, W.S. (1993). Philanthropy's paradox: Chicago school reform. *Educational Evaluation and Policy Analysis*, 15(22), 109–128.

Miller, L. (1993, December 1). California foundations urged to step up role in reform. *Education Week*, 13 (13), 3.

Mirel, J. (1993). School reform, Chicago style. *Urban Education*, 28, (2), 116–149.

Mitchell, S. (1984). Is progressive education the limit of possible reform in education? In Minnis, J.R. (Ed.), *Proceeding of the Alberta Universities Educational Foundations Conference*. Athabasca, Alberta: Athabasca University.

Mitchell, S. (1992). *Innovation and reform*. York, Ontario: Captus Press.

Moncey, D. & McQuillan, P. (1990). *Educational reform as revitalization movement*. Providence: The Coalition of Essential Schools.

Moore, D., Soltman, S., Manar, U., Steinberg, L., & Fogel, D. (1983). *Standing up for children*. Chicago: Designs for Change.

National Commission on Excellence in Education (1983). *A nation at risk: The imperative of educational reform*. Washington, D. C.: U.S. Government Printing Office.

National Education Goals Panel (1992). *The national education goals report*. Washington, D. C.: U. S. Government Printing Office.

O'Connell, M. (1991). *School reform Chicago style*. Chicago: Center for Neighborhood Technology.

Olson, L. & Sommerfeld, M. (1994, June 8). Annenberg gift may focus on 4 urban areas. *Education Week*, 3(37), 1, 14.

Olson, L. & Sommerfeld, M. (1994, December 14). Annenberg set to announce round of gifts. *Education Week*, 14(15), 1, 10–11.

Pearson, R. (1993, November 13). Last pitch accord on city schools. *Chicago Tribune*, Sec. 1, 1.

Rosow, J.M. & Zager, R. (1989). *Allies in educational reform*. San Francisco: Jossey-Bass.

Schumpeter, J.A. (1942). *Capitalism, socialism and democracy*. New York: Harper.

Selinker, M. & Weissmann (1993, October). Untangling government a mission impossible? *Catalyst*, 5(2), 1–6.

Smart Schools/Smart Kids: A Proposal to the Annenberg Foundation To Create the Chicago School Reform Collaborative (n.d.). Unpublished paper. Chicago.

Smith, L., Klein, P., Prunty, J., & Dwyer, D. (1986). *Educational innovators: Then and now*. London: The Falmer Press.

Sommerfeld, M. (1994, January 12). Annenberg gift prompts praise and questions. *Education Week*, 13(16), 1, 12.

Steinberg, N. (1993, June 15). Activist Karanja among 31 MacArthur fellows. *Chicago Sun*, Sec. 1, 14.

Texas Industrial Areas Foundation Network (1990). *Texas IAF network vision...values... action*. Austin, Texas: Texas Industrial Areas Foundation Network.

Timpane, P.M. & McNeill, L.M. (1991). *Business impact on education and child development reform*. New York: Committee for Economic Development.

Voice of the People (1993, October 8). Fairness in choice and voucher worries. *Chicago Tribune*, Sec. 1, 26.

Weissmann, D. (1993, October). Top city leaders dream big take tiny steps. *Catalyst*, 5(2), 1–9 .

Weissmann, D. (1933, November). Group aim to put street gangs on better path. *Catalyst*, 5(3), 6.

Wohlstetter, P. & Buffett, T. (1992). Decentralizing dollars under school-based management: Have policies changed? *Educational Policy*, 6(1), 35–54.

Wrigley, J. (1982). *Class policies and public schools*. New Brunswick, New Jersey: Rutgers University Press.

Chapter 3

Contradictions Confronting Advocacy Organizations

> The thirteenth rule: Pick the target, freeze it, personalize it, and polarize it. Go outside the experience of the enemy, stay inside the experience of your people. . . . There is just so much more than can be squeezed out of the Have-Not so the Haves must take it from each other. (Saul Alinsky, 1971, pp. 130, 139 and 149)

Before foundations came to eclipse them, the advocacy groups led the rush to major educational reforms. However, as they go about the business of trying to change education, organizations, even those in Chicago most influenced by Saul Alinsky, have stopped dealing with the school system and businesses as polar opponents. The two most influential advocacy organizations in Chicago, Designs for Change and the Chicago Panel on School Policy, have differed in the extent to which they represent specific constituencies who are trying to change educational policies. Designs for Change is more likely to represent interest groups, such as the families of special education students, while the Chicago Panel on School Policy is more prone to speak for a variety of liberal organizations with different concerns. The more specific the constituents, the more likely is the group to campaign in opposition to the educational establishment. National organizations are more likely to represent general interests and promote leadership for the larger sense of community than are parochial organizations; that is probably why Alinsky always stayed with local conflict groups. Two national advocacy organizations have been successful in providing broader leadership: the Canadian Parents for French, which has been the center for developing bilingual education in Canada, and the Coalition of Essential Schools, which has gained the support of ten states, and has been a recognized organization for its program of improved common learning in the United States.

These four organizations differ and continue to change because of the contradictions on which they have been built. How are their original constituents going to be affected as they become a part of larger alliances? How are their successes conflicting with the educational order? Is the organization of advocacy groups more important than the goals for which the organization was founded? How are those not included in the original struggles to learn the lessons of changing education? How are individual problems to be resolved while educational policies are also changed in the schools? These tensions are the heart of this chapter and the value of an Alinsky approach to change education will be repeatedly considered.

ORIGINS

Organizations that have wanted to influence schools have often had fairly limited aims; the four advocacy organizations that are our focus all have larger visions than those with the typical interests. Advocates from outside the schools have usually sought favors through selling goods or obtaining access to children in order to change their attitudes. Advocates within the system including teachers or trustees have usually wanted to influence salaries, tax rates, or employment practices (Gross, 1958). Pressure groups in this sense thought of themselves as disadvantaged; they tried to correct their situation by acquiring advantages for themselves. Pressure groups provide a contrast to groups that were showing civic leadership and were performing on the basis of a broader vision or greater public interest (Poyen, 1989, pp. 50–52). On this basis, the two pressure groups in Chicago are more limited than the Canadian Parents for French (CPF) or the Coalition of Essential Schools (CES). The latter have helped to develop new curriculum on a national basis, while the Chicago groups have opened a very closed, local system to outside ideas.

However, the spur for the development of advocacy groups, such as those in Chicago, was the civil rights movement in the United States. The civil rights effort led to the development of groups that acted to develop fairer policies for racial minorities in American cities in the 1960s (Moore et al. 1983, pp. 47–48). The civil rights campaign led, in turn, to movements to improve the rights of women, homosexuals, and the disabled. The Children's Defense Fund at a national level and Designs for Change in Chicago had attempted to improve the status of the handicapped. The racial crises in this one city led to the formation of a biracial group of businesspeople, Chicago United, so that Blacks would feel there were opportunities for them. The financial collapse of the schools in 1979 led the organizations for education to combine into the Chicago Panel on School Policy in order to monitor school finances and student achievement. These advocacy organizations that were directly or indirectly inspired by the demand for racial equality were hardly sheer pressure groups. Their leaders have been so personally dedicated and knowledgeable that they might be said to resemble Ralph Nader.

In the United States, there are an incredible number of advocacy groups that always seem to be multiplying even though some disappear as a result of the pressure in the campaigns for greater equality. The national study in the early 1980s analyzed fifty-two such groups in urban education (Moore et al., 1983). In 1993 a directory listed 105 projects in Chicago alone, most of which were formal organizations acting for clients. As a result of twenty years of conservative governments, many of the American advocacy groups have compromised with the dominant governments. Certainly, Danny Solis has made such an accommodation while he prepares to run for alderman and supports the remains of the Chicago machine. Designs for Change and the Chicago Panel have formed many alliances including one with their former opponents, the principals' association. However, some of the middle-level and local community groups maintain an idealistic stance. For example, the husband and wife team Bernie Noven and Joy Noven cannot be bought, as they operate under the revealing acronym, PURE, which stands for Parents United for Responsible Education (Diana Lauber, interview, April 28, 1994).

In Chicago, advocacy groups are generally viewed in terms of their status. Designs for Change and the Chicago Panel are now very dominant. Key observers have recognized the importance of a range of other advocacy groups. Peggy Gordon, the lawyer who worked with the reform group and provided other lawyers on a free basis to advise the school councils, calls Don Moore and Fred Hess "the fathers of reform" and their organizations were, as a result, more important (Peggy Gordon, interview, April 18, 1994). Gordon sees the organizations that are based in the neighborhoods with prominent individuals as interlocking with the two dominant groups. The organizations based primarily in neighborhoods include the Black leaders Coretta McFerren, Sokoni Karanja, and James Deanes, who leads a council of parents. An academic observer agrees with this characterization but stresses there is one hierarchy which extends from the two dominant advocacy groups to extremely local ones. This hierarchy of advocacy groups is seen as more distinctively related to class and racial positions (Dan Lewis, interview, April 13, 1994). Among the local, more stratified bodies is one originally built by Alinsky, The Woodlawn Organization (TWO).

The power of groups and the resentment against those with power mean that more is involved between these groups than status alone. Almost all Black leaders resent the white fathers of reform, although their opposition to the white female leaders, such as Ann Hallett and Diana Lauber, is more muted (James Deanes, interview, April 8, 1994). The dominance of the two leading advocacy groups results from the support they have acquired through grants from various foundations (William McKersie, letter, June 21, 1994) and their ability to negotiate the great racial divide (Lewis & Nakagawa, 1995). Opposition by Black leaders to White officers of foundations has not developed. The foundations have had to struggle to overcome guilt about their own White dominance, but they have not been pressured. The first protest organization in Chicago, the Citizens School Committee, is now largely irrelevant and is low on the list of both observers. The Citizens School Committee (CSC) has recently been denied even the right to apply for an extension of its grant through the efforts of Peter Martinez at the MacArthur Foundation. Marilyn Stephens, the executive director of CSC, does not show resentment of Peter Martinez at the MacArthur Foundation (interview, April 18, 1994). Martinez, who has $40 million to spend on Chicago reform, was said by others not to be very much "beloved by anyone;" perhaps the time has come that he should be challenged as his mentor, Alinsky, challenged other power figures in the past (Peggy Gordon, interview, April 18, 1994).

Advocacy groups have been linked to foundations and often, through foundations, to business groups. The rank of advocacy groups corresponds to the support provided by foundations, which reinforces such rankings, and the foundations do not seem able or willing to develop advocacy or research groups for specific purposes. Designs for Change was acting as a consultant to the biracial business group Chicago United even before reform began. Recently, the Chicago Panel has joined with businesses in applying for grants. The middle-level reform organization, PURE, maintains its original Alinsky style. The leaders of PURE have gone so far as to protest at the homes of their opponents in order to hold them up to ridicule and had created some bitter enemies (Diana Lauber, interview, April 29, 1994). The more dominant groups are, increasingly, using restrained tactics. During my observation of the fall 1993 and spring 1994 legislative sessions, there were no mass rallies or demonstrations even though significant changes in reform legislation were being made.

In Canada, the pressure to compromise with the establishment has never been as intense as it is in the United States, nor has the difficulty of relating to different power positions been as great, since government in Canada has supported many advocacy groups in their initial efforts, while, in the United States, similar groups have had to raise funds or obtain foundation grants in order to establish themselves. Organizations for women, trade unions, and natives have obtained support from the Canadian government. In education, advocacy groups exist for special, early childhood, and cross-cultural education. The Canadian Parents for French has been successful because it is based on official bilingualism; the American efforts for Latinos or Blacks cannot be said to match that success (Poyen, 1989). However, there is an American effort in which government is involved as a sponsor. The Coalition of Essential Schools has made the most important effort to engineer support from state governments.

Aside from the federal programs that support advocacy organizations, the combination of fiscal restraints and demands by parent and community groups has led to the emergence of a number of right–wing groups in both

Canada and the United States. Canadian groups have developed in Ontario and all of the western provinces (Organization for Quality Education, 1994, June). Similarly, in the United States, right–wing groups oppose progressive innovations and are organized into national federations such as the Eagle Forum (Harp, 1994, May).

These groups want choice among schools and oppose progressive education; they are organizations which use conflict as much as those founded by Alinsky. In later chapters, the opposition of the American right wing will be shown to be very important in considering opposition to new national programs. For now, we turn to the situation in Chicago, where advocacy groups tried to present a democratic challenge to the authoritarian operation of the schools.

THE LONG MARCH TO CHICAGO'S REFORM

Though local reform seemed to begin as a reaction to national efforts, the foundations of local advocacy groups were laid long before large-scale commissions for educational reform issued their reports. In Chicago, the two advocacy groups had developed their central direction before the appearance of the report *A Nation at Risk* (Chart 3.1). One advocacy group, originally called the Chicago Panel on Public School Policy and Finance, resulted from the financial crisis that struck after Chicago could no longer rely on a powerful mayor to obtain additional financing from the state legislature. The existing organizations that were concerned about improving public education, such as the League of Women Voters, American Jewish Committee, and Chicago Urban League, formed a coalition so that they could have accurate information to combat the misinformation manufactured by the school board. The resulting organization, now known as the Chicago Panel on Public School Policy, became a permanent organization that served its member organizations and the public as a watchdog on school finances (O'Connell, 1991, p. 6 and Kyle & Kantowicz, 1992, pp. 215–216). Only after a dozen years have links emerged with other cities in Illinois and the Midwest. The Chicago Panel has recently developed a statewide organization to focus on larger financial concerns. The Chicago Panel is similar to an organization in New York City that was founded earlier (Moore, 1990). Ironically, its executive director, Fred Hess, speaks of "having spun off our member service aspect and with a new division that concentrates on research in a much broader area" (letter, May 5, 1994). The organization has recently moved to much larger quarters on North Michigan Avenue and continues to add staff.

The other major advocacy organization, Designs for Change, started as a consulting firm and research agency. As a result of a national study of advocacy organizations Don Moore, the only Director that Designs for Change has ever had, decided that if his group was to ever have significant

Chart 3.1
Chicago Reform and Advocacy Organizations

1979 Chicago financial crisis leads to bailout plan by Illinois. The plan includes surveillance by a state-appointed financial authority.

1982 Two local advocacy organizations are founded: Designs for Change and the Chicago Panel on Public School Policy and Finance (Chicago Panel).

1983 National report, *A Nation at Risk*, released.

1984 Latino group in Northwest Chicago, Aspira, issues study of Latino dropouts. Local group stages march before a national committee with coffin, which symbolizes the problems of their youth.

1985 Hispanic Dropout Task Force leads to legislative recommendations. Design for Change issues more general study of dropouts. Two months later, Chicago Panel issues even more comprehensive study. Design for Change organizes School Watch program and starts parent training. Reflecting *A Nation at Risk*, a general bill passes the legislature which provides school report cards and creates Local School Improvement Councils.

1986 Chicago Board of Education holds local budget hearings as required by new law, but refuses to make any changes in its budget as a result. First general coalition formed to bring about educational reform, Chicagoans United to Reform Education (CURE) by Designs for Change and Save Our Neighborhoods/Save Our City. Mayor convenes first summit which focuses mainly on the business-education connection. School superintendent refuses to increase student achievement in return for business hiring more graduates.

1987 First report cards issued on schools under accountability legislation lead to the charge by the secretary of education William Bennett that Chicago schools are the worst in the nation. Chicago Teachers' Union and Urban League hold conference on school-based management in other American cities. Chicago teachers go out on strike for ninth time in eighteen years and stay out nineteen days. Longest teacher strike in Chicago history leads to organization and protests by parents. Strike settlement very similar to proposal made by Chicago Panel before the strike. Coretta McFerren leads People's Coalition for Education Reform, representing Black poverty groups, and forms a human chain around Chicago's central business area.   Parents establish links with advocacy organizations and open school alternatives. Peoples Coalition joins CURE as partner. General coalition, CURE, hires group that has expertise in developing legislation and lobbying for it, the Haymarket group. Mayor Washington convenes expanded summit but later dies of a heart attack. Advocacy groups focus more on state legislature after mayor's death.

Chart 3.1 (continued)

1988 CURE bill becomes basis for general reform act. Major Mexican organization, United Neighborhood Organization (UNO), announces support for CURE Bill. New mayor's summit has difficulty developing a working consensus for legislation; head of Chicago panel is fired by mayor's organization. Parent and teacher task force continue as separate organizations in the city. All dissidents and business organizations, such as Chicago United join CURE to form Alliance for Better Chicago Schools (ABC).

influence on educational practice, then it must become an advocacy organization much like those he had been studying nationally for the Carnegie Foundation (Kyle & Kantowicz, 1992, pp. 149-151 and Moore, 1990, p. 152). In this case, a national study led to a local project. Designs for Change would much later appear to be a key player in founding a national organization of advocacy groups in other cities (National Coalition of Advocates for Students, 1991). As a result of growing Republican influence in the suburbs, Designs for Change is working with groups in areas where a swing of a small vote could have a big impact; their closest ally is a militant group of parents with special education students (Diana Lauber, interview, May 5, 1995).

However, it is only in retrospect that the Chicago Panel on Public School Policy and Designs for Change would emerge as the most important general advocacy groups in Chicago. In the early 1980s, they were just being founded and they would have many rivals before they would emerge as the dominant organizations for changing Chicago schools (O'Connell, 1991, p. 13). Black and Latino groups were also involved in the political game. Along the way, each major advocacy group tried to build alliances and develop well–publicized positions.

At the start, publicity and reform efforts were all focused around the report of a national commission established by the U.S. secretary of education, the National Commission on Excellence in Education (United States Department of Education, 1983). This national report, combined with many others that followed it, highlighted the inferior international position of the United States that was thought to result from America's educational deficits. In Illinois, as in many other states, local efforts followed the national report in that they wanted education made more demanding and more related to science and technology (United States Department of Education, 1983, pp. 32–33). New legislation making schools more accountable was enacted in 1985. This legislation requires the yearly publication of the average scores of graduating students for each school in the newspaper.

Achievements and results are still a major thrust of the legislation of 1988; local concerns have, over time, led to more emphasis on the process of improvement than just on measurable results and accountability. Chart

3.2 shows the goals of the important 1988 reform law (Madigan, 1989, p. 27). None of these goals appears to have been achieved within the time lines specified. Although there may have been some improvement after the fifth year, 50 percent of students may never be near the national norm. The reformers might have accepted these overly specific goals out of frustration with the attempt to change a school bureaucracy that was covering up its own failures.

Originally, the Chicago Board of Education denied that there were major problems. The way the board calculated the annual school dropout rate, for example, made it appear far less than it was (9 percent vs. 47 percent). The specific concern of Latinos that less than half their students were completing high school was ignored. The first study by Aspira, a national Latino organization, was not even publicized until the community organized a demonstration with a coffin to symbolize the dropout and gang killings around one dominantly Latino school. Even then, the Puerto Ricans would have still been ignored if the parade had not been led by the bishop of Chicago. The Irish Catholic policemen would not stop such a parade. Furthermore, the parade culminated in a demonstration next door to a meeting of a national committee on dropouts and, as a result, a *New York Times* reporter wrote a story on the march for the Latin kids (Kyle & Kantowicz, 1992, pp. 15–19).

Perhaps it is because the Chicago Board, like most bureaucratic organizations, uses statistical norms to control their clients that the advocacy organizations used statistics to attack the controlling organization (Foucault, 1979). The legislation would also specify the individual responsibilities of teachers, principals, and top administrators so that the "jailers" would be controlled (Madigan, 1989, pp. 55–66). Initially, Designs for Change and the Chicago Panel built their reputations on uncovering the real failures of the public schools. The two advocacy organizations showed that the high Latino dropout rate reflected a general problem for all students. The schools ignored financial studies by an organization of Chicago Black and White business people, Chicago United (Moore, 1990, p. 161). The schools even stonewalled the local budget hearing results required by the 1985 law—no research or information would influence the Chicago Board of Education. When the Chicago Panel showed that students were regularly scheduled in study halls that did not exist, the system was shown to be absurd (Hess, 1991).

The two advocacy organizations that became most important tried to develop alternatives. Designs for Change developed more action programs based on research, particularly the effective schools literature, and worked with action groups that were mainly Black (Moore, 1990, p. 164). The Chicago Panel wanted instead to show more of the variety of programs that was possible; they continued to be a coalition of many varied organizations with different ideas (Fred Hess, interview, November 18, 1993). The Chicago Panel proposed limited trials of school-based management in a bill

Chart 3.2
Original Goals for Chicago Reform

Sec. 34—1.02. Educational reform. The General Assembly hereby finds and declares that educational reform in school districts organized under this Article shall be implemented in such a manner that:

1. the percentage of entering freshmen who 4 years later graduate from 12th grade from each high school attendance center within the district in each of the 1989–90, 1990–91, 1991–92, 1992–93 and 1993–94 school years exceeds by at least 5% the percentage of similar students graduating from that high school attendance center in the immediately preceding school year;

2. the average daily student attendance rate within the district in each of the 1989–90, 1990–91, 1991–92, 1992–93 and 1993–94 school years exceeds by at least 1% the average daily student attendance rate within the district for the immediately preceding school year;

3. by the conclusion of the 1993–94 school year, the percentage of students within the district failing and not advancing to the next higher grade or graduating is at least 10% less than the percentage of students within the district failing and not advancing to the next higher grade or graduating at the conclusion of the 1987-88 school year;

4. by the conclusion of the 1993–94 school year, at least 50% of all students—regardless of race, ethnicity, gender or income status—in each attendance center within the district score at or above the national norm on a standardized test; and

5. appropriate improvement and progress are realized each school year in each attendance center within the district, when compared to the performance of such attendance center during the immediately preceding school year, in advancing toward and achieving the objectives established by paragraphs 1 through 4 of this Section.

they sponsored in the Illinois legislatures (Kyle & Kantowicz, 1992, p. 218). Danny Solis and United Neighborhood Organization supported this trial. Designs for Change opposed the trial bill since it believed the whole system had to be changed decisively. Meanwhile, Don Moore with Designs for Change had begun running training programs for parents, school monitoring groups, and coalitions with other specific neighborhood groups, as a part of his more activist position. The actions of both advocacy groups were for democracy in the schools, but they rode off in two different directions.

The advocacy groups were transformed by the events of the great flood of protests that Chicago's longest teacher strike unleashed. Top administrators may have believed that they could break the union, but, in any event, they brought on broad and devastating attacks on themselves. At the summit mentioned earlier, which the mayor convened along the lines of the Boston Compact, school administrators painted themselves into a corner. The Boston-like plan would have had businesses providing jobs for high school graduates in return for improvement of student performance. The chief superintendent of Chicago asked the businesses to support more tax money for schools and to promise jobs for graduates whether or not there were any improvements in student performance (Kyle & Kantowicz, 1992, p. 187).

When Mayor Washington convened an expanded summit that involved parents, some very strange alliances started to form. Sokoni Karanja and Coretta McFerren had already emerged as leaders of parent protests against the teachers' strike (Kyle & Kantowicz, 1992, pp. 181–82). However, those two leaders of Black groups had also combined with Puerto Rican and White groups to form the Peoples' Coalition for Education Reform—the term "peoples' organization" is one Saul Alinsky had used repeatedly (Alinsky, 1969). However, some Black leaders, such as Jesse Jackson, who opposed reform and a legislature which was led by White leaders had to be persuaded to accept reform legislation (Lewis & Nakagawa, 1995, p. 89). During the mayor's expanded summit, the other leaders of the poorest Black and Latino parents discovered they could work with some of the top White business executives against the school board as their common enemy.

The informal relations between parents and business leaders could never have been brought off unless a broader coalition with a specific legislative bill had not emerged to provide direction. Designs for Change with Black organizers and local organizations in Black areas had much earlier joined with the dean of Loyola and a group of mostly White Catholics in the Save Our Neighborhood/Save Our City Organization to form Chicagoans United to Reform Education (CURE) (Moore, 1990, p. 164). The Save Our Neighborhood/Save Our City organization was led by two organizers trained by Saul Alinsky (Janet Hudlin, interview, April 11, 1994). CURE, in turn, found a financial backer whose generous support allowed them to hire the Haymarket group (Kyle & Kantowicz, 1992, pp. 212–215).

The Haymarket group had expertise in drafting legislation and in lobbying. But the group also had Al Raby, the Black man who brought Martin Luther King to Chicago. Raby had fought many civil rights battles and was an important supporter of Mayor Washington. The Haymarket group, with its charisma and political symbols, was more than a collection of experts. When the first reform bill was declared unconstitutional, the group helped to persuade a leading law firm to provide hundreds of hours of free work that would ensure an acceptable bill. Before 1989, Moore had hired his own lobbyist, Larry Sufferdin, who continued to represent the organization when the Haymarket group was no longer included.

While adapting to the external world of racial politics the advocacy organizations changed their internal structure as well. Designs for Change was becoming more than the base for one expert, its executive director, Don Moore. A White Ph.D. from Harvard, who is the brother of Susan Johnson, an academic at Harvard, Moore has had to try to cover his tracks and expand his organization's personnel. He is seen by some educators as remote, egotistical, and domineering (James Deanes, interview, April 8, 1994; Sokoni Karanja, interview, April 4, 1994; and Gayle Mindes, interview, November 23, 1993). In bringing in Black community organizers, such as Joan Jay Slater, as well as Latinos onto his staff, he has tried to counteract the remote bias charge. As we noted in Chapter 2, Joan Slater is remote compared to the more popular leader, Coretta McFerren.

Designs for Change has also developed alliances with the coalition of poor Black parents and provided resources for other parent groups such as Schools First. Schools First, for example, rather than Designs for Change, emerged as the leader of grass-roots protests against interference in local school councils (Bradley, 1994, March, p. 10). These organizations have had space in the offices of Designs for Change and have almost become a part of the more dominant organization. Strategic aims are sought from all of the coalitions developed and actions taken by Designs for Change (Eric Outten, interview, April 7, 1994). Unlike the studies by the Chicago Panel, research reported by Don Moore is always closely related to reform policy positions.

During the process of reform, Designs for Change was winning more battles than the Chicago Panel. The bill that the Chicago Panel supported gathered the support of Danny Solis and UNO, but it failed to pass. In the end, UNO and the Chicago Panel joined CURE to form an even broader alliance, Alliance for Better Chicago Schools (ABC). By those involved in the process, Don Moore was rated, together with Designs for Change, as the major influence in bringing about Chicago reform. The panel was only among the top five most influential in securing reform (O'Connell, 1991, p. 32). However, the panel ultimately survived and perhaps even surpassed Designs for Change because it balanced expertise with human concerns better than its rival. Its expertise was demonstrated in writing sections of the reform bill dealing with limitation on expenditures for administrators and with finances. No one would ever label the director of the Chicago Panel a "Fascist for reform" (Diana Lauber, interview, October 11, 1993). Hess has not usually been as personally involved in politics as Don Moore has been. People have doubted whether the leader of the Chicago Panel, Fred Hess, had the will needed to take a strong position and applauded when he did so during the last teachers' negotiations (Gert Westervelt, interview, September 2, 1993).

Between the Chicago Panel and Designs for Change there are sharp differences in how they relate to other people. The leaders at the Chicago Panel have been generalist intellectuals. Fred Hess is more than a specialist in finances; he has been a Methodist minister and holds a Ph.D. in anthropology (Fred Hess, interview, Nov. 18, 1993). His predecessor, Ann Hallett, was an activist from Washington who left the Chicago Panel to direct the Wieboldt Foundation. Ann has subsequently left Wieboldt to found Cross City, where she has been recently joined by Diana Lauber in the effort to expand urban reform, which was discussed in Chapter 2. These are interesting leaders who are neither overwhelmed by their own importance nor likely to adopt fixed positions.

Designs for Change perhaps is not aware of the social distance that it creates. In a short brochure *Network for Leadership Development* it uses the term expert or educator over ten times (Designs for Change, n.d). When asked about this focus, an important staff member insisted that the term community was mentioned often (Susan Davenport, interview, November 24, 1993). A number of educators see Designs for Change personnel as experts who are very fixed in their thinking (Lourdes Monteagudo, Interview, April 13, 1994 and Gerth Westervelt, interview, September 2, 1993). This organization is recognized for its achievements alone.

The limits of either advocacy organization were less important than what they were able to achieve in passing the Reform Act of 1988. The reform alliances among all interested organizations had to proceed from the very start on the basis of there being no additional funds for Chicago schools because of the opposition to giving state aid to Chicago by the rest of the state. Five groups with proposals met with the political leaders to work out a precise and acceptable bill. Usually, political leaders confine this process to their own inner circle. Large groups of supporters went to the capital, Springfield. UNO sent thousands of its supporters, executives flew down in company jets, and Chicago businesspeople, particularly Chicago United, paid for bus load after bus load of poor parents to travel from Chicago. Ceremonies were arranged; chants were recited and big yellow buttons proclaimed, "Don't Come Home Without It" (Kyle & Kantowicz, 1992, p. 253). Ironically, one leader of the reform movement would convince Danny Solis of UNO by saying, "We're going to win because we have more money than you" (Kyle & Kantowicz, 1992, p. 156). Money was still on the agenda for advocacy groups even if it was not for schools. An individual Black parent who could not get recognition said, "Legislation was forced through by power and money" (Lewis & Nakagawa, 1995, p. 90).

The goals of the reform bill reflect a very instrumental view of education (Chart 3.2). The tone of the bill does not capture human involvement. Elaborate calculations of dropouts, daily attendance, promotion numbers, standardized test results, and improvement of records are about as inflexible as you can get. The high and mechanical expectations were, according to one report, set to bring about any improvement in a terrible situation (Hess, interview, April 27, 1994). The editor of *Catalyst* recalls that these goals were forced on the reformers (Linda Lenz, interview, April 29, 1994). The actual process of reform involved people at the local level. Democratic involvement occurred in Chicago in securing legislation and implementing it in Chicago. Although the reform bill seeks to make teachers and principals accountable, in meetings during November 1993, reformers, such as Coretta McFerren, stated they wanted their educators to be more involved and inspirational, qualities that accountability cannot easily produce. The most concrete result of reform in Chicago is the school councils that select the principals and approve the school improvement plans and school budgets. Parents dominate the councils but community representatives, teachers, and student representatives at the high school level are also involved. Students and parents have been involved in various programs including a forum on April 21, 1994, where the new superintendent was offered a new specific constituency that the community organizers felt she did not have (Madeline Talbot, interviews, April 15 and April 28, 1994).

Just as reform appeared to be succeeding by involving so many interests, the victory began to be undone as the result of the appointment of an interim board that was notably lacking in experience. The reform act provided for the appointment of a regular board through the nomination of the elected school councils and their presentation of a list for possible appointment by the mayor. However, in the interim before a nomination procedure could be established, a board composed of business leaders and reformers, including Joan Slay from Designs for Change, was appointed (O'Connell, 1991, p. 27). Diana Lauber from the Chicago Panel was named head of the transition board's budget team. The group was very inexperienced and their inexperience showed very quickly. The mayor, the union, and those in the school bureaucracy may have wanted to have an inexperienced board in order that business as usual could be resumed (Vander Weele, 1994).

The decisions made by this inexperienced board created conditions that would constitute problems for the operation of the schools, if not the reputation of reformers, for many years to come. Teachers were given increases of 7 percent for each year of the three-year contract, and were paid bonuses in addition to educational increments usually received for advancing their education. Security for new certified teachers became a virtual lifetime guarantee, while generous payments for all health premiums were continued by the board for teachers (Vander Weele, 1994, p. 183). None of these conditions could be maintained for more than a year, and even today the teacher member of the board, Adela Greeley, who also helped found PURE, believes they made the right decisions then (Fred Hess, interview, April 27, 1994).

Decisions by the interim board, other than those which involved teachers, caused more problems. The interim board signed a contract with the engineers' union that allowed them to "work as substitutes during those days off and get paid twice for the same day—once for compensatory time and once for their substitute labor" (Vander Weele, 1994, p. 198). The interim board signed a contract for health insurance that was overpriced. It could have saved "15 to 20 percent had it done comparison shopping from the start" wrote Appellate Court Justice Mary Ann G. McMorrow (Vander Weele, 1994, p. 222). However, the most controversial decision made by the interim board was the appointment of a Black superintendent, Ted Kimbrough, who, even until his last days in the office, did not believe in the reform plan (Vander Weele, 1994, p. 167).

After two more changes in superintendent, Richard Stephenson and Argie Johnson, the process of spinning reform's wheels without improving education created intense pressure for conservative actions that were being accepted elsewhere in the country. Frustrations with both reformers and the opponents of reform led to a desire by the foundations to show some results that Chicago's educational reform has produced. The unloved Peter Martinez with the all-powerful MacArthur Foundation has probably been reflecting these pressures and has developed a counterrevolution in Chicago that reflects more acceptable national ideas rather than more controversial local concerns. Martinez wants programs for staff training, reorganization of the central board, and teaching standards (interview, Peter Martinez, April 27, 1994). A number of Black supporters of reform, including the closest ally to Sokoni Karanja, Ben Kendrick, came to doubt the future of reform during the interim board and subsequent moves to more conventional approaches (Ben Kendrick, interview, April 28, 1994).

The two dominant advocacy organizations, Designs for Change and the Chicago Panel, emerged from the interim board with a taste for power whether or not they had learned from the experience how to improve the educational lot of Chicago's children. One academic sees the two dominant White advocacy groups as setting themselves up as a shadow government to the school's governors and, at the same time, becoming more like the school's bureaucracy in the social distance they maintain between them and ordinary people (Dan Lewis, interview, April 13, 1994). The Black leader of the Parent Community Council, which was originally formed by the summit of Mayor Washington, James Deanes, believes that Designs for Change "really messed up when they had a chance to run the interim board" and is biased in favor of changes as its name shows (James Deanes, interview, April 13, 1994). Deanes thinks that the Chicago Panel, in general, is more helpful and makes a limited contribution through the financial analysis it has always provided. He believes that there is an enormous difference between his Black groups and any of the White advocates.

In Chicago, advocacy organizations, for all their success in bringing about reform, have made a critical sacrifice of private gains for public policy (Dan Lewis, interview, April 13, 1993). Advocate groups still have not found a way to increase financial support for schools though their own budgets have risen dramatically (discussed in Chapter 2). Increased foundation support has meant much higher levels of activity for research and community action. The two leading advocacy groups, Designs for Change and the Chicago Panel, have a larger number of people on staff and more impressive offices, the physical signs of their success. However, the children of Chicago have not gained, nor have they found their education more meaningful; certainly, the extremely overcrowded and dilapidated schools for Latino children offer a startling contrast to the opulence of the advocacy organizations (Charles Kyle, interview, November 10, 1993).

VOICES FROM A GROUP WHOSE MISSION IS ACCEPTED

Groups that are not involved in altering the governance of schools or the divisions between them and their constituents have more legitimacy and can be supported by the larger government. In Canada, a number of advocacy groups have received funding and support from the federal government since World War II. No other advocacy group has received more consistent support for education than the Canadian Parents for French (CPF). The founding conference and first newsletter for CPF were supported by the federal Office of the Commissioner of Official Language (Poyen, 1989, p. 89). Support for this organization's total financing was continued by the federal secretary of state. At no time between its founding in 1977 and 1989 did the federal support fall below 64 percent of the organization's total financing (Poyen, 1989, p. 102). In 1982, the secretary of state began funding provincial branches of the organization, an unusual, if not unprecedented, move (Poyen, 1989, p. 106).

The organization was never a tool of the federal government. Rather, CPF was able to lobby effectively with broader political bodies representing all the provinces, such as the Council of Ministers. CPF has also targeted other key federal departments such as the Treasury Board, where decisions that affected bilingual education were made (Poyen, 1989, p. 77). CPF became as much an advocate as those involved in the Chicago reform, though lobbying is less frequently done with legislators; CPF lobbies the bureaucrats more than legislators since its mission is accepted by government.

No American group has shown the degree of involvement with those who develop knowledge for the curriculum than the CPF has displayed. The parents in CPF often go beyond concern with their own child in local groups. As parents advance to the provincial or national organization, they become caught up in the causes that the organization supports (Poyen, 1989, p. 154). For students, the program developed a sense of identity and even a separate high school diploma so that CPF offers meaningful programs for students and parents, but CPF is not a homogeneous group itself. The federal support for the provincial and national organization means that there are alternative leaders. As a result, parent members show less resentment against a single isolated elite who is running the organization; this is a frequent problem when hierarchies dominate as they do in Canada.

Because of the wide-scale involvement of experts with parents in the CPF, the organization provides a critical focus for the development of research and not just for the dissemination of truth. The organization has been repeatedly seen as the clearinghouse for research on bilingual education (Poyen, 1989, pp. 87, 141). However, the parents have been more than critical of the positions of experts, as was found in a California study of gifted programs (Fetterman, 1988). Unlike the parents of gifted students, parents in the CPF give answers to bilingual researchers and do not confine themselves to asking questions (Poyen, 1989, p. 140). It is possible that when Chicago advocates move beyond changing the governance of schools they will be concerned about changing the schools' missions in a similar way.

It is clear that a separate kind of education, one based on knowledge of linguists, became the focus in the French program for parents, teachers, and researchers; this type of focus is rare. The major political battles of Canada in the 1960s involved the acceptance of French as an official language and the promotion of immersion programs in French for English-speaking children. Budget cuts in the 1980s, as well as today, have made the maintenance of these programs a continuing controversy. French immersion has appealed to a minority who have been dominantly upper middle class and who supported learning the French language because of the program's cultural rather than utilitarian aims (Mitchell, 1992).

As the budget crunch has become worse, a number of fringe groups have emerged as advocates for educational excellence in Ontario as well as the western provinces. These organizations have questioned the French program, though the program is not their prime concern (Dan Levson and Colin Penman, interviews, May 26, 1994). Rather, organizations such as Albertans for Quality Education support choice among education programs and act through public forums, roundtables, and conferences. It is difficult for such organizations to implement changes in the educational system when they are focused on individual problems and consciousness-raising experiences with the system. However, the Alberta government has included their ideas in the agenda for reform, while consulting them more than the teachers' union, superintendents, or trustees.

CPF has long been able to reach political leaders at the local and national levels; it has prevented cuts to the French immersion program in Alberta and provides leadership for the educational debate. The CPF suggests how important an advocacy group can be. There are, varied political efforts that promise changes in goals and national competitive efforts by students. These efforts are increasingly seen by the governments and foundations that support them as being removed from the local situations in which they try to bring about change (Warren Chapman, interview, November 22, 1993). The large-scale efforts at reintegration of community services with schools have recently faltered, showing, again, the importance of leadership by an advocacy organization (Cohen, 1994).

RE-LEARNING

One large-scale American effort does appear to be an exception in that it relates national and local efforts on a continuing basis. The program of the Coalition of Essential Schools, centered at Brown University, leads local schools to a humanistic common core of education through the cooperation of some ten state governments (Educational Commission of the States and Coalitions of Essential Schools, 1990). The program was developed in 1984 by Ted Sizer, who had previously been associated with a call for great books in education, the Paideia proposal. The new effort by Sizer was designed to have a wider appeal and to focus on doing the essentials well. Foreign language, physical education, and most electives have been omitted so that there is a focus on mathematics and science together with English and social studies (Sizer, 1984). Essential schools often have four teachers from each area to form a team around which students are grouped.

Unlike other national programs, Sizer's Coalition of Essential Schools has attempted to become involved with state governments. The state governments typically provide about thirty thousand dollars, ideally fifty thousand, for a summer program for individual schools to plan their program. Additional funds for planning and provision for critic teachers and substitute teachers are sought from foundations and businesses so that the teachers involved in the program can learn and travel to other sites (Coalition of Essential Schools, 1992, November, p. 5). Over a million dollars was obtained to get such schools started in Chicago (Lourdes Monteagudo, interview, April 14, 1994). The programs, renamed by Sizer as Re-Learning, provide a direction for education reform. The Educational Commission of the States (ECS), which represents all of the state governments except Montana, has become a sponsor of Sizer's organization for Re-Learning.

In each state, Re-Learning is governed by a steering committee that usually includes the governor, state legislators, representatives of governors from higher education, and teacher unions. In Illinois, the group is chaired by the state superintendent of education and Re-Learning is housed at the Illinois State Board of Education (Illinois Alliance of Essential Schools, 1991–92). In Chicago, the deputy mayor for education, Lourdes Monteagudo, saw the program as a way of clustering schools and relating the usually separate city and state policies.

The involvement of government with education extends in many directions. The steering committee is supplemented by working members, a "cadre" from professional organizations that are involved at the top level and provide more specific technical and program support than their superiors. In Illinois, only the University of Illinois does research on the Re-Learning project (Warren Chapman, interview, November 22, 1992). Each of the two competing teacher organizations has been persuaded to be involved so that they could watch their competitor. The staff officer for the Educational Commission of the States particularly helped local schools obtain grants from foundations as well as advised on negotiating with state government offices and professional organizations.

Re-Learning, with the involvement of ECS, is particularly helpful in building a structure for obtaining support from foundations and business.

In states that do not sponsor Re-Learning, such as California, much more diverse networks are needed to support cooperating schools (Coalition of Essential Schools, 1993, March, p. 4). The California picture is now very complicated since ECS has been called on to redesign that state's educational program. ECS is also planning to become more politically active and to promote some model programs as well (Harp, 1994, January, p. 11).

However, the political support cuts two ways. The Coalition of Essential Schools is often pulled into political wars as a result of the alliance with political bodies. The Illinois Alliance has seen its growth limited to twenty schools because the Illinois State Board of Education is dominated by rural areas. The demand for new school affiliates for Re-Learning has come from suburban schools. The crisis in Chicago has been in the inner city schools (Warren Chapman, interview, November 22, 1993). The development of a system in Chicago is further compounded by the lack of feeder schools that operate on similar principles to the high schools in Chicago since there are few junior highs or middle schools there. In the suburbs of Illinois, as well as more generally, the essential school concept is more attractive to the less specialized middle schools than it is to high schools because of their departmental specializations. The coalition has probably opened itself up to even more attacks by jumping into the unknown world of charter schools (Celis, 1994, March). The coalition's vision has not been extended to the political process.

Besides politics, the curriculum for Sizer and CES presents problems. The lack of specializations is the largest difficulty for the CES. The emphasis on integrating specialists means that the oracle, Sizer, does not want just generalist teachers (Sizer, 1984, p. 191). However, a state, such as New Mexico, is defined by CES as making progress when it reduces the number of recognized specialties from 134 to 25 (Coalition of Essential Schools, 1993, March p. 7). The further problem remains that arbitrary exclusions of foreign languages or vocational education are justified on the basis of pedagogy rather than knowledge. The pedagogy calls for a new vision of teaching less or applying conceptual ideas through exhibitions rather than a focus on the organization's methods and principles of knowledge (Sizer, 1984, p. 135). A broader philosophy and more specific expectations for teachers are both needed for CES.

Unlike the Canadian Parents for French, the Coalition of Essential Schools has not focused on a particular kind of knowledge, nor has it caught the research interest of scholars who care about the same problems as do teachers and parents. CES also seems to reinforce the division between educational and related fields of research. To go beyond a first faltering attempt at educational reform through political involvement, one needs a more integrated curriculum to complement the teaching approaches and schedules. Cross-disciplinary integration is more than being "unbounded by disciplines"; it is being framed by concerns and claims to know (Coalition of Essential Schools, 1992, November, p. 4).

The CES has sponsored studies of itself, particularly, by staff ethnologists who have produced some very critical reports. It appears that only concepts related to teaching, such as the student as a worker and teacher as a coach, have been widely accepted by schools in the confederacy (Muncey & McQuillan, 1992). Changes in the curriculum and in the school structure appear more imaginary than the concrete changes teachers can initiate (Muncey & McQuillan, 1992, p. 65). Even the teacher vote to join the coalition is frequently not very meaningful for those involved. When only one part of the school joins CES, the divisions between that part of the school that takes up even a few of the program's ideas and those who do not are often intense. The critical studies of CES have not led to a change in the principles around which Sizer expects the program to develop.

The state politics and the school power struggles are frequently compounded by community controversies over the particular pedagogy advocated by Sizer. Extreme right-wing groups have frequently objected to the inductive learning and relativism of values that they have detected as a form of inquiry-based learning (Coalition of Essential Schools, 1993, May, p. 3). In Alton, Illinois, one such right-wing religious and political leader was outsmarted; the Alliance leaders successfully labeled her before she could stereotype them in the media and in group meetings (Warren Chapman, interview: November 22, 1993). However, local victories have not established a more general claim to acceptance for this educational program.

The program seems ethnocentric as well as politically naive. Though CES sought one of its initial schools in Calgary, according to John McCarthy, who was the separate school superintendent at the time, no other school in Canada joined subsequently. Nor has the program been copied in other English-speaking countries. In contrast, the National Writing Project, which spread to Canada within a year of its start in Oakland, has also been widely adopted in Australia as well as other countries (Batiuk, 1993). Within the United States there seems little sense in ignoring vocational education, as CES does, because vocational education has the most tightly organized lobby of any teacher group (Toch, 1991, pp. 107–110). Vocational educators could also be helpful in the practical assessments of general ideas that Sizer wants.

This coalition needs to go beyond connecting with everything that is going on politically (Coalition of Essential Schools, 1992, November, pp. 1 & 2). The Educational Commission of the States, CES's partner, has not seemed to be aware that they need greater direction either; they are only aware that they have gone beyond a limited function of information exchange and have crossed "the line into advocacy" (Jennifer Crandall, letter, April 30, 1993). ECS is reportedly planning to become a more active political organization. In the case of Kentucky, which is discussed in the next chapter, ECS provided general advice, helped select a consultant, and then disappeared (Harp, 1994, January, p. 11).

At the school level, the greatest concern of Re-Learning is to provide support for local teachers who are attempting change along the lines of the coalition's principles. The local teachers are provided with training sessions, a national faculty, and outsiders who serve as critics, as well as a large number of other teachers who are supposedly further along in understanding CES rules (Coalition of Essential Schools, 1993, January, pp. 4, 9). The support of other teachers can be a part of a year-long "trek" process between neighboring schools (Coalition of Essential Schools, 1992, November, p. 5), and schools in many states are just beginning to hold these treks (Holly Bartunek, interview, April 27, 1994). All of the procedures by CES are ways to deal with the problem of teacher isolation during change. CES has not suggested a critical base for deciding what changes need to be made in education and how commitment to those changes needs to be nourished. The culture of educational change in the United States has perhaps been accepted too much by Sizer and his organization. Even when they attempt to change, they assume the problem is one of how to do it, not why we should want it done. The Annenberg Foundation, with its enormous gift, has provided Sizer with a great opportunity to develop the coalition, but as Chapter 8 will show, the National Writing Project is more meaningful for those involved even though it has less money.

A FOOTNOTE FOR FREIRE

Meaningful programs are the aim of Paulo Freire. The Brazilian educator has combined work with peasant groups becoming literate and theorizing about the empowering process since 1940. The Chicago reforms could sense that their social movement, like those in underdeveloped areas, can provide a model for education in schools. Their leadership could make them into more than an interest group which is preoccupied with criticizing the bureaucracy. Because education in schools will always be rather ritualized, involvement in the social movements is a necessary supplement to formal education (Shor & Freire, 1987, p. 3). Cooperative programs and teacher advocates for cultural minorities would be related to cooperative efforts and advocacy organizations in society.

The Canadian Parents for French represents an educational innovation that is blessed by the powers that control the government and the class structure. When I discussed the bilingual program with Danny Solis in Chicago, he asserted that it could only occur as an option after the French had scared the dominant English group; only in opposition did he see it as a model for Spanish-English programs (Dan Solis, interview, November 24, 1994). Knowledge and education are a result of the dominant groups' hegemony, and their resistance from subordinate folks, counterhegemony (Freire & Macedo, 1987, p. 78). The development of a program that links with those resisting French immersion for their children is the challenge of CPF. The new advocacy groups are from constituencies where French immersion has not yet been organized. Articulations of separate interests appear to precede any effective cooperation.

Finally, the Re-Learning project is a result of dominant groups who are ignoring the ordinary people while seeking a global integration of school knowledge. Disciplinary language of experts can be combined with the commonsense language of peasants (Freire & Macedo, 1987, p. 72). Such combinations often occur through the use of Bible-like proverbs. Such proverbs are richer than the slogans of "student as worker" or "teacher as coach." In teaching literacy to children or adults, Freire insists that the poor and the experts both have language and both can improve their understanding by working with each other. He stresses the need for structure and correction, but states, "Practice needs evaluation like fish need water and farming needs rain" (Freire & Macedo, 1987, p. 91). Freire suggests a poetic vision for education which contains contradictions and these conflicts are overcome by living in a community. Visions for Sizer are goals that are only a part of a single-dimensional and rationalistic approach to education in which education becomes instrumental and fragmented in its realization.

LESSONS FOR STUDENTS

Creative thinking is involved in seeing and understanding the dilemmas that confront an advocacy organization. The experience of reform organizations can itself be a significant source for students to learn how to deal with conflicts. Reform groups have not seized the opportunity that Freire has suggested to use their own movement and the differences among their own advocacy groups for the school's curriculum. Rather, reformers have taken ideas from all over the country and have promoted programs based on experiences other than their own.

The closest alternative to using the heightened aspirations from movements of reform has probably been the Algebra Project that the former civil rights leader Robert Moses, as a concerned parent, developed originally near Boston (Moses et al., 1989). Moses believes that motivation is more important than ability for achievement levels to rise in mathematics among minority groups. To foster this motivation for achievement among the minorities, he draws on analogies to community efforts in the civil rights movement. Cooperative learning is stressed and the students develop an intuitive understanding that is based on physical events and moves to models of the events where symbolic reasoning is used.

In order to translate physical events to mathematical symbols, Moses has drawn from the civil rights movement the three parallels of "cast down your bucket where you are," the centrality of families for organizing, and the empowerment of people. From the local scene, physical changes, such as riding a city transit train, are used to teach "number line, displacements and the use of integers as position coordinates and as displacements" (Chicago

Panel on Public School Policy and Finance, 1992). The students' ordinary language is transformed into very structured language and the structured English to mathematical symbols. Families and community members who act like families have become supporters of the programs by teaching in a community center. They have parents learning algebra along with their children, and promote algebra as a tool against racism. Students are empowered as they and their families learn that, for inner city children particularly, the decision to take algebra in grade seven will open doors for advancement and learn that being "parked" in basic mathematics closes off future opportunities. Teachers, as well as students, cease to be afraid to show that they are learners in mathematics. Though supplemented by a standard textbook, the current grade six program is being extended to grades seven, eight and nine (Moses et al., 1989, p. 429). Just as a civil rights leader without political experience, Fannie Lou Hamer, knew she could ask the right questions of the Democratic party's politicians in 1964, students can ask direct questions and turn their potential limitations into actual strengths in today's classes for minority children.

The Algebra Project has shown how analogies to social movements can be turned into a curriculum program. The three-year program came to Chicago in 1992 and 150 schools sought to be among the 7 schools that would be included. Robert Moses says that, as a result of school reform, there were community groups of grandparents, parents, and teachers in community centers such as the South Austin Community Coalition that were doing sample lessons in Chicago (Chicago Panel on Public School Policy and Finance, 1992). Moses also believes that, since Chicago reformers had focused so much on governance, they were ready to turn to curriculum. The community led the reformers and educators in Chicago to support the Algebra Project. To learn algebra would be like learning to read so that the people could qualify to vote in the American South; freedom would be the result of education in both cases.

Aside from the Algebra Project, the experience of advocacy organizations has not been used as a model for the curriculum where you would expect it, social studies and English. Reform groups have repeatedly reacted to current practices rather than developing their own curriculum program. Indeed, one approach to dilemmas defines them as a sense of alternatives to current school practices (Berlak & Berlak, 1981). Critical teaching of the school dilemmas never seems to move beyond conflicts of alternatives with present practices to an integration with past traditions. Only the Algebra Project has done this.

The dilemmas that organizations must face and that advocacy groups must learn to think about can be grasped more clearly by the following example:

Shawn and his sister Tish tried to enroll in a Chicago high school when school opened in the fall. There was one little problem. The school nurse sent them home with a note saying that Shawn and Tish would not be allowed in school until they received measles vaccines.

Weeks passed and the children did not return to school. Finally, the children came with a note from a clinic documenting that they had received their vaccinations. The school attendance clerk accepted the note and told the children their mother would now need to come into school so they could be reinstated. Shawn explained that their mother had some problems, mainly with drugs, and was not around much. The children often stayed with their grandmother, he explained, and suggested the attendance clerk could call her. The clerk informed Shawn and Tish that their mother, as their legal guardian, was the only one who could get them reinstated in school and she had to do so in person. (Carter, 1993)

The problem of relating individual families to schools is so substantial that a whole host of reforms will be reviewed in Chapter 6.

The problem now is the conflict for advocacy groups that integrated services pose. Don Moore, with Designs for Change, long ago concluded that advocacy groups must focus their resources on changing the system because individual cases are too time-consuming (Moore et al., 1983). Organizations that are more idealistic, such as PURE, do try to write letters in an attempt to advise concerned individuals. There is also the obvious alternative of developing ombudsmen to help people. In addition, there is the long tradition in social work, which finds that both individual and structural approaches are needed.

In considering both individual and system changes, there is the general issue that compromise involves a choice between principles rather than between good and bad (Eby, 1954). Another set of principles involves the good of the organization and the good of students in the system; hypocrisy alone can justify attention to the private interest of the organization over the needs of those it claims to serve (Mitchell, 1966). For students, as for advocates, there can be "a dynamic relationship between thinking and acting" in developing school improvement plans (Moore et al., 1983, p. 79). However, if we listen to Simone Weil, a person's greatest temptation is a desire to live in a perfect world and the tension between acting and thinking is to be valued (Blum & Seidler, 1980).

Learning to discuss dilemmas that are exemplified in advocacy organizations, as well as in life, would be an enormous step over conventional approaches where the schools' programs still seem to be a museum of morality (Waller, 1967). Conflicts in social and human affairs are ignored (Massialas, 1969). Classes often consist of lists, definitions, defensive simplifications, and mystifications to avoid discussion of controversial subjects (McNeil, 1988). Schools might yet be more than places where teachers tell lies about the way the world ought to be rather than deal with the conflict within even the most dedicated attempts at reform. As the amount of money for education reform grows enormously, these issues become more critical; the Annenberg Foundation's gift raises the question of the results which can be expected from their gifts to reform (Olson & Summerfeld, 1994, June). The benefit for the students is something that reform advocates, as well as the community, need to consider. The involvement of students in the movement can energize their education; borrowing the dilemmas from reform can make their education more realistic.

REFERENCES

Alinsky, S. (1969). *Reveille for radicals*. New York: Random House.
Alinsky, S. (1971). *Rules for radicals*. New York: Random House.
Batiuk, M. (1993). The National Writing Project. Unpublished course paper. The University of Calgary.
Berlak, A. & Berlak, H. (1981). *The dilemmas of schooling*. London: Metheun.
Blum, L. & Seidler, V.J. (1989). *A truer liberty*. New York: Routledge.
Bradley, A. (1994, March 2). Chicago board rescinds order aimed at local councils. *Education Week*, 13(23), 10.
Carter, J.(1993). Parents must be seen as true partners. *Catalyst*, 5(3), 21–23.
Celis, W. (1994, March 19). Private groups to run 15 schools in experiment by Massachusetts. *New York Times*, 1, 8.
Chicago Panel on Public School Policy and Finance (1992, April). The Algebra Project. *Reform Report*, 2(8), 1–11.
Coalition of Essential Schools (1992, November). What works, what doesn't: Lessons from essential school reform. *Horace*, 9(2), 1–7.
Coalition of Essential Schools (1993, March). What's essential? Integrating the curriculum of the essential school. *Horace*, 9(4), 1–7.
Coalition of Essential Schools (1993, May). Essential collaborators: Parents, school and community. *Horace*, 9(4), 1–7.
Cohen, D.L. (1994, June 1). Demise of Pew project offers lessons to funders. *Education Week*, 13(6), 1, 9.
Designs for Change (n.d.). *Network for leadership development—the network advantage*. Chicago: Designs for Change.
Eby, K. (1954). *The God in you*. Chicago: University of Chicago Press.
Educational Commission of the States and the Coalition of Essential Schools (1990, Fall). Re-Learning orientation packet. Denver and Providence.
Fetterman, D. (1988). *Excellence and equality*. Albany: State University of New York Press.
Freire, P. & Macedo, D. (1987). *Literacy*. New York: Bergin & Garvey.
Gross, N. (1958). *Who runs the schools?* New York: John Wiley.
Gross, N. & Herriot, R.(1965). *Leadership in public schools*. New York: John Wiley.
Harp, L. (1994, January 26). New challenges seen as key tests of E.C.S.'s political muscle skills. *Education Week*, 13(18), 11.
Hess, G. A. (1992). *School restructuring, Chicago style*. Newbury Park, California: Corwin.
Hess, G. A. (1994, May) Outcomes of Chicago school reform: Introduction. *Education and Urban Society*, 26(3), 203-219.
Illinois Alliance of Essential Schools (1991–92). *The Illinois alliance of essential schools*. Chicago: Author.

Kyle, C. & Kantowicz, E. (1992). *Kids first - primero los niños*. Springfield: Illinois Issues.

Lewis, D.A. & Nakagawa, K. (1995). *A study of school decentralization*. Albany: State University of New York.

Louis, K.S. & Miles, M.B. (1990). *Improving the urban high school*. New York: Teachers College Press.

Madigan, M. (1989, September). *Chicago school reform*. Springfield: General Assembly, State of Illinois.

Massialas, B. (1969). *Education and the political system*. Reading, Massachusetts: Addison-Wesley.

McNeil, L.M. (1988). *Contradictions of control*. New York: Routledge.

Mitchell, S. (1966). The people shall judge. Presentation for Annual Meeting of the Alberta Home and School Association.

Mitchell, S. (1992). *Innovation and Reform*. York, Ontario: Captus Press.

Moore, D. (1990). Voice and choice in Chicago. In Clune, W.H. and Witte, J.F. (Eds.) *Choice and control in American education*, Vol. 2 (pp. 153–198). London: Falmer Press.

Moore, D., Soltman, S., Manar, U., Steinberg, L., & Fogel, D. (1983). *Standing up for children*, Chicago: Designs for Change.

Moses, R., Kamii, M., Swap, S. & Howard, J. (1989). The Algebra Project; Organizing in the spirit of Ella. *Harvard Education Review*, 59(4), 423–443.

Muncey, D. & McQuillan, P. (1992). The dangers of assuming a consensus for change: Some examples for the coalition of essential schools. In Hess, G.A. (Ed.), *Empowering teachers and parents* (pp. 47–70). Westport, Connecticut: Bergin & Garvey.

National Coalition of Advocates for Students (1991). *The good common school*. Boston: The National Coalition of Advocates for Students.

North Central Regional Educational Laboratory (1992). *1992 Chicago School Reform Study Project*. Oak Brook, Illinois: North Central Regional Educational Laboratory.

O'Connell, M. (1991). *School Reform Chicago Style*. Chicago: The Center for Neighborhood Technology.

Olson, L. & Summerfeld, M. (1994, June 8). Annenberg gift may focus on 4 urban areas. *Education Week*, 13(37), 1, 14.

Organization for Quality Education (1994, June). *Forum*. Waterloo, Ontario: Organization for Quality Education.

Poyen, J.M. (1989). Canadian Parents for French: A national pressure group in Canadian education. Master's Thesis, The University of Calgary.

Sarason, S. (1971; 2nd ed., 1982). *The culture of the school and the problem of change*. New York: Allyn & Bacon.

Shor, I. & Freire, P. (1987). *A pedagogy for liberation*. New York: Bergin & Garvey.

Sizer, T.R. (1984). *Horace's compromise*. Boston: Houghlin Mifflin.

Sizer, T.R. (1992). *Horace's school*. Boston: Houghlin Mifflin.

Toch, T. (1991). *In the name of excellence*. New York: Oxford.

United States Department of Education (1983). *Meeting the challenge: recent efforts to improve education across the nation*. Washington, D.C.: U.S. Department of Education.

Vander Weele, M. (1994). *Reclaiming our schools*. Chicago: Loyola University Press.

Waller, W. (1967). *The sociology of teaching.* New York: John Wiley.

Chapter 4

Political Myths and Individual Awareness

> When some 400 local organizers for the town forums gathered in Lexington to discuss the details of the event, Mr. Prichard told them they were "the shock troops in the battle for educational improvement." "As long as I draw breath," he said, "I will give everything to the cause." And he kept his word, working diligently until the day the forums were to take place, even though he had lost his sight from complications of diabetes and was on dialysis for kidney failure. On the day of the forums, he entered the hospital and was unable to deliver the televised address. He died a month later. Mr. Prichard's long-time friend, former Gov. Bert T. Combs, stepped in that night for Mr. Prichard and the forums went on as planned. (Walker, 1988, May)

Edward Prichard's dedication to education in Kentucky has made him into a martyr for educational reform in that state and for the advocacy group that continues to carry his name there. The committee that Ed Prichard founded has become a much more inclusive advocacy group than those in Chicago. In Chicago, Mayor Washington and the various mothers and fathers of reform have been somewhat similarly eulogized by the movement which has used more confrontational tactics there. In western Canada, Premier Ralph Klein has reached new heights of popularity as the Conservative leader in a province that has reduced governmental expenditures and reorganized the educational system. The alliance in Canada is built on informal relationships among business, religious, and political groups. Premier Klein has listened to right-wing groups which have developed as local advocacy groups; several Canadian provinces have begun to move away from a primary reliance on federal advocacy organizations.

Each of the three heroes has been linked to radical reforms. Each of the drastic transformations has been a reaction to crises. Kentucky had its entire educational system declared unconstitutional and the Prichard Committee reacted by creating a new system of education which is based on the advice of national experts so that they would be recognized as one of the most progressive states in the United States. After a series of such strikes, Chicago's residents confronted the longest teacher strike in their history; a variety of groups attempted through their alliances to take control of their educational system while they worked with Mayor Washington. In Alberta, a conservative coalition responded to a growing government debt and accepted Premier Klein's plan to take the control of educational and governmental services away from professionals, promising future participation to parents and citizens.

In Kentucky, an exceptional individual and an elite committee helped launch a systematic program of innovations. In Alberta, radical reductions in education have come from a top-down effort by government, but that effort has coincided with the emergence of new interest groups, particularly when their representatives were invited to roundtable discussions. In contrast, Chicago has been more of a grass-roots effort; business has been part of the unstable pattern of alliances that has been trying to find additional funding for reform. The more unified efforts in Kentucky and Alberta both show the dominance that business can exert over education. Kentucky shows business as part of a unified advocacy group which is working for greater funding and improvements in education. Alberta subordinates education to a merger of business and political interests which sees education as a priority among governmental expenditures, all of which are undesirable.

In all three of the large-scale innovations, marginal and alienated groups emerge. Right-wing fringe groups have been previously mentioned, but, in Alberta, they join with business to set policy. The marginal group that appears to be the most alienated in each of these revolutionary changes is teachers. School-based management, which is supposed to focus on empowering people in local schools, seems to ignore the central teacher-student nexus. Right-wing political and religious groups are challenging the reforms in Kentucky and Illinois. No one is speaking very strongly for teachers and students; teachers in all three situations are withdrawing as their way of controlling change. Parents are most influential in Chicago, while educational experts have become very important in Kentucky. The educational experts are subordinated to business people and politicians in Alberta and in Chicago; only through broader advocacy groups can they hope to affect innovations.

Because of the alienation of teacher and student groups, the meaning of any innovation is more fragmented for them than it is for the dominant decision makers in schools. Specific innovations, as well as the general experiences with reform, reveal that local school boards are losing power in the innovation game. Power conflicts and fragmented perspectives occur in spite of the claims for autonomy, such as charter schools. Empowerment for the have-nots may have to develop through confrontation, as Alinsky suggested, but the early history of the Prichard Committee in Kentucky shows that consensus and support for education can be developed by an elite association.

A COMMITTEE IN KENTUCKY

Edward Prichard was initially asked, in 1980, to head a thirty-member Committee on Higher Education for Kentucky's future by the state government. Prichard had become a legend in Kentucky after his work for the New Deal and a subsequent, ill-fated campaign for the Senate. In his later years, "Prich" had become a dazzling and brilliant statesman for Kentucky in order to bring about social change (Walker, 1988). From their initial quasi-governmental position, Prichard and the Committee on Higher Education completed their task and published the report, *In Pursuit of Excellence*. In order to ensure that its report did not remain on the shelf, the committee reconstituted itself as a private, nonprofit citizens' group known as the Prichard Committee on Academic Excellence. Its original report on higher education seemed to require a complete change in basic education from kindergarten to high school. The committee arranged public forums and one night in November 1984, they heard the voices of over twenty thousand Kentuckians echoing throughout the state (Adams, 1993).

After these efforts, the Prichard Committee was able to obtain new legislation and make modest improvements in selected high schools; also, they arranged publicity campaigns of educational needs together with the largest employers in the state. Suddenly, all progress seemed to halt when a new governor, Martha Collins, refused to increase taxes for education (Parish, 1990). The committee then challenged the state's entire educational system since it believed that the state was failing to provide financing that would make possible a reasonable education for all school districts as required by the state constitution. The Prichard Committee was a powerful force in Kentucky as it was identified with a number of prominent individuals, including four former governors. One of the former governors, Bert Combs, led the team of lawyers that argued the constitutional case against the state's educational system. Combs had brought Prichard back from oblivion and opened the town forums on Prichard's death (Dove, 1991). Ultimately, the decision of the court went further than either Combs or Prichard had ever expected. The courts mandated that a new educational system must be established. The higher funding that Collins had refused was obtained; a host of new programs were required to meet the court's demands.

By convening forums to influence the new legislation, the Prichard Committee had come a long way. They had come from simply serving as an

arm of impersonal government to becoming an advocacy organization that
was trying to articulate personal visions for the future. In the statewide
television forums, citizens offered ideas for reforms and dramatized the need
for a drastically new kind of education (Adams, 1993). These
teleconferences led to a permanent increase in the number of people
involved in Kentucky's reform initiatives. The Prichard Committee doubled
in size, going from thirty to sixty members. A Prichard Alliance of five
hundred local leaders was launched after the teleconference.

The committee was becoming a social movement that allowed otherwise
alienated people to voice their views (Parish, 1990). The people in the
mountains, those of Eastern Kentucky in particular, distrusted their local
school boards. The boards were seen to be unresponsive since people
believed they were controlled by friends and relatives of board members.
Floyd County, a county especially torn apart by partisanship and alienation
in the past, developed both a new nonpartisan organization as well as a new
political one (p. 22). To overcome the fears of people, such as those in
Floyd County, the Kentucky Education Reform Act (KERA) was designed
to eliminate nepotism within school boards.

The 1990 act also led to a more extensive series of networks and activities
designed to involve a lot of ordinary people in the movement. Local
branches of the Prichard Committee were organized in school districts so
other local problems would be recognized; by 1993 there were sixty districts
with organized committees (*Education Week*, 1993). Businesses and
foundations which are supporting the Prichard Committee are shown on
Chart 4.1, but there are many other indirect connections. In collaboration
with the national organization of business leaders, the Business Roundtable,
a coalition of business, public, and private leaders was organized. This
organization of business, civic, government, education, and union leaders was
called the Partnership for Kentucky School Reform and operated along with
the Prichard Committee. The leaders of the partnership made a ten-year
commitment to educational reform and contributed to a public relations
campaign about KERA. Over $1.5 million was raised for the campaign,
which included newspaper inserts, a KERA school bus, and a "fly around"
for four sites in the state in one day by CEOs of the largest businesses in
Kentucky (Adams, 1993, p. 6). The Prichard Committee also brought
together groups other than those of business to support KERA. The
Education Coalition of the major state educational organizations was
formed. Collaborative relations were established with numerous
organizations that were indirectly concerned with education, such as the
Kentucky Council on Science and Technology. Discussions with the
Kentucky Council of Churches were also held (Adams, 1993, p. 8). Plans for
further meetings with the Council of Churches have been made (Cindy
Heine, interview, May 8, 1995). In order to deal with these varied
relationships, the Prichard Committee had a staff of sixteen by 1993 from its
original lone executive director, Robert Sexton (Adams, 1993, p. 4). Mr.

Sexton is a historian with great concern for details; he has provided continuity for the organization even when he was supposedly on sabbatical leave at Harvard.

The Prichard reformers attempted to link Kentucky with the nation rather than allowing it to remain a marginal area or island. Contacts have also been maintained with several of the Chicago organizations, including the United Neighborhood Organization directed by Danny Solis. The national organizations involved include Ted Sizer's Coalition of Effective Schools and the Educational Commission of the States. Consultants, such as David Hornbeck, were selected from a national pool. Hornbeck has emerged as the great advocate for comprehensive reform in education. The first appointed state commissioner of education, Thomas Boysen, was brought in from California. As the previous commissioner had been elected, the change was meant to enhance educational expertise as opposed to political ties. All members of the State Department of Education were fired and then rehired, if qualified, so that, at the state level, as well as in local communities, expertise was emphasized. The Prichard Committee has attempted to mobilize citizens and experts in order to ensure that the promises of KERA are fulfilled. The Prichard group wants to be more than a narrow group that performs a task. The committee has been enlarged to its legal limit of 100 members (Adams, 1993, p.18). Most importantly, one must realize that the Prichard Committee has never wanted to be an interest group which would remain a permanent part of Kentucky politics. The committee was originally seen as a temporary organization and has only gradually become a continuing alliance. Membership on the Committee is still expected to change. When older members have chosen to retire, the committee has become a training ground for new leaders. The current governor and lieutenant governor are former members, as are a large number of board and commission members for the state.

In developing public leadership, the Prichard Committee has crossed the line between public leadership and private groups in society (Berger, 1979, p. 4). It has moved from a government-appointed agency to a catalyst involving the many groups in the Kentucky reform. The committee has linked local communities, particularly in eastern Kentucky, to the educational establishment. Recently, it has become more of a monitor of change, determining the effectiveness of reform (for the primary school in particular), overseeing school-based management, and evaluating the integrated services for children built around the school (Rath et al., 1992 and Rath et al., 1993). The Prichard Committee attends meetings of educational groups around the state, has organized district committees to monitor as well as support school reforms, and has hired outside consultants to do studies of the implementation process (Business Roundtable, 1992, p. 23).

Chart 4.1
The Prichard Committee Contributors

The Annie E. Casey Foundation, Inc.
Ashland Oil, Inc.
Bell South Foundation
Business Roundtable
Carnegie Corporation of New York
General Electric Foundation
Humana Inc.
James Graham Brown Foundation, Inc.
Knight Foundation
Lexmark International, Inc.
Liberty National Bank and Trust Company
South Central Bell Corporation
Toyota Motor Manufacturing, U.S.A., Inc.
The UPS Foundation, Inc.
and numerous Kentucky citizens, businesses, Prichard Committee members, and
Prichard Alliance members.
(Raths et al., 1992; and Raths et al., 1993).

The Prichard Committee moved to this more informal type of influence
in order to secure the promise of the KERA reforms. It has conceded
modifications in the law that prevented right-wing groups from claiming that
KERA emphasized affective goals rather than academic aims before the
opposition could make these and many other changes (Harp, 1994, May, p.
24). Through such social sensitivity as this, the Prichard Committee can be
said to articulate the values of families rather than impersonal institutions
(Glazer, 1979). The committee's position appears to correspond closely to
the model of mediating structures which is advocated by right-wing theorists
(Berger, 1979). As a mediating institution, the committee avoids partisan
politics and casts its legislative ideas as general ideas rather than specific
proposals, as the advocacy groups in Chicago have done. Again, unlike the
Chicago groups, it does not lobby but attempts to involve influential leaders.
The committee members see themselves as volunteers and do not claim
expert status. However, the committee has increasingly relied on experts
whose language and behavior have been noticeably different from those of
its founders, "Prich" and Bert Combs (Dove, 1991, p. 66).

Because of their reliance on educational experts who are progressive, the
committee has been opposed by local right-wing organizations in Kentucky
who assert support for more accepted goals. The Eagle Forum founded by
Phyllis Schlafly, does not see the Prichard Committee or KERA as
representing its families' values. The vice president of the Eagle Forum,
Donna Shedd, objects to the whole-child philosophy in KERA (Harp, 1994,
May, p. 22). Local groups organizing petitions against KERA have included
Families United for Morals in Education, America Awaken, Parents and

Professionals Involved in Education, and the Southern Exchange Foundation. Most of these groups want a voucher plan of choice rather than an improvement in public education such as KERA. More vocal supporters of right-wing positions want instruction in phonics, a mandate to spend state funds only in classrooms, and open enrollment (Harp, 1994, February, p. 14).

Within the educational establishment, the school board association in Kentucky has seen the school site-based management councils as invading their turf; a number of school superintendents see the Prichard Committee as elitist, and many teachers feel that they are being forced into a march that is much too fast (Adams, 1993, p. 11 and Appalachia Education Laboratory, 1992, September, pp. 2–3). These educational groups want only a slight modification of the status quo. The Prichard Committee is mediating between very opposite positions. It builds its support both by training parents and involving important decision makers while maintaining its own nonprofit tax status. The jargon used by the commissioner of education, Thomas Boysen, as well as other educators, had become a problem (Harp, 1994, May); the committee has had to try to make the positions of educational experts more intelligible for ordinary people while eliminating the objectionable aspects of KERA.

THE SILVER BULLET OF SYSTEMIC REFORM

The passage of the Kentucky Educational Reform Act in 1990 meant that the educational establishment became increasingly involved with the Prichard Committee in implementing reform, while the Prichard Committee did studies of reform's success. As Chart 4.2 shows, KERA has reinforced both expertise and credentials of all personnel and governors of education in its path of comprehensive changes. The former secretary of labour under Jimmy Carter, Ray Marshall, praised the system of rewarding high-performing schools while assisting those that do not make progress (Marshall & Tucker, 1992). Nepotism by school board members is no longer possible, though friendships still influence the appointments of teachers. Board members themselves must be minimally educated for their job. The operation of the school is removed from the control of the school board members by the appeals procedures for teachers that are fired and by the establishment of school councils.

Aside from school board members, education and specific requirements are specified for everyone in the school system. Education programs for superintendents, principals, and teachers include assessment procedures to monitor their behavior even before new performance tests for students were developed. The principals spend one year in an internship similar to that of teachers after passing a generic exam on communication skills, general knowledge, and professional concepts as well as current instructional and administrative practices in Kentucky. The program for superintendents must provide and assess the core concepts of management, school-based decision making, Kentucky school law and finance, and school curricula and assessment. The new professionals are to be well groomed educators! The extensive in-service program for teachers includes affective awareness and sensitivity training (Commonwealth of Kentucky, n.d., p. 21). The term "distinguished educator" is applied to teachers who are selected to assist poorly performing schools or whom the department wishes to recognize as "distinguished." Unfortunately, no similar name is given to parents who are expected to be involved in the wide-ranging set of reforms.

The Kentucky reforms have been widely praised outside Kentucky. A national publication has called them "the most comprehensive and integrated piece of school-reform legislation ever enacted" (*Education Week*, 1993, April, p. 3). The former editor for education of the *New York Times* has, similarly, seen Kentucky's program as a climax to current reform efforts (Fiske, 1990, April, p. 8). The Business Roundtable has said that only in Kentucky have they completed the immense task of establishing state learning goals, developing curricula and student testing programs aligned with those goals, trained educators to use them, and held schools strictly accountable for progress (Business Roundtable, 1994).

Parent involvement was an important goal for KERA, a goal that is not being achieved. Many parents do not believe in KERA because they still report that they do not know very much about the four-year-old act and they do not believe they can change schools even if the schools aren't performing well (Raths et al., 1992, p. 12). Parents have not consistently been involved in school-based management, nor have they taken the bait of the family centers which were supposed to get them involved with the schools (Appalachia Educational Laboratory, 1993, December). Perhaps parents must take some sort of exam before they can become parents—a performance based test, of course!

Undoubtedly, it is exams and national standards that have focused national attention on Kentucky. When Kentucky develops portfolios as an alternative to traditional testing with contractors who are thousands of miles away, or when it retreats from its goals of self-sufficiency or sociability because of attacks from right-wing groups, it is major news (Harp, 1994, May). The attraction lies in the systemic and calculating character of the reforms, characteristics that make KERA very appealing to educators as well as experts (Mitchell, 1992). The integration of governance, finance, curriculum, testing, and licensing of all professionals has made systemic reform the in-thing, thereby the consultant that Kentucky originally picked, David Hornbeck, has become the in-man (Bradley, 1994, June p.13). Hornbeck was also the consultant for a similar plan in Alabama, a reform idea that did not pass the legislature because of the strong opposition from the right wing (Harp, 1994, February, p. 14). The Brave New World in Kentucky stands out because of the language used. A language of calculation is constantly used by educators in promotion of their procedures.

Chart 4.2
KERA Reforms: A Summary of Features

Finance: Support Education Excellence in Kentucky (SEEK) provided in 1991 per pupil increases between 8 and 25 percent based on land assessments and number of at-risk students. Even larger capital increases were made as well as increases in per pupil grants in following years. In any year, district can receive additional grants up to 15 percent of the norm and further grants for specific costs and new programs. Performance standards are set for all schools and additional rewards are provided for schools that exceed the standard.

Governance: An appointed Commissioner of Education replaces an elected one and all members of the existing Department of Education were dismissed. Employment of relatives by the school boards is prohibited. School Board members are required to have a high school diploma or the equivalent and they must receive up to 18 hours of training for their positions. Teacher firings are subject to review by special committees composed of one administrator, one teacher and one lay person, all from outside the district. Alternative routes are provided for the hiring of teachers with bachelor's degrees from outside the faculties of education. New teachers are expected to have a year of classroom experience in their training. Distinguished teachers are appointed to assist the Department of Education and low performing schools.

Councils: Councils are established over several years and must consist of 3 teachers, 2 parents and the principal. A set amount of discretionary income is provided to councils and the councils are charged with hiring staff including the principal, adapting the curriculum, and scheduling and establishing disciplinary procedures. Non-certified employees are on the committees only if they were on the committees or councils before KERA; new councils may apply to the state board of education for alternative structures. High performing schools can be exempt from all school-based management requirements. All schools who have not met their target scores must have implemented school decision making through councils.

Centers: The programs attempt to locate physical and emotional problems of youth that will hamper academic achievement. Family Centers in elementary schools offer day care and the training for day care workers, health services or referrals, and services for new parents. Youth Service Centers in middle and high schools take on the additional tasks of counseling for employment, drug and alcohol abuse and family crises, and part-time and summer work projects. The two programs are jointly administered by Service Centers at a cabinet level position for Human Resources and the Commissioner for the Department of Education. Most schools that have 20 percent or more of at-risk sstudents now have centers. Surveys of all students at grades 4, 8 and 12 are planned.

Pre-School: Required for all at-risk students beginning at age 4. At-risk students are those qualifying for the free lunch program. Handicapped students are to begin at age 3 and all others at age 4 if places are available. The program is for a half day only as is kindergarten.

Chart 4.2 (continued)

Primary School: Kindergarten is a part of this program that extends through grade three. Active involvement is sought through education that is "developmentally appropriate," age and ability groups are to be mixed, continuous promotion is used to avoid a sense of failure, and a host of progressive education approaches are recommended including whole language, cooperative learning, thematic teaching and writing as a process.

Testing: Superintendents, principals and teachers are tested as well as students. For students' continuous progress, authentic assessments and qualitative reporting is being emphasized; a new exam was developed, the Kentucky Instructional Results Information System (KIRIS). KRIS consists of writing and math portfolios, a test with open-response patterns, and group performance events with an individual written component. Passing the new exam is required for leaving primary school. However, additional time is provided for students to stay in primary school as well as to have additional instruction after school, on Saturdays or during the summer months. Letter grades are abandoned and student performance is judged as novice, apprentice, proficient or distinguished. Restructuring is voluntary at the high school. (Legislative Research Commission 1991; Commonwealth of Kentucky n.d.; Appalachia Educational Laboratory, 1991, May; and Appalachian Educational Laboratory, 1996, February).

For example, the Council on School Performance Standards is to define successful schools: The formula is to be a combination of factors such as "attainment of learning goals, attendance, dropout and grade retention and a successful transition from school to work" (Commonwealth of Kentucky, n.d., p. 25). With some allowance for threshold effects, rewards and punishments are handed out stringently. A decline of 5 percent in the proportion of successful students in a three-year period leads to the label of "school in crisis," all staff are placed on probation and Kentucky Distinguished Educators are assigned to the school at 50 percent more than their usual salary to make recommendations in regard to the retention of staff after a six-month period. Parents are notified that they can transfer their kids from a school in crisis.

In order to ensure the entire reform act was implemented and reviewed critically, the Office of Education Accountability was created; this office reports directly to the legislature rather than to one department of government. The reports of the office are amended by the special Subcommittee on Educational Accountability. The entire amended report has virtually no limit. Concerns for inflexible bureaucracy, alternative bases for teacher certification, relationships between school councils and advisory councils for family resource centers are all considered in its most recent report. The director of the office urges that she be considered a "critical friend" by all of those involved in implementing reforms in Kentucky. Like similar decentralization efforts in Chicago and Alberta, superagencies, such as the Office of Accountability, led to spectacular growth in the number of staff with these new central agencies. After four years, the office in Kentucky has grown from two people to seventeen full-time and six contract employees (Kentucky General Assembly, Office of Educational Accountability, 1994, p. i).

THE AMERICAN DREAM: LISTS OF GOALS

Parents and even teachers seem unable to see more than single aspects of KERA, and see instead only small parts of the entire package (Chart 4.2) that make up the systematic reform effort in Kentucky (Appalachia Education Laboratory, 1993, May). As was noted, national organizations appreciate the total effort that KERA involves. The Business Roundtable (BRT) has put together a synthesis of reform from many sources. This collection of nine principles for education, shown in Chart 4.3, claims the Business Roundtable, matches Kentucky's program perfectly.

These principles are drawn from the recommendations of educational reformers and legislative acts from across the United States. The mixed ability plan in Kentucky is seen to support the assumption of goal one that all students can learn, and the second assumption of goal one that all students can be taught. Student success is provided for in the opportunities for instruction after school, on Saturdays, and in additional years of schooling (Business Roundtable, 1992, pp.14-16). Equitable funding in Kentucky presumably makes possible a high expectation, a third assumption of goal one, through some type of unexplained link. Parental involvement, which Kentucky attempts, is not even mentioned, since the Business Roundtable is so certain Kentucky meets all of the assumptions.

Any questions about Kentucky's meeting the basic assumptions of component one are lessened by the extent to which Kentucky clearly meets goals two through eight. Goals of applying basic communications and math skills, the aim of using concepts from the other academic and vocational areas, as well as thinking, problem solving, and integrating knowledge around the outcomes of the program are clearly spelled out. With exams planned for grades four, eight, and twelve, performance portfolios have been partially developed (Viadero, June 8, 1994, pp. 26–27). KERA combines rewards and punishments for schools. School-based decision making is intended to give the school the freedom to implement the outcome-based goals for all schools. After the third year, $16 per pupil for staff training and training for reform is provided in modular courses for each grade level. The seventh and eighth components show that Kentucky provides the essence of Head Start programs for almost all its at-risk students, along with the health and community services that are to make education, in itself, possible.

As for the final aim, that of technology, Kentucky, as well as the federal government, is full of promises and plans. These are accepted at face value

Chart 4.3
Essential Components of a Successful Education System

1. A successful education system operates on four assumptions:
   -Every student can learn at significantly higher levels;
   -Every student can be taught successfully;
   -High expectations for every student are reflected in curriculum content, though instructional strategies may vary; and
   -Every student and every preschool child needs an advocate—preferably a parent.

2. A successful system is performance or outcome based.

3. A successful system uses assessment strategies as strong and rich as the outcomes.

4. A successful system rewards schools for success, helps schools in trouble, and penalizes schools for persistent or dramatic failure.

5. A successful system gives school-based staff a major role in instructional decisions.

6. A successful system emphasizes staff development.

7. A successful system provides high-quality pre-kindergarten programs, at least for every disadvantaged child.

8. A successful system provides health and other social services sufficient to reduce significant barriers to learning.

9. A successful system uses technology to raise student and teacher productivity and expand access to learning.
(Business Roundtable, 1992, December, p. 26)

by the Business Roundtable; $200 million has been set aside, but it should be mentioned that no major expenditures were made before 1995 on the master plan. There have been a number of achievements in technology including software options for textbooks in social studies, professional development through computers, and an annual conference for parents, teachers, and students on technology. There have also been a number of delays, problems with administrative systems, and disagreements about the extent to which selected computers meet the previously agreed standards (Kentucky General Assembly, Office of Education Accountability, 1994). An Advisory Council for Education Technology in Kentucky has sought three major system-design firms to develop the flexibility for a winning plan at the school and district level. The pie-in-the-sky quality of technology in Kentucky is not criticized by the Business Roundtable. This is similar to the way the BRT glossed over the extent to which KERA meets the basic assumptions. The view of Kentucky as a prize by the BRT may result from the fact that Kentucky's consultant, David Hornbeck, is the author of the nine-component plan for the Business Roundtable (School Management Study Group, 1994, p. 3). The BRT and Kentucky are so close that the new education director of the elite business group went to Kentucky as a part of her orientation (Cindy Heine, interview, May 8, 1995).

Among the allies for the Kentucky plan is the National Center on Education and the Economy, which helped develop the assessment program. Marc Tucker, the president of that national organization, has been working with Kentucky's reform supporters (Harp, 1994, February, p. 14). Kentucky represents one of the largest groups of schools in the alliance of schools that the same Carnegie Foundation group has assembled. Though Alabama is the only state to try to follow Kentucky's program, national organizations of businesspeople, educators, and economists have been intensely following Kentucky's progress. Business professionals and economists support Goals 2000, but most educators are lukewarm to the new federal program (Pitsch, 1994, March). Kentucky is the link between professional educators and the new federal programs. If educators can have specific programs with progressive aims, as in Kentucky, Goals 2000 is the beginning of a beautiful new world. At present, Kentucky and Delaware see themselves as closer to Goals 2000 than any other states (Pitsch, 1994, April, p. 21).

All of the assumptions and the nine principles in Chart 4.3 are not questioned since they are based on either legislative acts from states other than Kentucky or significant educational projects. The first assumption that a successful system requires, that is, every student can learn at higher levels, for example, is based on the Accelerated School Project at Stanford, which takes approaches used with gifted students and applies them to lower achieving ones. The assumption that all students can learn more effectively is written into law in the 1991 Maryland School Performance Program and 1992 Utah Strategic Planning for Public Education. It is also related to the National Goals for the year 2000 that all children in America will start school ready to learn and that U.S. students will be the first in the world in science and mathematics achievement, reproduced in Chart 4.4. National Goals in Chart 4.3 are now a part of the Goals 2000, Educate America Act, that the American Congress passed in April 1994 (Pitsch, 1994, April, pp. 1, 21). Goals for better teacher education and parent participation were added to this legislation. Unlike all other federal legislation since World War II, Goals 2000 is not a required program by which states must abide. Its emphasis is on "getting states to establish clear standards and to develop strategies for helping students meet them" (American Federation of Teachers, 1994, July, p. 20). States are provided with a limited amount of funds to monitor plans which they develop. Right-wing political and religious groups are very critical of Goals 2000.

This integration of reforms, legislative acts, state practices and plans makes it possible for business leaders to be absolved of any charge of ignorance about education. The clearest realization of this shield is the

Kentucky Educational Reform Act. Kentucky is claimed to be the only state that has all nine of the essential components (Business Roundtable, 1992, pp. 14–16). KERA may not be supported by that many business leaders; the number of small business people listed with the Prichard Committee is small. In Chapter 7, the business support for integrated services is shown to be limited, and integrated services is an important part of the national campaigns that have been discussed. Kentucky is almost a shrine for national organizations that support such broad reforms.

Whether it is from the perspective of new national legislation or the direct advocacy of the Business Roundtable, the Kentucky program constantly attracts outside attention. Within the state the downward trickle of reform has reached few parents, teachers, or students. The language of the educational experts has become a barrier as the Kentucky reforms have evolved. In the early period, both Prichard and Combs communicated through parables and stories; the experts recruited into Kentucky have not followed these earlier examples. Furthermore, the alignment of the Kentucky program with progressive ideals has led to the opposition of those who express a right-wing ideology. The Eagle Forum claimed the Family Centers would be "Nazi child snatchers" (Dryfoos, 1994, p. 165), though its anger and opposition is now directed more against the new type of exams (Marsha Morganti, interview, May 5, 1995). The Prichard Committee has become, at times, a lightning rod, although its many attempts to mediate conflicts would not have suggested this role. Key institutional alliances within the state as well as the nation, particularly with businesses, have been the major achievement of the Prichard Committee and KERA.

REINVENTING GOVERNMENT IN ALBERTA

Over two thousand miles away from Kentucky, an equally large-scale and drastic set of reforms is being implemented. In western Canada, just east of the Rocky Mountains, the government of Alberta has begun to remake its educational system. This reshaping started on the basis of budget cutting although ideological positions are increasingly becoming involved. While the right-wing protestors want traditional education in Kentucky, right-wingers are themselves in power in Alberta. Evidently, they have no intention of listening to established educators or administrators of the systems as they attempt to remake education on a more restricted, if not more private basis.

In a country that regularly follows American change practices, it is still a huge step for one province to undertake so many revolutionary changes at once. There had been no serious court decisions involving tax equity among school districts, yet the Alberta government has moved, following American decisions as in the Kentucky case, to take over all property taxes from the school districts in order to achieve greater equality (Ken Jesse, interview, May 16, 1994). The same provincial government in Alberta pushed ahead with the integration of the handicapped, to the point of eliminating special

Chart 4.4
National Education Goals

By the year 2000:

1. All children in America will start school ready to learn.

2. We will increase the percentage of students graduating from high school to at least ninety percent.

3. American students will leave grades four, eight, and twelve having demonstrated competency over challenging subject matter, including English, mathematics, science, history and geography.

4. U.S. students will be the first in the world in science and mathematics achievement.

5. Every adult American will be literate and possess the knowledge and skills necessary to compete in a global economy and exercise the rights and responsibilities of citizenship.

6. Every school in America will be free of drugs and violence and offer a disciplined environment conducive to learning.
(National Education Goals Panel, 1992, pp. 4-5)

education teachers. These types of governmental efforts are mirroring an earlier American initiative with current budget cutting pressures. Without precedent in their own country and following only American examples, the Alberta government has adopted charter schools which appeal only to small, recently organized groups of conservatives in the area, all but ignoring the teachers' union, trustees, and parent-teacher associations. The slashing becomes more random as this province cuts early childhood education in half while the premier claims he is following all the research evidence, which to him is selected American studies (Dempster, 1994, April and Martin, 1994, April). The cuts in early childhood education were not supported by the initial meetings, the roundtables, that the government itself convened (Lisac, 1995, p. 145).

All of these events began when a government with a heavy conservative majority and public support introduced comprehensive school legislation on April 1, 1994 (Collins & Dempster, 1994, April). The legislation promises to change the face of Canadian education. The national newspaper for Canada, *The Globe and Mail*, has suggested, editorially, that Alberta should be the model for all of Canada (Campbell, 1994, May). The changes in education in Alberta are part of a program to privatize and reduce government; the larger province of Ontario is now following a similar course. Hospitals are being closed; private care hospitals, initially for American visitors, are being considered; and home and community services as a replacement for hospital care are being planned. If federal guidelines preventing changes in the state health care system can be avoided, patient fees and private hospitals for Albertans will be introduced. This broad policy on health, social welfare, and education is influenced by another American plan to reinvent government. Budget reductions are recognized as part of an ideological change to alter the direction of government. All these changes are presented by Premier Ralph Klein, a former television newsman reminiscent of President Ronald Reagan, a former actor. Premier Klein has recently called himself "Newt of the North" identifying himself with House of Representative Speaker Newt Gingrich who has championed fiscal and conservative political reform in the United States (Jeffs, 1995, January, p. A1).

These recent developments in Alberta have to be considered against a pattern of social structure and values that are substantially different from those that affect American education. Religion and related ethnic and language differences have larger effects on education in Canada than in the United States. Canada, with the exception of one province, British Columbia, publicly supports religious education as a part of its educational system. In one province, Newfoundland, religious schools still constitute the public system (Mitchell,1992).

The strongest opposition to the current educational reforms in Alberta came from the Catholic separate system, which planned to challenge, in court, the state collection of their parishioners' property taxes for the government coffers. It is opposed to charter schools that are planned to be nonreligious (Jeffs, 1994, April). The government has retreated and exempted the Catholic, separate schools, but the public schools have now charged religious discrimination and believe they can win in court and prevent the government from collecting their taxes (John Hogan, interview, June 13, 1994). The inclusion of the nonreligious requirement for charter schools may be an accident of copying American language too closely. Religion and language diversity is the core of Canadian resistance to American dominance, but in a variety of ways Catholic schools in Alberta believe that their separateness is being undermined. Strangely enough, this diversity is the core of the Canadian need for greater order and control of people in both private and government organizations than those in similar groups in the United States. Dualism in religion and language in Canada makes it more necessary to manage and limit the system. The bureaucrats, particularly the former deputy minister for education, Reno Bosetti, were blamed for failing to anticipate the Catholics' resistance (John Ballheim, interview, May 17, 1994).

A greater emphasis on hierarchy in Canada than in the United States contributes to the cultural difference, since bureaucratic rules are used to keep the Canadian educational system together, whereas the American model is more diverse and fragmented even within individual states. Catholics are not the only established group being ignored. However, in the present crisis, the Albertans for Quality Education, a very new group, was reportedly more influential than the teachers' union or the trustees' association (Dempster, 1994, February, p.14). Common business values and moral concerns have led to the emulation by Albertans of extreme policy alternatives, such as American charter schools.

THE EXPLOSION IN ALBERTA

As has been true of all cuts in government, Alberta has followed New Zealand in using the "earthquake method" of rapid, substantial, and widespread changes while pursuing the American idea of reinventing government as well as specific reforms (Barrington, 1991). The number of government offices, hospital boards, and school boards has been reduced to save money. Grass-roots organizations that have been sought to provide support for reform in Alberta have had a revolution led by the government. Some small groups have been mobilized to support the reforms, including those wanting the teaching of values and character education (Dempster, 1994, February). Charter schools have been sought as a means to provide character education by the same supporters. These groups are only the tip of the iceberg for the silent majority that the premier claims support his efforts. Certainly, because of the perception of a financial crisis to which all government employees must contribute a 5 percent salary reduction, the premier's popularity has soared. Business groups support these actions and believe that the premier will always listen to them.

In opposition to the drastic changes, mass meetings of Catholics forced the government to modify its position. All Catholic school boards united in opposition. Groups other than the Catholics have been less successful in mobilizing resistance against the government. The teachers' union, the Alberta Teachers' Association, spent over half a million dollars on a television campaign, but was ignored and has had only one meeting with the premier since the campaign; small right-wing groups receive far more of his attention. The hopes of other labor unions for a general strike fizzled and now even the retirees, badly hurt by revenue reductions, have trouble finding more than one leader to represent their position (Collins & Dempster, 1994, April). Other than among the Catholics, the lack of advocacy groups has enormously handicapped those in Alberta who would oppose these innovations.

School boards and superintendents are viewed as barriers to innovation by the government. The number of boards has been reduced and the provincial government must now accept the appointment of new superintendents. The Alberta government wants, however, to expand school-based management throughout the province so that parents and local school personnel are involved. Parents, apparently, are not very interested in running the schools (Dempster, 1994, July 9). The government intends to monitor school reform in terms of the views of parents and employers as well as students' achievement. The monitoring process can be as much a limit on local decision making as are the superagencies in Kentucky and Chicago (Mitchell, 1995, January).

The councils are part of a business plan in Alberta to widen support for changes that are based on the involvement of business. Business supports the reduction in school expenditures and business is sought as a partner in education. The premier, who lacks business experience, admired those who did; the chartered (certified public) accountants were listened to very closely (Lisac, 1995, p. 147). Education is expected to match the productivity increases that business has achieved, particularly through distance education and television (Alberta Education, 1994, p. 6). Business partnerships are to be promoted to support and direct schools while employers are to provide education to students (pp. 15 & 19). "Efficient use of services" is to be promoted by the integration of schools and community services so that the cost and effectiveness of all public services can be regulated (pp. 13 & 19). The overall educational success is to be measured by the satisfaction of employers, parents, and public representatives with the work of schools as well as by the achievement scores of students (p. 14). Such results are the guide for politicians who claim to follow the guidelines of *Reinventing Government* (Dempster, 1994, February, A14 and Osborne & Gaebler, 1992).

It is the dissatisfaction with the existing situations in schools that characterizes support for the business plan for Alberta. Perhaps the most telling remarks about the disturbance in Alberta are the letters to the editor in which citizens express their individual resentments against teachers or other professionals whom they had to endure when the experts were in short supply (Webber, 1995). Among those opposing reforms, similar expressions of blame are directed against the premier or any other supposedly guilty parties (*Calgary Herald*, 1994, February and *Calgary Herald*, 1994, March). Albertans are said to want people in other provinces to suffer as much as they have (Braid, 1994, October). A resentment against intellectuals is also expressed by members of the governing party (Lisac, 1995, p. 222). The silent majority and the ruling elite both feel a deep alienation that appears to be brought out by the current crisis.

CHARTER SCHOOLS AND CORPORATISM

The resentment in Alberta is expressed by a number of groups which have been developing their position on the far Right. As mentioned in Chapter 3, moral absolutists have opposed relearning because of Sizer's emphasis on process alone. Economic individualists have wanted a voucher plan so parents could control their own program in the public school system. Charter schools are the alternative whereby the grant can follow the child for new or renewed schools organized for special purposes within the public system. The Alberta Chamber of Commerce has endorsed the plan of Premier Klein that will enable "funding to follow the child" and transfer "decision making to individual schools and communities" (Birdsell, M. & Salloum, M., letter to Premier Klein, February 1, 1994). Since running a charter school seems to require the skills of operating a small business, there is consistency between this innovation and the overall approach adopted by Alberta since the government wants schools to operate similarly to businesses (Richardson, 1995, August).

Politically, charter schools allow for a development in education that may well represent a transition to a more private system. In Alberta, the government floor leader, Stockwell Day, is a declared right-wing ideologist who runs the People's Church in Red Deer, Alberta, and who had problems with the Alberta Department of Education over a private school that he used to run (Ken Jesse, interview, May 16, 1994). On the basis of his own situation, Mr. Day has obvious reasons for supporting charter schools. However, charters are granted for only a limited period and charter schools can be reviewed by a state agency. The government has problems controlling the right wing on other issues, such as abortion, and it may have difficulty preventing them from establishing private schools under the heading of charters for character training.

In most places, including Alberta, the local school board must first review the proposed charter school. Charter schools are associated not only with the decline in confidence in schools run by the school boards, but also with a loss of confidence among members of the Alberta government in superintendents, who are responsible for the local systems (Olsen, 1986, November 12). The appointment of superintendents by the Alberta government, rather than local boards, was added to the government plan very late in December 1993, as a result of frustration from trying to get more equal distribution of taxes among school boards (John Ballheim, interview, May 17, 1994). The removal of taxes from local boards and the assertion of control over superintendents have made the creation of charter schools easier by removing supporters of the established school systems.

Charter schools frequently have emerged in the United States from liberal, not right-wing supporters. There have been a number of liberal groups who have organized these schools in Minnesota, the first state to offer them. The Association of Community Organizations for Reform Now (ACORN), which is politically on the Left, is attempting to organize such a school in Minnesota and has formed an independent school in New York City (Madeleine Talbot, interview, April 28, 1994). In Alberta, government leaders are following Minnesota's example and ignoring British experience (Ken Jesse, interview, May 16, 1994). It has been proposed by an expert on charters that teachers could cease being employees entirely and establish teacher-partnership schools (Public Services Redesign Project, 1993, p. 4). In Alberta, right-wing groups who follow a radiologist, Dr. Joe Freedman, have shown a strong interest in charters without teacher or left-wing controls (Collins & Dempster, 1994, April). Business leaders would like to change the culture of the schools and would like to see teacher partnerships. The charter schools are a part of a program in which the government's treasurer, Jim Dinning, has proclaimed, "It is now Armageddon;" the crisis justifies any of the varied changes that the government wants (Lisac, 1994, February).

However, the initial thrust in Canadian education has come from Alberta with a coalition of government, business, and religious groups that hold common ideological convictions, including a belief that the raising of oil prices will not be a solution to the current financial crisis (Hesch, 1994). A clever use of financial restructuring, which includes equalization of payments to school boards, appears to make the charter schools the only alternative for those who want any control over their local schools (Dempster, 1994, March). Similar groups seem to be most involved in Colorado, a state to which the media of Alberta have looked most directly for examples. The Academy School in Colorado is an elementary school with a tight dress code and a strong emphasis on business virtues. Colorado's second operating school, Connect Middle School, exchanges a relaxed dress code for a strong emphasis on technology, core subjects, and cooperation; it has been a scene of controversy, as the first dean was removed by what she considers right-wing Christian parents (Dempster, 1994, March). Native Albertans, who have gone to Colorado for jobs, were teaching in these schools and others were reading about them in Alberta's newspapers.

The most important characteristic of charter schools is the local involvement that it encourages while allowing the state to maintain control. This combination of centralization and decentralization has been particularly puzzling to Albertans who have just been introduced to charter schools. While school autonomy is supported, greater controls via testing of student achievements are introduced, as in the case of home schooling (Dempster, 1994, July). The central state takes responsibility for testing, but it gives decision making on how to bring about these goals to those on the site, as also occurs in Kentucky (Center for Policy Studies, 1993). The charter schools focus on outcomes, as does systemic reform in general. The first charters in Minnesota were a variation of alternatives or schools without walls for students that the ordinary schools were not successful in educating. School boards, it is argued, accept charter schools with programs for students that they cannot serve and reject programs for more mainstream kids they want to keep (Sautter, 1993, p. 9).

It is possible to see charter schools as a part of an evolution from small schools within larger schools to a voucher system whereby parents choose the type of education they prefer (Sautter, 1993, p. 1). Philadelphia used the term *charter* school for smaller schools in a larger school; the more typical use of the term is to refer to schools with legislative authorization that gives choice for schools to run different programs. Independent clusters of schools or school districts might develop a consistent pattern just as Catholic schools have done, so that they can have the same consistency in their school climates from elementary to higher education. Following the choice idea alone, home schooling or vouchers would be a logical development.

Pursuing the school option conception means that, as in Philadelphia, many students do not have a choice of programs since schools are assigned to them (p. 17). Unless autonomy is secured from the larger system, any optional program may be illusory as it has become in Philadelphia. The combination of autonomy and choice is the crux of the educational issue and charter schools can achieve that combination.

A host of different organizations, including businesses or even programs for drug addicts, can sponsor charter schools by obtaining board or state approval. The Minnesota legislation required teachers to be, at the very least, cosponsors of such schools. Albert Schanker, president of the American Federation of Teachers, originally called for charter schools in 1988 as a cooperative effort of school board-union panels to establish schools to achieve aims such as cooperative learning. However, the situations have since become much more confused and teacher unions have many doubts about charter schools. The Alberta Teachers Association sees charter schools as "the best education for a select group of students" (Committee on Public Education and Professional Practice, 1994, p. 9). The encouragement of any and all groups to run schools while the government sets the general direction has been shown to be similar to the way Russia is now approaching education (Kirkpatrick, 1994, p. 254).

BACK TO CHICAGO

The opposition between central control and democratic participation that charter schools seem to permit is better shown by the establishment of learning zones: schools within the existing school systems. Schools in learning zones are given the same freedoms and clear expectations for student achievement as charter schools. New schools are not contemplated and existing elementary and high schools are clustered, but, otherwise, the learning zones are similar to the charter schools. Significantly, this program of options within the existing system is supported by the Educational Commission of the States, an advocacy group discussed in Chapter 3 which is attempting to bring about a consensus along with the Coalition of Essential Schools. In a new law for Chicago, approximately 10 percent of Chicago schools would become a learning zone with state tests, Chicago-wide exams, and local assessments. The greater freedom will be secured through an acceptance of this proposal by the state. A majority vote by teachers in the schools, as provided under the current reform act, is sufficient to start the learning zones (Chicago Learning Zone Advisory Committee, 1994). The future will tell how learning zones are used in Chicago; they may be a part of a breakup of the system, particularly if a voucher plan is eventually introduced.

The similarity between the learning zones and charter schools is that both would provide control and approval by the state for limited periods together with greater variation and participation than now occur among all those involved in the schools. In order to modernize the instrument of control, governments must bring about both control over education and involvement in education so that its legitimacy is renewed (Hannaway & Carnoy, 1993). This new legitimacy is said to combine centralization and decentralization, and intermediate levels of governing, such as school boards, are eliminated. The superagency in Chicago was reluctantly accepted with the expansion of the School Finance Authority whose legislative life was continued until this year. There have been interesting additions, such as the hiring of a former FBI agent to be the inspector general, in order to find thievery among educators. However, with a permanent superboard now appointed by the mayor, the full separation of the elected councils, who are to make local decisions, and the appointed boards, who are to supervise the councils and their decisions, has been brought into the open (Harp, 1995, June).

As the state draws upon the greater resources of private corporations, the division between local units and central plans is increased, though not realized, because of the involvement of citizens in local schools. Government and corporations tend to become united because of the increased influence of business, and the power of other competing groups is diminished (Lindbloom, 1977). In the United States and, increasingly, in Canada, business influence has grown. Business in Chicago has allied itself, initially, with community groups and has, more recently, decided to support the school system and curtail its own advocacy organization, as will be discussed in the next chapter. Unlike in Chicago, the business influence in the Canadian West is more right wing and more openly concerned with business self-interest, as opposed to broader approaches, including those focusing on human resources (Lawrence Howe, interview, April 25, 1994).

The dominance or hegemony of business in any one place can clearly be contested by the creation of new options. Charter schools provide a basis for creating such options for both business and competing community groups. Left-wing groups may want the charter schools as much as those who follow the ideology of the far Right. Both groups risk the controversies that can bring the opposition between control and participation into the open. The learning zone alternative allows the same independence of schools and focuses on academic results as does the charter proposal. However, with the learning zone, a consensus position is maintained in the public system as a basis for reform; creating more alternatives within the system is even more of a unified approach. In contrast, charters are similar to voucher plans in that they separate schools with only ideological supports.

Massachusetts, the American state that has adopted charters to the greatest extent, recently has seen the charter movement lead to a profusion of competing groups which want to be approved to run charter schools (Celis, 1994, March). Boston University is running a school which should complement the school system it has been directing for several years. The Coalition of Essential Schools has two entrants. Parents and teachers have planned a number of schools. However, the most controversial new schools are the three that are sponsored by the private company Project Edison. Project Edison as well as other for profit schools will be discussed in the next chapter.

Aside from promoters of profit-making schools, the religious Right is the group that is most interested in founding charter schools so they can extend their influence in many directions. The government of Alberta is currently balancing the two groups, businesspeople and religious advocates. In Kentucky, right-wing groups are attacking systemic reform, which business supports. Nationally and internationally, business leaders are, increasingly, distancing themselves from the extreme right-wing groups (Harp, 1994, June). Aside from charter schools in the United States, the extreme conservatives have won control of school boards and branches of the Republican party.

The conflict is whether or not the far Right is a disruptive influence for educational reform. Jeanne Allen says that business doesn't really understand how nonacademic standards or outcomes, including things like "children will learn to reason better, work in specific classroom practices;" she believes businessmen are "not real savvy about education policy and they end up getting snookered" (Harp, 1994, June, p. 12). Ms. Allen is the president of the Washington-based Center for Education Reform and a former policy analyst with the conservative Heritage Foundation. However, Christopher Cross, with the Business Roundtable until recently, believes business leaders have long been involved, and they "have rolled up their sleeves and worked on this issue" (Harp, 1994, June, p. 12). Rae Nelson, with a U.S. Chamber of Commerce program, believes that standards and results are the way to improve education. John Ballheim, president of the Alberta Chamber of Commerce, is very concerned about Albertans for Quality Education and right-wing ideologies within the Conservative party (interview, May 16, 1994). The right wing often threatens a corporate alliance between business and education. The left wing, on occasion, can also represent this opposition, as in the case of Kentuckians for the Commonwealth (Robert Sexton, interview, May 4, 1995).

The American battle is joined by the American civil liberties group People for the American Way, which is opposing the conservative organization Focus on the Family (Harp, 1994, June 15). Paul Hetrick, vice president of the latter group, believes that conservatives must defend the family and traditional values because their turf has been invaded by politicians. With the Kentucky family and youth centers, the right wing has a case for claiming that they have been invaded. However, how can the conservatives explain the Chicago situation where parents have invaded education in the view of principals in the Chicago system? (Kyle & Kantowicz, 1992, pp. 274–76) Teachers see the challenge from parents for control of education and researchers see parent and professional control of school-based innovation as major alternatives for site-based management (Murphy & Hallinger, 1993).

PARENTS AND TEACHERS

Certainly, the lack of parent and teacher involvement is the Achilles heel of the systemic reform in Kentucky. Aside from their limited involvement with the family resource centers and school-based councils, the parents show the extent to which the Kentucky reform is based on traditional conceptions of educational experts. The experts are likely to want a logically consistent system that replaces the inefficiencies of the existing partial and inconsistent approaches (Mitchell, 1992). Of course, the subordinates see only one part of the new system and resist any abstract conception that does not correspond with their own experiences. Teachers in Kentucky may be like experts in sensing an increased professional involvement, but they see only one part of the system and want more information about the assessment by portfolios that are so removed from their experiences (Appalachia Education Laboratory, 1992, September, p. 3). One teacher in Kentucky wrote to every newspaper in Alabama to warn them against following Kentucky's example (Harp, 1994, February, p. 14).

It is perhaps surprising to learn that in Kentucky primary teachers are so fixed to a hierarchy that the inclusion of kindergarten students in a class with those from grade one sparked fears that grade one children would be permanently damaged because of the coupling. The extent to which kindergarten and grade one had to be combined showed a process of shopping around for the answer that teachers would find "modest and less threatening." The acceptable answer from Department of Education officials in Kentucky would then be broadcast as the answer when it was found. For teachers so insecure there was never any notion that parents could be partners with their schools (Raths et al., 1993, pp. 11-13).

Parents are more subordinated to experts than to teachers in Kentucky. It is hardly surprising that parents were infrequently involved in school-based decision making (Appalachia Educational Laboratory, 1993, December). One sample of ten schools found that parent voting was close to the 4 percent voting record for councils in a widely publicized survey (Raths et al., 1993, p. 33). No voting results in Chicago are as low as the reported figures in Kentucky. However, the participation in Chicago is far less guided by the influence of experts. One can only guess that the voting in school elections would be greater in Alberta than in Kentucky only because it would be set at the same time as general elections for other political offices in exactly the same way as school board elections are now scheduled. However, because of the small number of advocacy groups, which increase parent involvement, Alberta will probably show a very low voting percentage.

SCHOOL COUNCILS AND SCHOOL BOARDS

The involvement of parents and teachers in councils is justified as part of a basis for holding professionals accountable (Hill & Bonan, 1992).

However, the professional and bureaucratic systems of education are critically challenged. Bureaucracies are fragmented and make a variety of demands on individual schools (Hill & Bonan, 1991, p. 9). Conflicts between a unified central board and autonomous schools can be prevented by a new approach. The conflicts between schools can be mediated by a more efficient central system that can collect statistical information better than can a local council. The autonomous councils are presumably limited to "information assessments and expert judgements" (p. 64). Even teacher unions can become a partner in this grand plan (p. 72). The scenarios are not from outer space; they are the work of Paul Hill, whose writings are distributed by Peter Martinez of the MacArthur Foundation as a model for the new central board in Chicago. Certainly, Hill, writing as one who is currently involved in a national study of school-based decision making, has had an influence in Kentucky, and his work is consistent with that of other experts, such as Hornbeck, who have practiced the approach that Hill preaches.

However, a system-based model for schools may be more structured and more like a business approach to education. It is questionable whether the new consistent model will make schools better able to deal with future changes than the present system. Schools in Salt Lake City are said to "possess their own identities, and older staff effectively socialize new additions to each school's culture" (Hill & Bonan, 1992, p. 17). It is just such assimilation into existing systems that has been the mark of socialization into school boards in the past. It is this type of socialization that we should be measuring reform actions against, if we are to have the greater variety and social support in individual schools which is the mark of creativity in any organization (Mitchell, 1971, pp. 131–143).

School board members, like others in the school system, are socialized to fit into that system. The most striking result of their socialization into the organizations is the extent to which they are overwhelmingly influenced to talk about procedures, including finances and buildings, rather than educational ideas (Nowakowski & First, 1989; Kerr, 1969; Olsen, 1986, November 12). However, school board members were elected because they promised new ideas of good education, rather than routine procedures. Members who want to change policy are isolated through either divide-and-conquer techniques or co-optation into the old boys' network of previously elected members. The striking result is that school board members are often alienated from the people they are elected to represent. When conflicts within boards become apparent, confidence in the board declines dramatically as a result. Professionals and business leaders have, conversely, become unwilling to serve on school boards. Experienced school board members often make jokes about the ignorance of the public even though they were just as ignorant before joining the board and even though there is no way for the public to learn about the board's realities because so many of its decisions are made in closed meetings.

The largest segment of the public are parents, and it is this group, as well as other community representatives, in whom Chicago has put its faith for a bottom-up approach to reform. In the Chicago councils, the principal dominates discussion of the school's program but shares authority with the council chair. In most other areas, the principal brings in more people than are involved in most school board meetings (Hess & Easton, 1991, p. 164.) In the Chicago councils, there also appears to be slightly more discussion of the curriculum than the usual dominance of topics, finances and procedures, during school board meetings (pp. 169–173). Still, parents are less experienced and less expert than educators; they are, however, capable of learning if opportunities are provided (Mitchell, 1992). Parents can and do develop political consciousness, but reformers often treat them in a paternal manner and state that parents are likely only to be interested in matters such as school uniforms or discipline (Susan Flinspitch, interview, October 8, 1993). Uneducated parents on Chicago's councils may indeed have a long way to go, but it hardly helps for them to be told to "trust the teacher." Researchers for school-based management who put politically aware parents down as divisive are even less helpful (Hill & Bonan, 1992). It is from organizing a variety of ideas that the people can come to see the possibilities of education. It hardly seems advisable to limit the educational options to what is organizationally sound. It is certainly not surprising that some parents object to KERA as turning their children into guinea pigs, or that others join right-wing groups. It is probably surprising that many parents are still so supportive of KERA and that other parents and even some students support the experts' reforms when they are recognized by such titles as "Kentucky Scholars" (Raths et al., 1993, p. 15 and Harp, 1994, May).

THE NEXT GENERATION

In many senses, the future of reform is unknown and may be a circle of more and more reform efforts. There would be a more promising prediction if more students were involved in their own education in these efforts. In Kentucky, in the model that professional educators seem to promote, only a few parents and students have been involved in the political efforts to maintain reform. The strategies of the expert reformers have been more effective than those of the right-wing opposition. In Alberta, the right-wing government has used a crisis to bring forth reforms such as charter schools, which most of the public object to or give only limited support for (Angus Reid Group, 1994). Demonstrations by students are ignored by Premier Klein, who doesn't meet with demonstrators and relies on the silent majority for authoritarian rule. Premier Klein has stated that students should be in classes rather than in demonstrations. Reported discussions among teachers in Alberta seethe with resentment against the government, which appears no longer to respect them as individuals (Webber, 1995).

Though there are more signs of student involvement, there are other indicators of student resentment. In a chapter on teachers with a title, "Caretakers of Our Children," suggested by a student activist, a Chicago reporter finds that children in Chicago schools have little desire to be there (Vander Weele, 1994, p. 74). The same author notes that the students who would make arbitrary decisions to get rid of the unfit teachers would in the future become, in many cases, unfit teachers themselves. In the past the reform magazine *Catalyst* has covered involvement by students only when they were directly linked to reform activities, such as going to the capital in order to participate in a rally. Currently student leaders believe that they are used by reformers to increase the numbers attending a meeting (Philip Bleicher, interview, May 2, 1995).

Most Chicago teachers have been passed by in the parade of reform. The transition from student to teacher is one of many links that need strengthening between these two groups. Programs to recruit liberal arts graduates to teach in Chicago as in Kentucky may make some difference, and the teachers' union is involved with its own Quest Center to develop reforms that are well accepted or that enhance teacher status, though not in richer contact with students (Vander Weele, 1994, p. 82). The Quest Center has developed a focus on standards and their implementation that is significant (Bradley, 1994, June, p. 34). Teachers are probably more shocked by the seemingly arbitrary actions of parents in firing well-regarded principals than by the statistical norm that most principals are rehired (Weismann, 1994 and Pick, 1994). The teachers in Chicago have not matched the success of parents as the parents make their first tentative steps to empowerment. The failure of teacher professional committees to work effectively is one of the biggest problems in Chicago (Hess, 1994). Reform in each of these cases requires the active cooperation of teachers with students as the core activity of education.

All reformers seem caught in their own webs and these webs are dominated by abstractions rather than the perspectives of constituent groups involved in schools. The perspectives of parents, teachers, and students need to be included along with those in the hierarchy of experts and administrators. The concern for reconciliation of conflicts in any part of the system needs to be matched with a concern for minorities who may be smothered by those who love their reforms too much. There are more considerations than the choice of withdrawal or participation for the clients of professionals (Hill & Bonan, 1992). The point of participating is to acquire a voice in order to state a position that represents a minority with rights, not just one group finding itself welded into a larger whole. School reformers, particularly those writing about school-based management, might do well to think about civil liberties. The reformers might also do well to see conflicts such as minority rights as part of an agenda for developing new and more creative alternatives to traditional socialization. With the mayor's replacement of the school board in Chicago or the acceptance of any cuts for a balanced budget in Alberta, there is an increased likelihood that democracy will be considered less important than the need for security. Unfortunately, business requirements often compete with the political development of education; neither minority rights nor creative alternatives are seen as important to those who focus on the bottom line.

REFERENCES

Adams, J. (1993). *The Prichard Committee for Academic Excellence.* New Brunswick, New Jersey: Consortium for Policy Research in Education, Rutgers University.

Alberta Education (1994). *Meeting the Challenge. Three Year Business Plan (1994/95–1996/97).* Edmonton: Alberta Education.

American Federation of Teachers. (1994, July). The promise of Goals 2000. *Quest Line,* 2(4), 1–7.

Angus Reid Group (1994, May 24). *Education in Alberta.* Calgary: Angus Reid Group.

Annie E. Casey Foundation (1992, Fall). Equity and excellence: Education reform in Kentucky. *A.E.C. Focus,* 2(3), 5.

Appalachia Educational Laboratory (1991, May). Education reform in rural Kentucky. *Notes from the Field,* 1(1), 1–8.

Appalachia Educational Laboratory (1991, September). Special feature: School-based decision making. *Notes from the Field,* 1(2), 1–13.

Appalachia Educational Laboratory (1991, December). Family resource/youth services centres. *Notes from the Field,* 1(3), 18.

Appalachia Educational Laboratory (1992, April). Special Feature: KERA finance measures. *Notes from the Field,* 2(1), 1–8.

Appalachia Educational Laboratory (1992, September). Special Feature: KERA through the eyes of teachers. *Notes from the Field,* 2(2).

Appalachia Educational Laboratory (1993, May). Kentucky's primary program. *Notes from the Field,* 3(1), 1–8.

Appalachia Educational Laboratory (1993, December). School-based decision making after two years. *Notes from the Field,* 3(2), 1–8.

Appalachia Educational Laboratory (1996, February). Five years of education reform in rural Kentucky. *Notes from the Field, 4(1), 1–4, S1–S4.*

Barrington, J. (1991). Educational reform in New Zealand. In M. Ginsburg, (Ed.), *Understanding educational reform in global context* (pp. 285–316). New York: Garland.

Berger, B. (1979). Introduction. In Berger, B. & Callahan, S. (Eds.), *Child care and mediating structures* (p. 1–4). Washington, D.C.: American Enterprise Institute for Public Policy Research.

Bradley, A. (1994, June 22). Hornbeck, prominent consultant, is tapped to head Philadelphia schools. *Education Week,* 13(39),13.

Bradley, A. (1994, June 22). A quest for change. *Education Week,* 13(39), 34-35.

Braid, D. (1994, October 6). Reform will spread and thrive. *Calgary Herald,* p. B1.

Business Roundtable. (1992, December). *The essential components of a successful education system.* Washington, D.C.: Business Roundtable.

Business Roundtable. (1994). *A new architecture for education reform.* Washington, D.C.: Business Roundtable.

Calgary Herald, (1994, March 26). Letters, A6.

Calgary Herald, (1994, February 6). Letters, A7.

Callahan, S. (1979). Report on the Conference. In Berger, B. & Callahan, S. (Eds.), *Child care and mediating structures* (pp. 68-80). Washington: American Enterprise Institute for Public Policy Research.

Campbell, D. (1994, May 7). Ralphonomics, *Calgary Herald*, D7.

Celis, W. (1994, March 19). Private groups to run 15 schools in experiment by Massachusetts. *New York Times*, 1, 8.

Centre for Policy Studies (1993, September 26). *Charter schools: The states begin to withdraw the "exclusive"*. Saint Paul: Public Services Redesign Project.

Chicago Learning Zone Advisory Committee (1994, March 31). *Report and Recommendations*. Chicago: Chicago Learning Zone Advisory Committee.

Collins, R. & Dempster, L. (1994, April 2). Education in Alberta, new chapter. *Calgary Herald*, B5.

Committee on Public Education and Professional Practice (1994). *Trying to teach: Necessary conditions*. Edmonton: Alberta Teachers' Association.

Commonwealth of Kentucky (n.d.). *Educational reform in Kentucky: A new beginning*. Frankfort, Kentucky: Commonwealth of Kentucky.

Dempster, L. (1994, February 11). Inner circle re-draws classroom. *Calgary Herald*, A14.

Dempster, L. (1994, March 20). School reform sweeping North. *Calgary Herald*, A1.

Dempster, L. (1994, April 15). Catholic cry out, school protest packs corral. *Calgary Herald*, A1, A2.

Dempster, L. (1994, July 6). Parents hope for fewer restrictions by province. *Calgary Herald*, B3.

Dempster, L. (1994, July 9). Parents want to be seen, heard. *Calgary Herald*, B5.

Dempster, L. & Bicknell, D. (1994, March 20). Charting a new course. *Calgary Herald*, B3.

Dove, R. (1991). *Creative constitutional law: The Kentucky school reform law*. Lexington: Prichard Committee for Academic Excellence.

Downey, L. & Associates. (1975). *The social studies in Alberta—1975*. Edmonton: L. Downey Associates.

Dryfoos, J. (1994). *Full-service schools*. San Francisco: Jossey-Bass.

Education Week (1993, April 21). Charting a course for reform: the next 10 years. *Education Week*, Special Report, 3.

Fiske, E.B. (1990, April 4). Lessons: In Kentucky, teachers, not legislators, will be writing the lesson plans. *New York Times*, B6.

Fiske, E.B. (1992). *Smart schools, smart kids*. New York: Touchstone.

Glazer, N. (1979). The lawyer and the child. In Berger, B. & Callahan, S. (Eds.), *Child care and mediating structures* (pp. 56–67) Washington, D.C.: American Enterprise Institute for Public Policy Research.

Graham, P.A. (1992). *S.O.S., sustain our schools*. New York: Hill and Wang.

Hamilton, S. (1990). *Apprenticeship for adulthood*. New York: The Free Press.

Hannaway, J. & Carnoy, M. (1993). *Decentralization and school improvement*. San Francisco: Jossey-Bass.

Harp, L. (1994, February 9). Kentucky, Alabama: Seen barometers of state reforms. *Education Week*, 13(20), 1, 14.

Harp, L. (1994, May 18). The plot thickens. *Education Week*, 13(34), 20–25.

Harp, L. (1994, June 15). A G.O.P. divided: O.B.E. drives wedge in party. *Education Week*, 13(38), 12.

Harp, L. (1995, June 7). Governor signs bill pushing mayor in control of Chicago schools. *Education Week*, 14(37), 11.

Hesch, R. (1994). Klein kuts and control in Alberta. Paper presented to Canadian Learned Societies Conference.

Hess, G. (1994). The changing role of teachers: Moving from interested spectators to engaged planners. *Education and Urban Society*, 26(3), 248–263.

Hess, G. & Easton J. (1992). Who is making what decisions: Monitoring authority shifts in Chicago school reform. In Hess. G. (Ed.), *Empowering teachers and parents*. Westport, Connecticut: Bergin & Garvey.

Hill, P.T. & Bonan, J. (1992). *Decentralization and accountability in public education*. Santa Monica: Rand.

Jeffs, A. (1994, April 28). Catholic deal dead says grit. *Calgary Herald*, A1.

Jeffs, A. (1995, January 19). Klein tells feds: "follow us". *Calgary Herald*, A1.

Kentucky Education Association and Appalachia Educational Laboratory (1993, March). *Finding time for school reform: Obstacles and answers*. Charleston, West Virginia: Appalachia Educational Laboratory.

Kentucky General Assembly, Office of Educational Accountability (1994). *Annual Report*. Frankfort: Kentucky General Assembly, Office of Educational Accountability.

Kerr, N. (1969). The school board as an agency of legitimation. In Rosenthal, E. (Ed.), *Governing education* (pp. 137–177). New York: Doubleday Anchor.

Kirkpatrick, D.W. (1994). Magnet schools/Charter schools. In Greenwalt, C.E. (Ed.), *Education innovation* (pp. 241–260). Lanham, Maryland: University Press of America.

Kyle, C.L. & Kantowicz, E.R. (1992). *Kids first - primero los niños*. Springfield: Illinois Issues.

Lauber, D. & Warden, C. (1992). Edmonton plans one way to set schools free. *Catalyst*, 4(1), 11–12.

Legislative Assembly of Alberta (1994). *Bill 19, School Amendment Act, 1994*. Edmonton: Legislative Assembly of Alberta.

Legislative Research Commission. (1991). *The Kentucky Education Reform Act of 1990*. Frankfort, Kentucky: Legislative Research Commission.

Leighton, M. & Sykes, G. (1992, October). *The professionalization of teaching: Centerpiece of Kentucky reform*. Charleston, West Virginia: Appalachia Educational Laboratory.

Lindbloom, C. (1977). *Politics and markets*. New York: Basic Books.

Lisac, M. (1994, February 11). Provincial tories hiding a big secret. *Calgary Herald*, A4.

Lisac, M. (1995). *The Klein revolution*. Edmonton: NeWest Press.

Marshall, A. (1994, April 4). The wrath of grey power has yet to surface. *Calgary Herald*, A1, A2.

Marshall, R. & Tucker, M. (1992). *Thinking for a living*. New York: Basic Books.

Martin, D. (1994, April 28). Kindergarten research major hokum. *Calgary Herald*, A3.

Mitchell, A. (1995, January 10). Grading of schools planned in Alberta. *Globe and Mail*, A1, A2.

Mitchell, S. (1971). *A woman's profession - a man's research.* Edmonton: Alberta Association of Registered Nurses.

Mitchell, S. (1992). *Innovation and reform.* York, Ontario: Captus Press.

Murphy, J. & Hallinger, J. (1993). *Restructuring schooling.* Newbury Park, California: Corwin Press.

National Alliance of Business (1991). *The Business Roundtable participation guide: A primer for business on education.* New York: Business Roundtable.

National Alliance for Restructuring Education (1993, June). *The Alliance,* 1(10), 1–4.

National Education Goals Panel. (1992). *Executive Summary, The National Education Goals Report.* Washington, D.C.: National Education Goals Panel.

Nowakowski, J. & First, P. (1989, Winter). A study of school board minutes: Records of reform. *Educational Evaluation and Policy Analysis,* 11(4), 389–404.

O'Connell, M. (1991). *School reform Chicago style.* Chicago: Center for Neighbourhood Technology.

Olsen, L. (1986, November 12). Local school boards lose power, prestige: New study asserts. *Education Week,* 6(10), 1, 16.

Olsen, L. (1994, January 19). Varied laws raise a question: What is a charter school? *Education Week,* 13(17), 14.

Osborne, D. & Gaebler, T. (1992). *Reinventing government.* Reading, Massachusetts: Addison-Wesley.

Parish, T. (1990). *The Prichard Committee for Academic Excellence: The first decade 1980-1990.* Lexington, Kentucky: The Prichard Committee for Academic Excellence.

Pick, G. (1994, April). LSC learns from '90' uproar. *Catalyst,* 5(7), 8–9.

Pitsch, M. (1994, March 30). Stage set for senate showdown on Goals 2000. *Education Week,* 13 (27), 16.

Pitsch, M. (1994, April 6). With students' aid, Clinton signs Goals 2000. *Education Week,* 13(28), 1, 21.

Prichard Committee For Academic Excellence and The Partnership for Kentucky School Reform (1993, October). *KERA Updates: Watch for....* Lexington: Prichard Committee for Academic Excellence.

Public Services Redesign Project (1993, September 23). *Charter schools, the states begin to withdraw the "exclusive".* Saint Paul: Public Services Redesign Project.

Raths, J., Katz, L., Fanning, J., David, J. & Roeder, P. (1992). *First Year Reports of the Prichard Committee.* Lexington, Kentucky: Prichard Committee for Academic Excellence.

Raths, J., Katz, L., Fanning, J., David, J. & Roeder, P. (1993). *Second Year Reports of the Prichard Committee.* Lexington, Kentucky: The Prichard Committee for Academic Excellence.

Richardson, J. (1995, August 2). Flushed with victory, charter-school advocates share words of wisdom. *Education Week,* 14(4), 16.

Salamon, L. M. (1987). Of market failure, voluntary failure and third-party government: Toward a theory of government non-profit relations in the modern welfare state. In Ostrander, S. & Langton, S. (Eds.), *Shifting the debate* (pp. 30-49). New Brunswick, New Jersey: Transaction Books.

Sautter, R.C. (1993). *Charter Schools: Policy Brief, N. 2.* Oak Park, Illinois: North Central Regional Educational Laboratory.

School Management Study Group (1994). *Partnership assessment: St. Charles Parish/ Union Carbide model school reform agreement.* Salt Lake City: Union Carbide.

Sommerfeld, M. (1994, January 12). Annenberg gift prompts praise and questions. *Education Week*, 13(16), 1.

Staff (1993). *From risk to renewal.* Washington, D.C.: Education Week.

Toch, T. (1991). *In the name of excellence.* New York: Oxford.

Vander Weele, M. (1994). *Reclaiming Our Schools.* Chicago: Loyola University.

Viadero, D. (1994, June 8). The little firm that could. *Education Week*, 13(37), 25–27.

Walker, R. (1988, May 11). The legacy of 'Prich': Bluegrass roots reform. *Education Week*, 7(33), 1, 12.

Webber, C. (1995, July 9). Educational change in Alberta, Canada. *Education Policy Analysis Archives*, 3(12).

Weismann, D. (1994, April). New council in, prize-winning principal out. *Catalyst*, 5(7), 5–7.

Chapter 5

The Transformative Powers of Business

Many companies are concerned that they will not be able to find employees who can even read or do simple arithmetic. *Business Week* reports $210 billion is spent annually by American companies to train and upgrade their workers, which exceeds the $195 billion annual expenditure for public elementary and secondary education. Because $20 billion of that private sector budget is already earmarked for remedial education (a total that can be expected to increase), companies are forced to pay twice for education—first through taxes and then for internal remedial programs—for what the schools could not or did not achieve. (National Alliance of Business, 1990, p. 3)

It is fashionable today to be in favor of such active partnerships, although far more often than not such assent on the part of educators means: "How can we get them to support what we are already doing?" (Seymour Sarason, 1990, p. 156)

Business influence on education has increased and partnerships for education have become a fad. The venerable American investment house, Lehman Brothers, has proclaimed that education "may replace health care as the focus industry" (Walsh, 1996, February, p.15). Both possible influences and actual relationships will be examined critically here, but the present focus is on mapping the major activities that are involved and the reasons why these activities have evolved. The separate entities of business and education have very different values, but the conflicts are best seen in specific contexts. The long-term effects of business demands on education also need to be considered; this is the focus of this chapter. For example, neither business nor education anticipates that it will change as a result of the new partnership. As was the case in the first Chicago summit, business expects to see improvement in the skills of new graduates, and school administrators expect business to provide jobs for their graduates. Alternatively, members of partnerships may experience a mutual change based on a shared commitment, as in Kentucky (Sarason, 1990, p. 177). The joint involvement of business leaders and community activists also showed such dedication in opposing the educational bureaucracy and securing the Chicago Reform Act.

However, neither reforms in Chicago nor elsewhere have proved that executives are either reliable or knowledgeable partners. In Alberta, for example, partnerships with schools have not constituted a significant part of the dramatic political or educational changes that have occurred. In all of the cases, business is assumed to be superior because of its generally dominant position in our society. However, business has proved to be erratic both in its involvement in education and in its positions taken regarding the school system. It has alternated between private school challenges to the public schools and cooperation through joint committees to improve the public system. In either case, the rational and instrumental way of thinking of businesspeople and the predictable planning that results from their business model of the world dominate and subordinate the efforts of those involved in educational reform.

Rather than altering its position on change or its own limited ways of understanding reform in the educational system, business is, increasingly, transforming the kind of power that is involved when it attempts to change education. The economic power of business can be changed into political capital, as well as other, more varied forms of power. The business advocacy group in Chicago as well as the national business organizations in Canada and the United States have attempted to develop their respective legislative influences. Attempts by maverick business leaders to start individual schools represent an attempt to develop personal power. Attempts to develop systems of private schools and to develop entrepreneurial efforts by teachers are intended to transform the political authority of schools into the original image of business, namely, economic power. The more indirect forms of business power exercised through foundations, and the symbolic control over educational activities shown by awards and model schools, represent still another, probably more frightening, direction that business has tried to take. None of these power shifts has been consistent. Business power is distant from the world of the young and may force students to be too realistic too soon as they are caught up in the power moves. Alternatively, business can, if it chooses, direct its many powers toward the transformation of the education of students into more meaningful and comprehensive directions.

IDEOLOGY FROM THE OUTSIDE

The pattern-setting Boston Compact has had to be renegotiated three times because the educators and business leaders could not achieve a working consensus. The initial goals were unrealistic; business was providing jobs, rather than offering incentives to improve the educational program itself (Farrar & Cipolline, 1988, p. 111). The most recent plan is framed in terms of annual improvements in the school program (Walsh, January 26, 1994). With the new incremental approach, business leaders and teachers should see each other as partners.

Originally, in the most famous agreement between business and education, business leaders were seen by educators as very strange. The characters, in a very revealing incident, are Bob Schwartz as the Boston Compact's executive director; Edward Doherty, as the Boston Teachers' Union president and Cay Stratton, as the executive director of the Boston Private Industry Council, a nonprofit organization that develops employment training. Though none of these actors was a business representative, they all act on their shared understanding of the motives that they believe characterize corporate leaders. None of the three seems to consider a creative meeting of private interests and public education.

"It's always a tough choice whether to begin with something at the grass-roots level and get a lot of participation or, particularly with something of this complexity, to negotiate behind closed doors with a limited number of people and then deal with the flack you get from those who weren't included," Bob Schwartz admitted. The compact staff felt they had to operate the latter way because the business community had little understanding of, or tolerance for, the processes required in working with the public sector. "If we had said to the business leadership that, in addition to having to negotiate with the Superintendent, we would have to go out and consult with 25 different community-based organizations and interest groups, they would have said, 'Hey, sorry.'" The staff also felt that securing the business community's commitment first would help to deliver the cooperation of other groups.

Still, at the time, the union had "no major objections to the Compact. The schools need money to operate, and that's tax money. If business is lobbying against the schools or being silent, it doesn't get legislators to vote favorably. If business cooperates, it's easier to get money from elected officials." Ed Doherty also liked the Compact's goals. "They're ones that no one can object to: improved attendance, jobs for the kids, reducing dropouts, increasing college attendance. They are simply and clearly spelled out." Cay Stratton believes that attaching numbers to these goals and putting them in the form of a bargain was essential to winning wide endorsement. "This concept was easy for the business community and the public to understand. When you talk about school improvement as a bargain, it's less abstract. They can grab it. Businesspeople do not relate to terms like institutional change." (Farrar & Cipolline, 1988, pp. 98–99)

Though recognizing that businesspeople have different language, beliefs, and values, those who are responsible for establishing educational policy have never challenged the culture of business. From the start in Boston to copies in Chicago and Canada, businesspeople were partners who, like colonial masters, were to be manipulated for benefits that could be immediately gathered. There are benefits for those at the bottom of the educational order who are not even aware of the arrangement made by policy makers at the top. In Chicago and Boston, the sponsorship programs have been shown to produce a more positive attitude toward school among students (Hess, 1991 and Timpane & McNeill, 1991). Furthermore, those teachers directly involved with business partnerships do have a greater sense of empowerment, probably because they are no longer so isolated as are the more typical teachers (Trachtman, 1988, p. 199).

Teachers do not understand the influence that business can have on work opportunities for students, political changes in education, or teachers' daily work. Businesses may be most effective in developing a knowledge of jobs and careers through the exposure of students to work (Timpane & McNeill, 1991, pp. 15-18). In North America, work experience is not seen by teachers as relevant to the teaching of basic subjects (Jones & Maloy, 1988, p. 80). In Germany, in contrast, apprenticeship programs reinforce academic goals, including moral education, so the contribution of work education to academic goals seems more obvious (Hamilton, 1990). In Chicago, teachers do not see business as a major contributor to school reform in spite of an incredible amount of activity by the business advocacy group (Day, 1993, p.16). The teachers are more likely to see and understand the more political advocacy groups as active players even when such protest groups are working hand in hand with business organizations. For their daily problems of classroom discipline, few teachers ever consider an increase in the unemployment rate as being related to discipline problems of high school students. The students who would prefer to have jobs, but cannot find them, act out in the teachers' classrooms as a result (Mitchell, 1967).

One might expect teachers to see the significance of business policies and economic changes, but they could also come to understand the difference between their values and those of business. Unfortunately, teachers usually do not sense the different values of businesspeople even when they are involved in partnerships (Trachtman, 1988). Teachers might sense the dangers and advantages of involvement with business if they took a broader view.

There are many reasons why any form of business partnership may be suspect. Sponsorship can be as self-serving as giving away pizzas for reading a book or donating computers to schools when families purchase their groceries from a particular chain (Rigden, 1992, p. 43). In New Zealand, advertisements have been used on students' examination booklets to the point of becoming distracting. Closer to home, at a Fairfield, Connecticut, company, Lifetime Learning develops programs for a variety of companies so that they can have their films or booklets used in the schools (Barlow & Robertson, 1994, p. 81). Chris Whittle's Channel One has put his advertisements on the television programs that are provided to schools, while Youth News Network has tried the same thing in Canada (Walsh, 1994, August). The tax write-offs for support of special education in the United States are a major reason for business to support work experience programs (Brennan, 1990). The Canadian Chamber of Commerce has long sought similar tax advantages (John Ballheim, interview, May 17, 1994).

Teachers can come to see that the economic interests of some businesses, more than others, may coincide with their interests. For example, knowledge of health is important for Metropolitan Life, since prolonging lives saves them money. Metropolitan Life also has broader interests; it wants to develop relationships with teachers, and that is apparently why it carries out studies for its teacher profiles (Levy, 1988). Technological literacy is necessary for the sales that Hewlett-Packard makes and so their employees work jointly with teachers in advanced classrooms. It is in their best institutional interest to develop a summer program that employs twenty-five thousand mathematics and science teachers. *Time* magazine has an interest in literacy and, consequently, has trained volunteers and developed a curriculum for this purpose (Conference Board, 1988, p. 26). Many other magazines and newspapers are involved in literacy efforts since they are in very competitive markets. There are a host of overlapping purposes that include immediate improvements as well as long-term relationships between businesses and educators.

IDEOLOGY AS AN ANSWER TO CRISES

Teachers, or others who are caught up in a set of beliefs about how business can change education, do not weigh the advantages and disadvantages of their value position. Unlike proponents of traditional cultures or values, modern managerial ideologists see science or reason as the basis for establishing policy in education or other institutions (Boudon, 1989, p. 25). A cost analysis makes it possible for Canadian business, for example, to determine the benefits of participating in an educational partnership (Conference Board of Canada, 1993). There is little doubt in the minds of those who support such actions that they are capable of solving the problems of education. Those who are accepting such new answers are accepting ideologies which are "endowed with excessive and unjustified credibility" (Boudon, 1989, p. 33). Other positions are put down while the new faith is upheld. Righteous claims are reinforced by a perception of crises. For the Boston Compact, racial and urban changes are the underlying sources of this, the first business compact, as racial conflicts have affected educational and social policies in many other American cities. For Alberta, with little concern for racial conflicts, it was the perception of governmental debt that led to new plans for fundamentally altering the role of government, as discussed in Chapter 4. As will be shown in the next chapter, Kentucky tried to alter its position as near last among the states in terms of educational achievement or educational expenditure. The specific cases that are discussed in the next chapter will further clarify the meaning of ideology, which is used here to refer to differences in thinking, not just emotional feelings and value judgments. Whether it is Kentucky, Boston, Chicago or Canada, the perception of a moral crisis in education made the legitimacy of education questionable and the answers from business acceptable (Carnoy & Levin, 1985).

Generally, business joined the educational war to prove its might after the *A Nation at Risk* report focused attention on educational excellence as the remedy for international economic decline; it was only after this that there was a call for higher academic standards. It has been assumed, rather than proved, that greater competitiveness will be secured by an educational revolution. Claims are made that business interests and educational aims are the same (Frank, 1992 and Corporate-Higher Education Forum, 1991a). In these reports, all educators and businesspeople are said to endorse the goals of academic skills, personal attitudes, and teamwork. Right-wing groups and others may object, but are we not all to become entrepreneurs in the postindustrial world? If so, teachers, businesspeople, and even students as workers will all be cut from the same corporate cloth. Ideology incorporates various interests so that "a fusion of disparate groups" occurs (Kenway, 1990, p. 177).

If any other group in our society dared to make such an exclusive claim, there would be a huge outcry. The values of unions, women's organizations, natives, or churches are seen as "typical" of special interest groups. If an exchange, such as the Ryerson plan between school and business personnel, was proposed between schools and these other organizations, there would be a crisis (Apple, 1982, p. 132). Economic power, together with a perception of crisis, allows business to have a disproportionate amount of influence on society. Interests other than business can resist their position but, without an alternative ideology, the dominant ideology cannot be actively contested (Knight et al., 1990, p. 136).

The acceptance of a business view of education leads to an expansion of the claims that such an ideology will make until it is opposed. Business has, for a long time, had an ally within education, educational administration. Since educational administrators accept many business values, they, apparently, cannot blame businesses for their problems (Evans, 1994). Business leaders see administrators in education as people whom they can train and whose institutions they can reorganize, since their tasks are similar to those of businesses (Conference Board, 1989). In contrast, for educational administrators, students' low achievement results from a lack of family support, low motivation of students and teachers, and inadequate financing, while, for business executives, the problems result from a lack of emphasis on teaching skills, inadequate teachers, and low standards

(Graham, 1992, p. 140). Recent plans for restructuring the central office in Chicago show how potent the alliance of administration, research, and business may become, in contrast to local community groups (Diana Lauber and John Ayers, interviews, May 11, 1995).

New advocates for business can claim new territories, including the family. At an earlier time, the efficiency movement tried to extend its measurements to the family after applying them to education, health, and social agencies (Callahan, 1962). It has been asserted that, in a partnership situation, businesspeople are just like parents (Doug Clovechok, interview, August 3, 1994). In fact, business leaders have a lot more power than parents, and they also have an interest in profits that parents lack. Parents are concerned about their individual children in a way unknown to firms. It might help teachers to understand that parental values and business values are at least as different as family values and school aims. Businesses influence families by laying off household heads or by supporting the education of male employees, while ignoring similar programs for their spouses (Corporate-Higher Education Forum, 1991).

Since business has made claims of restructuring schools and families, it is hardly surprising that claims are made as to how teachers should teach and how knowledge should be organized. A study for the national Governors' Association suggested that functional integration in business is a justification for integration across instructional areas of either curriculum supervisors or teachers (Lewis, 1989, p. 101). Scientists together with engineers are not always in favor of integrating the sciences. Scientists or related groups are seen by business as being able to transfer their knowledge to teaching in schools. The Teachers Academy for Mathematics and Science in Chicago particularly showed the problems that this simple approach can produce. Lourdes Monteagudo, (who was discussed in Chapter 2) a principal, not a scientist, was hired as a result of the initial problems. Business or the Business Roundtable, at least, supports class projects because such project activities are similar to their use of groups in decision making; there is similar support for cultural sensitivity since it is seen as required by the society's changing ethnic and racial composition (National Alliance of Business, 1991).

LIVING WITH THE PAST

To continue the expansion of claims, ideologies must both fit the present social milieu and adapt to past ideas and values (Bendix, 1956, p. 115 and Boudon, 1989, p. 168). There is no precedent for business's present support for academic programs, and there is no recent precedent for the level of educational activity that national business organizations are now sustaining in search of the Holy Grail. For the first time, specialists in ideological development have emerged, such as the author of the nine-point plan of the

BRT discussed in chapter four (Boudon, 1989, p. 195). The party line of such a specialist will be discussed at length in this chapter.

Business has not followed a consistent path in its relationship with the schools. Today, businesses are supporting a largely academic curriculum as a basis for developing thoughtful and cooperative employees. The academic interest corresponded with the publication of *A Nation at Risk* in 1983. In the past, companies have supported vocational education and the streaming of different student programs (Levine, 1988). At the turn of the century, companies wanted employees who were more adjustable than skilled workers and let many apprenticeship programs disappear as a result of major strikes with early unions (McNeil, 1988, pp. 8–9). However, the companies' support for vocational programs was so controversial that many withdrew from education for a long time (Kyle & Kantowicz, 1992, p. 220). The early interest of business in vocational education was strongly opposed by unions.

After the open battle over vocational education, business executives often tended to work behind the scenes on school finances and to limit their direct involvement to participation on school boards and committees (Wrigley, 1982). After 1960, in the United States, the controversies caused by student activists and racial resistance led to a withdrawal of business participation in the boards and committees (Trachtman, 1988, p. 207). In Canada, at the same time, there were fewer crises, but business involvement in the organizational structure of public education is also said to have declined (Canadian Chamber of Commerce, 1990). The increased involvement of teacher unions, advocates for special education, lawyers, and organized community groups is claimed to have led to the Canadian withdrawal (p. 9). Only later, when allies could be found, did business in either country overcome its ingrained fear of educational conflict.

However, just before the current era of partnerships and the reign of academics, there was a return to vocational aims that is still practiced in some places. In the late 1970s, some companies supported career education and competency-based training. These programs had such a decidedly vocational direction that they alone could have accounted for the declining performance of students in schools (Shor, 1986). Support for career programs had declined well before *Nation at Risk* heralded academic failures as the source of productivity decline and a fall to a less competitive position.

Ironically, just before the current rediscovery of the importance of educational excellence, companies let their concern for profits get the best of them. Declining profits had led to a fingering of education as one of the causes of high taxes, which were believed to reduce profits (Carnoy & Levin, 1985). Of all the provinces in Canada, Alberta has kept business most happy by keeping corporate taxes lower than in most provinces and, as well, lower than personal taxes (Hesch, 1994). The limitation of taxes or new bonds led to the decline of California; it went from being one of the highest spending states to one of the lowest (Berman & Clugston, 1988). Currently, the Educational Commission of the States has been brought into California in order to redirect the once proud educational system (*Education Week*, 1994, February, p. 12).

Even in Chicago, school reform is an alternative to greater financial support for schools by the state. While school taxes were being squeezed by corporate concerns, there was another push that would bring forth greater business efforts for education: the racial explosions. In most large northern American cities, including Chicago, racial riots would signal a new corporate involvement as being preferable to large-scale destruction; such involvement would, over time, lead to greater action for education (Berman & Clugston, 1988). The business concern for riots did not, apparently, transfer into educational reform in the South, but the call to arms of *A Nation at Risk* would put education on the agenda of companies all over North America.

A WORKING CONSENSUS

One inheritance that business cannot discard is its attachment to vocational education and the divisiveness that it has introduced into modern education. Current work experience programs have been shown to bring out contributions that business can, rather distinctively, make to education (Timpane & McNeill, 1991, pp. 15–18). Students develop more realistic perceptions of jobs while employers screen and select potential employees. Work experience programs are like vocational educational programs in that they are removed from the academic work of teachers. This is likely a result of the fact that vocational education has been developed, proportionately, more by school administrators than by teachers (Daft & Becker, 1978, p. 113). Recent attempts to integrate academic work with vocational education have dramatically raised the test results of vocational students (Olson, 1994 and Bottoms et al., 1992, January). From the same studies it can be seen that the aspirations of vocational students have also risen remarkably, though in 350 schools, not a single vocational student has yet taken physics!

Vocational education has led to a whole series of stereotypes about vocational and academic students and teachers. Academic students see vocational students as being in the zoo while vocational students see their academic peers as being in the country club (Rosenbaum, 1976). The streaming has not improved the performance of such differing groups and has lowered the aspirations of the more subordinated ones. Similar separations between teacher groups have been shown to lead to misunderstandings and antagonisms (Sarason, 1982). Academic teachers are likely to see business as mainly interested in vocational education.

The difficulties with work experience and vocational education are only part of the separation of education and business. Involved, as they are, in the separate fields of education and business, the players are not even likely to recognize their mutual contributions to educational reform. For example, the school's staff and business partners learn to work together through tutoring or sharing of resources. Joint training in the use of the computer for teachers and company employees, or printing of school materials by the company print shop, reduces the stereotypes that business leaders and teachers have of each other (Jones & Maloy, 1988, p. 82).

Aside from the greater mutual understanding that can result from such sponsorship programs, it is possible to develop specific educational achievements in other ways. When corporate leaders can transfer the experience of reorganizing their own business to changing the schools, they can be a very valuable asset for school reform. In Chicago, it was a man with great experience on both sides of the business-education divide, Warren Bacon, who spearheaded the formation of a business advocacy group for education (Lawrence Howe, interview, April 25, 1994). Also, opportunities for a meaningful partnership are greater when business uses more than the single criterion of profits in thinking about school change (Jones & Maloy, 1988, p. 82 and Graham 1992, p. 153). Partnerships are most productive when both groups rethink their roles, change their positions, and develop common aims. Such changes are difficult for partnerships to develop unless the shared purposes are based on accepting the distinctive purposes of each institution rather than simply subordinating the interests of the weaker party.

Businesspeople misunderstand teachers and schools in even more varied ways than teachers misunderstand business leaders. Executives often see school administrators as indecisive and rule–bound bureaucrats (Jones & Maloy, 1988). Business leaders are even urged to approach schools with "controlled impatience" (Timpane & McNeill, 1991, p. 34); rigid school structures are expected to frustrate results-oriented business executives (National Alliance of Business, 1991). Corporate executives have seldom learned to approach the reorganization of schools with the same attention to bottom-up thinking they practice in restructuring companies (Sarason, 1990, pp. 17–24). Furthermore, only 25 percent of companies have adapted to more highly skilled graduates as employees (Barlow & Robertson, 1994, p. 58).

Educators and business leaders generally have trouble overcoming stereotypes because they have little, if any, experience in working with each other. Large companies do not often recruit local school graduates, even in middle-size cities such as Guelph, Ontario (Hall & Carlton, 1977). With such an arms-length stance, both are likely to misread each other. Educators have often pigeonholed new interest of business into the area of vocational education and limited business to serving only as a resource for money and assistance (Timpane, 1984, p. 390). But if partnerships are to provide both parties with an opportunity to rethink their roles, then both parties must be able to help each other. Educators can help business develop employees who are creative and sensitive; this will enhance the long-term future of these companies. Executives for Citibank who have successfully served the Coalition of Essential Schools as outside critics have shown how business can advise without hindering reform (Coalition of Essential Schools, 1993, January, p. 3). Businesspeople need no longer see educators as rule-bound, timid, and rigid, while educators, in turn, should not view business executives as dominating and unconcerned (Jones & Maloy, 1988 and Graham, 1992 p. 138). Each may see the other as a partner in making improvements.

INDIVIDUAL MAVERICKS AND CORPORATE SCHOOLS

The possibilities of both cooperation and conflict are experienced by a number of school systems confronting businesses that are entering education directly. Corporate organizations are either running schools for public systems or competing with the systems through private corporations. In Minneapolis, beginning in December 1993, a for-profit consulting firm, Public Strategies Group Inc., took over the entire forty-four thousand-student district. This firm's contract is unique in that it is paid for the tasks it achieves. For example, by negotiating employee contracts within a budget, it earned $6,000. In its first six months, the company completed thirty of forty-one tasks and earned $165,000 of a possible $244,000 (Richardson, 1994, August, p. 18). Over $100,000 of the possible pot involves student achievement, in which large gains have not yet been made.

The people of Minneapolis have hired a man whom they trust as superintendent, Peter Hutchinson. Hutchinson and his partner, Babak Armajani, are the heart of the firm that was said by the school board president, Ann Kaari, to have provided a new way to achieve the goal of improving performance for all students. Mr. Huchinson had, in the previous year, cleaned up the school finance-and-operations division, where the financial blunders of a previous superintendent and one of his top aides had led to a scandal (Richardson, 1994, February, p. 32).

Hutchinson had successful experiences with private industry as well as government before becoming a consultant. Managing the Minneapolis Zoo prepared him to manage the school system! He believes in reinventing government and spending as much time as possible with the customers, students and parents; his approach is direct with no jargon and he is willing to tell the most "brutal truth," which is "I don't know" (p. 33). His previous clients were located largely in Minnesota, though the Province of Manitoba also has a contract with him. His other clients have also paid him by the number of services performed. Only an early-learning service project for families in Minneapolis has not been satisfied with his results; in that case, he swallowed $430,000 in costs (p. 33). Peter Huchinson is neither an expert nor a corporate builder. His goal is to provide temporary leadership. His partner, Armajani, tries to develop leadership so that, when the contract with Public Strategies is completed, there will be good school people to carry on. While the two partners are running the school system, they believe that they are members of the community where they work, and they will have to live with any mess they make.

In contrast to the community commitment of Public Strategies, a corporate school in Chicago was supposed to be a model for other efforts by corporate sponsors, but franchises in Houston and St. Louis never developed (Corporate/Community School of America, 1991). The corporate school in Chicago is the lone product of this effort and the work of one individual, Joe Kellman. Mr. Kellman, unlike Mr. Hutchinson, never planned on withdrawing from the school, but has, recently, found that he has no choice but to join the Chicago public system. His school has attempted to be a part of the cluster project discussed in Chapter 2. Mr. Kellman has tried to obtain money from the Annenberg Foundation but, apparently, has been unsuccessful (Joe Kellman, interview, April 27, 1994).

Mr. Kellman's school has had a promising start and has become an important example of integrated services that will be discussed in Chapter 7. Joe Kellman made his fortune in the auto glass industry and has used his position to raise $12 million from corporate sponsors for a school in one of the poorest sections of Chicago, Lawndale. Even after joining the Chicago public system, the school has $750,000 a year, which is pledged by corporate sponsors, to provide an extensive schedule of health and welfare services. Seventy-five community agencies are coordinated with the school's own services. The school operates from 7:00 a.m. to 7:00 p.m. eleven months a year for children beginning at age two. The children are chosen by lottery and will continue to be chosen that way even after the public school board takes over. Staff who lack formal certification will be provided with an opportunity to acquire their credentials.

Ironically, Mr. Kellman has always believed that experts should replace school boards. A number of problems have compounded so that he is no longer able to be the sole judge of experts for his school. His expert principal, Elaine Mosely, chosen for the job after a national search, has left. This school's initial burst of high scores among its students has not been sustained, and the high scores may have resulted from testing an atypically stable group from an area where transiency is the norm. There have also been morale problems among the teachers who continued on staff and who may suffer from burnout (Diana Lauber, interview, October 11, 1993).

A close ally of Joe Kellman, Marva Collins, has also, recently, turned away from individual efforts to government involvement. Mrs. Collins runs a private school in the same area of Chicago as Mr. Kellman. Her school, Westside Preparatory, stresses individual responsibility and high academic work for poor Black children. She is unlikely to return to the school board from which she departed after being a teacher there for a number of years (Collins & Tamarkin, 1992). She has become involved with a government project after rejecting a more direct political role. Prior to her current involvement with this special project, she had, supposedly, turned down offers by both Presidents Reagan and Bush to be secretary of education, as well as an offer to be superintendent of the Los Angeles school system. For many years, she had preferred to remain an independent entrepreneur in education, while teaching her students to be independent of governmental help.

Recently, Marva Collins has changed her stance and has developed a school in a Chicago public housing project where she is administering a nonselective program from kindergarten to grade four. Before Mrs. Collins extended the program, it had been limited to preschool activities. The new effort is a private school but it is also a joint partnership of the U.S. Justice Department's office for juveniles and delinquency prevention, the Chicago Housing Authority, and Marva Collins (Cohen, December, 1993). This combined effort is the Beethoven project.

Both Mrs. Collins and Mr. Kellman have been outside the circle of the reformers who had worked to implement the 1988 Illinois Reform Act. Kellman was viewed as a competitor for corporate donations and Collins was seen as a person who had given up on Chicago schools long ago (Diana Lauber, interview, October 11, 1993). Though there is still no dialogue with the reformers' groups, the mavericks, Kellman and Collins, have started to move to a focus in which some common action may be possible.

Though Peter Hutchinson, Joe Kellman, and Marva Collins are remarkable pioneers of private contributions to education, none has inspired more potent reactions than Christopher Whittle has with his Edison Project. Teacher unions are particularly aghast about the profit-motivated schools that Mr. Whittle has proposed. Whittle has had the greatest success with his Channel One, that provides television equipment to schools, along with news that includes paid advertisements to which students must listen (Walsh, 1994, August, p. 18). Originally, Mr. Whittle was going to build new schools and operate them for profit at the same cost per student that most public systems are now charging. Investors included Philips Electronics and Time Warner, who put up $40 million. However, far more money would be needed and, without the money that a voucher system could provide for its schools, the Edison Project has turned to charter schools which will be operated through contracts with school systems.

Aside from the money, Whittle and other corporate managers are challenging the way schools are governed. Walt Disney Enterprises fiddled with the idea of investing in Project Edison and having Whittle operate the new school that Disney is building in its Orlando community. But Disney, instead, decided to run its own school as a model for training teachers from all over the country (Walsh, 1994, June, pp. 16). Both Disney and the Edison Project want to show they can run schools better than democratically elected school boards; they are sounding the autocratic call much as the robber barons did in the past century.

With clearer operational plans than either Whittle or the managers at Disney, Educational Alternatives Inc. (EAI) became an important player in the educational scene when it contracted to run nine schools in Baltimore in 1992. After over a year of negotiating, it is now taking responsibility for some of the schools in Hartford, Connecticut; EAI was, originally, to run the entire school system.   Before obtaining the Baltimore and Hartford contracts, John Golle, the CEO of EAI, was a retired salesman who had come out of retirement to run three schools in his hometown of Minneapolis and in the Miami Beach area. Mr. Golle believes that he must invest in new technology and building repairs, since he wants to bring about systemic reform with "more disposable income to spend on the students" (Schmidt, 1994, August, p. 19).   In Hartford, Mr. Golle has won out over Public Educational Services Inc. of Woodbridge, Virginia, presumably one of his competitors, whom he has elsewhere described as a "mom and pop" consulting firm (Golle, 1994, June p. 44).

Though the mavericks have developed some individual approaches to curriculum, the more corporate groups want to offer packages of other people's ideas. Marva Collins has, for example, rather uniquely combined classics and parables with personal consulting and moral training.   Joe Kellman has instituted an integrated curriculum, merging social values and integrated support services (Klonsky, 1994, September, p. 31). However, the EAI seems to act as if there is an "it" to be taught, while the Edison Project almost entirely draws on the ideas of others.   EIA claims to use innovative methods, which include no grades, a personal education plan, computers, and a low student-teacher ratio. At least, in an evaluation done by the Maryland State Teachers' Association, EAI was very traditional with none of its proclaimed innovations amounting to much more than the usual dominance of teacher talk in the classrooms (Edmonton Public School Board Custodial Workers, 1994, pp. 2–3). In its proposal for a charter school in Massachusetts, the Edison Project has ideas that are surprisingly similar to other educational approaches, such as a Great Books program (Schmidt, 1994, August, p. 1). The planners who were recruited by Chris Whittle have also adopted a number of other reform ideas, including cooperative learning, experiential science work, use of computer networks, and even character training. If the mavericks join the public systems, it may be hard to find a creative thrust for the curriculum from the businesses that compete with public education.

Perhaps because of its inflated ambitions, EAI has drawn the repeated fire of teacher unions (Schmidt, 1994, August, p. 190).   Complaints by the teachers' union led to the finding that EAI failed to follow some federal mandates for special education, but many other charges by the American Federation of Teachers proved to be unfounded.   EAI and Baltimore officials complained that checking out the many charges required an inordinate amount of time and that the problems the investigators did find had begun before EAI's involvement and stemmed from one middle school. The same people claim that evidence from the Miami Beach school, South Pointe, shows improvement in the students' performance. Mr. Shanker, president of the American Federation of Teachers, says that the test results in Baltimore have declined and that there are financial irregularities in the accounting of funds for poorer students, the Chapter 1 allocations (Shanker,

1994, June, pp. 43–44). *Education Week* found that the issue was so controversial that "superintendents of several of the largest school districts in the country declined to submit commentaries on the subject" (Education Week, 1994, June, p. 41).

The superintendent of Baltimore City Schools, Dr. Walter Amprey, who has continued to support EAI, explained this corporate approach to the Edmonton Public Board and that board, subsequently, voted to explore the contracting out of one or more schools (Edmonton Public School Board Custodial Workers, 1994, p. 1). Another company, Ombudsmen Educational Services, has contracts with over sixty districts in Arizona, Illinois, and Minnesota; it limits education to three hours a day so that teachers can handle several clusters of students in rotation to make its program more effective and less expensive than the public schools (Hopchin, 1994). A Canadian corporate group, Akademia Enterprises, is listed on the Alberta Stock Exchange, operates an international school in Banff and is planning a combination of a school and hotel in The Waterton National Park (Barlow & Robertson, 1994, p. 145 and Carmalita Capco, personal communication, March 25, 1996). The Canadian experience has been less publicized than the American.

THE NATIONAL ROUNDUP

Many business and education organizations have tried to sidestep controversies and have not taken any specific stance on private business operating schools. These organizations have developed programs with educators which include curriculum changes. The large number of business organizations try to achieve some coordination so that they do not appear to be competing with each other (National Alliance of Business, 1991). Chart 5.1 shows the broader business organizations that are concerned about education. The Business Roundtable has been rated by the other leaders of business organizations as the most influential group in educational reform in the United States (Council for Aid to Education, 1994). In Chicago, the branch of the BRT is less important than the Civic Committee and its related organizations, such as Leadership for Quality Education; this Chicago case is discussed in the next chapter. In Canada, the Business Council on National Issues (BCNI) is similar to the Business Roundtable in that it is composed of the executives of the twenty-five largest corporations; as well, organizations in question can be very influential on specific national issues (Ted Mieszkalski, interview, August 24, 1994). The BCNI was a crucial supporter of free trade debate and even influenced the number of televised debates on the subject, but, in terms of education, has limited itself to a few studies such as one on job retraining and a position paper on competitiveness. BRT, on the other hand, has a ten-year commitment to keeping educational reform one of its highest priorities.

The BRT collaborates with the National Alliance of Business as well as a host of other organizations (Council for Aid to Education, 1994, p. i). The Business Alliance considers any company that pays its dues a member, in contrast to the BRT, with its eighty-nine select members. However, the alliance often does the work of writing publications and offering conferences that the BRT supports. Both of these American organizations are members of the Business Coalition on Education Reform, as are the Committee on Economic Development and the Chamber of Commerce; Black and Spanish business organizations are also members. The Committee on Economic Development includes 250 CEOs and senior managers, grant makers, and community leaders. The Center for Workforce Preparation of the Chamber of Commerce raises its own funds and provides studies and conferences to individual chambers on school financing and technology.

In Canada, there are neither the broad coalitions nor the specialized business centers that exist in the United States. The Conference Board of Canada, through its National Business and Education Centre, has tried to become the dominant organization for influencing educational policy in Canada. It represents the one hundred largest corporations in Canada. Through well-advertised conferences, extensive publications, and its award programs for the best local partnerships involving business, the Conference Board has become the country's most important group for bringing educators together with business ideas for education.

In the United States, an extensive program of awards, the Anderson medals, is given by the Business-Higher Education Forum. The forum, which is an affiliated organization of the American Council on Education, is limited to a hundred members who are university presidents and chief executives of selected Fortune 500 companies. The forum, with its award program, is part of a far greater commitment to education among American businesses for financially supporting schools than among Canadian groups (Corporate-Higher Education Forum, 1987). The Canadian Forum gives two awards on behalf of two companies. The very influential Council for Aid to Education reflects this greater corporate support for education. It has 230 corporate members who are making grants for public and higher education; as well, it tries to direct reform. The Council on Foundations takes a somewhat different approach in that it does not attempt to influence policy and is composed of independent foundations that respond to funding requests.

There are many more American business organizations than Chart 5.1 begins to show. The Americans have a number of organizations involved with technology, though they are not well known or, as yet, influential. The Triangle Coalition for Science and Technology, which is listed, tries to link national organizations with local action (National Research Council, Memo, September 1, 1993). It is an organization that includes the three sectors of business, science, and education; this coalition seeks to become a major force

Chart 5.1
Dominant Business Organizations

United States	Canada
Business Roundtable (BRT)	Business Council on National Issues (BCNI)
Council for Aid to Education	
	National Business and
Committee on Economic Development	Education Centre of
	Conference Board of
Center for Workforce Preparation,	Canada
Chamber of Commerce	
	Corporate-Higher
Business-Higher Education Forum	Education Forum
Conference Board	Chamber of Commerce
	Information Technology
National Alliance of Business	Association of Canada
Council on Foundations	
Triangle Coalition for Science and Technology Education	

in the reform of science education. The American Business Conference, which is not on Chart 5.1 because of its low rating, views itself as the voice of the midsize, high-growth sector of the economy. It has launched the Vital Link program for students to meet specific achievement expectations as judged by portfolios or passport displays of their work. For students in the program, incentives and rewards are provided.

For more specialized education, there are a number of organizations (some of which are not listed) whose influence is more limited. The Corporate Council for Mathematics and Science Education is a program of the National Research Council that is intended to magnify the voice of individual corporations in developing standards in math and science. Canada has only one organization that is active in this area, the Information Technology Association of Canada (ITAC). The ITAC claims that its focus is on advocacy, networking, and information exchange, but its work in education is limited to one publication (Verma & Irvine, 1992). ITAC has developed a synthesis of American ideas, including those of the current U. S. secretary of labor, Robert Reich. The proposed program of this group is organized in a hierarchy from adopt-a-school efforts at the elementary school level to cooperative research in higher education.

Though ITAC advocates partnerships with schools, it does not seek to develop alliances among business groups any more than any other Canadian organization does. The American organizations not only form alliances in the United States, but also export their organizations to other countries. The Conference Board has exported its organization to Europe and Canada. The Corporate and Higher Education Forum in the United States has helped found parallel organizations in Australia and Eastern Europe as well as in Canada (Business-Higher Education Forum, 1994, September).

LOCAL EFFORTS

While national efforts are very remote and may provoke resistance, local activities are usually more accepted and are influenced by local conditions. Local foundations show how the relationship between education and business has evolved. The local public foundation in Boston, for example, developed as a way of evaluating adopt-a-school programs there, while the program in Chattanooga is a contrasting case that evolved to support Paideia (Public Education Fund New York, 1994, February). In Calgary a local foundation was developed in 1991 to enable sixty businesses to share resources with five school districts (Calgary Educational Partnership Foundation, n.d.).

The Calgary effort was modeled on a partnership in the Ottawa-Carleton area in eastern Canada, but it developed its own agenda (Doug Clovechok, interview, August 3, 1994). Common activities, such as a conference on students' choices, have created more activities than most Canadian efforts by individual companies (Canadian Chamber of Commerce, 1990). The joint business and educator training programs and executive exchanges that Ottawa-Carleton has developed have not been replicated in Calgary (The Ottawa-Carleton Learning Foundation and the Ottawa-Carleton Research Institute, n.d.). On the other hand, Ottawa-Carleton has, reportedly, not been able to match the exchange of resources that Calgary has achieved (Doug Clovechok, interview, August 3, 1994). In working on the employment skills program that the Conference Board of Canada has promoted, the Ottawa-Carleton effort had a three-year lead over Calgary. The Ottawa-Carleton coalition has been much more directly linked to the Conference Board of Canada; that connection may be reflected in the larger number of awards they have received from that organization (Ottawa-Carleton Learning Foundation, 1993, April, p. 4).

None of the Canadian efforts has come about as a result of the crises that have led to some of the American coalitions at the local level (Lies & Bergholz, 1988, p. 82). The financial crisis in Alberta has, supposedly, increased corporate donations, but this was not related to the establishment of foundations. In the United States, most of these local foundations were influenced by the Ford Foundation, which, initially, supported the Public Education Network, the national organization of local foundations (Lies &

Bergholz, 1988, p. 75). Many of the local foundations developed in response to problems related to desegregation. Some twenty-three cities have local foundations in the United States, but there are only a handful in Canada. In Chicago, there is no organization affiliated with the national network because of the dominance of large foundations, particularly MacArthur. The large foundations in Chicago do, however, find it convenient to distribute small grants through a local foundation, the Fund for Educational Reform (Peggy Gordon, interview, April 18, 1994).

However, the Chicago approach lacks the major advantages of a local foundation. The local foundation provides an easier way of developing trust between business and education; the most immediate handicap for these foundations occurs when they are not independent and are housed at the school board (Lies & Bergholtz, 1988, p. 86). The trust developed by such foundations means that business, for its part, does not have to establish a separate advocacy organization. The foundation is also able to deal with the distribution of gifts in an equitable manner that, apparently, produces few complaints (p. 81). Finally, the local foundation allows for continuing discussion between business and education, which can lead to a change of roles that was earlier suggested to be desirable.

THE VIEWPOINT OF THE BUSINESS ROUNDTABLE

Local foundations may try to incorporate groups other than businesses in the same way that the Boston Compact was expanded to include unions and higher education (Farrar & Cipollone, 1988). National organizations are more able than even a collection of local ones to develop a broad cover that combines their interest with that of their allies (National Alliance of Business, 1991). In fact, the involvement of health, welfare, and social agencies is seen as a reason for expanding the content of the reform movement to include integrated services (p. 7). The controversial nature of many reforms led to the recommendation that business not identify such reforms with individual companies (p. 6). Since those left out can "often stymie later action," it is argued that neighborhood and religious leaders, together with parents and social service providers, should be included in the business-led coalition (p. 8). Business goals may become the nucleus for nonprofit civic foundations (p. 6a). The existence of many different power groups within education and protracted negotiations among these groups mean that business executives must learn patience. Executives must also develop ways of maintaining interest in the reform process for themselves as well as from other businesspeople who want rapid results (p. 9). Meaningless long-term goals, without check points, will destroy a coalition.

Though a dominant player in such coalitions, business, nevertheless, seems to accept many innovations that educators have developed, such as cooperative education, when they correspond to the corporate value of team work (p. 20). The majors concern of business is to find some standards

which can function in education in the same way that profits do in business
(p. v). The development of standards and incentives based on the standards
is the reason for the support of the wide-ranging plan in Kentucky, as well
as the appeal of its systemic character and economic rewards to successful
schools.

Since standards are needed to judge the innovations of educators, the
business leaders seem very confident that their approaches to management
development or special knowledge, particularly from the sciences, can be
applied to education without any serious modification (pp. 18 and 33).
Areas in work that are perceived to be the most important include "science,
mathematics, technology and multicultural understandings" (p. 19).
Furthermore, the integration of subject areas is to be pursued by a "common
core of active learning and problem solving" (p. 20).

Business involvement in the curriculum is recognized as "one of the most
controversial areas" (p. 22). However, as educators develop a recognition
of their common goals with corporate entities, trust will emerge. Better
evaluations will be developed; because of their similarity to assessment
procedures that are used in business, they will relate to the expertise of
executives and ensure accountability (p. 41). Business will be able to
interpret performance data, communicate the data through public relations,
and help increase the funding for assessment instruments.

From this business perspective, education is an underdeveloped area to
which economic concepts need to be applied. Schools spend less than
$1,000 per teacher on technology, while businesses average over $50,000 per
employee in similar investments (p. 53). Teachers are more likely to have
a computer than they are to have a telephone (p. 63). A number of
approaches can add to the economic value of education. The BRT claims
that Chris Whittle has shown how information can be delivered into the
classroom and Apple's Classrooms of Tomorrow have discovered that
independent and cooperative student activities were increased while teacher-
led activities drastically declined (pp. 60–61). The teacher is the "employee
who adds the most value to a school's product—learning" (p. 11). Incentive
systems are needed for teachers and students (p. 36). Improvement must
always be measured in terms of the value added to the educational process
(p. 39).

For those at the bottom of the educational hierarchy, empowerment can
occur through decentralization just as it has for business (p. 25). "Educators
frequently have a factory model in mind when they think of business and are
not as familiar with the shared decision-making strategies that are,
increasingly, common in today's corporate environments" (p. 33). From the
medical model, education could borrow paraprofessionals, who would be one
more subordinated group to whom participation could then be offered.

Though reforms that have worked in business are supported, very
controversial plans that will draw the fire of educators are to be avoided
through moderation. School choice is, for example, "an emotionally charged

issue" (p. 29). A moderated view allows for distinctive schools within existing school systems, which are developed through school-based management with a final goal that all schools will become excellent (pp. 103–104). However, even parent participation in schools is seen as a source of dreaded controversy (p. 77). Opponents argue that parents lack expertise in education or management and they may use their power in schools for patronage or political purposes. The Business Roundtable and Business Alliance state that it is possible for communities to avoid these dangers and reap the benefits of parental involvement, just as other good things can be accomplished without serious conflict.

BEWARE OF THOSE WHO BEAR GIFTS

The BRT plan needs to be seen in the context of other symbolic influences on education. Other national organizations that are attempting to bring about business goals are particularly revealing about the ways in which corporations may control education (Corporate Higher Education Forum, 1987 and 1991). These organizations provide signals for success in education in many ways other than those of the usual awards and gifts. Progress toward common goals can be measured by "indicators," and companies should continuously "monitor" gifts that are given to educational institutions. Recommendations for educators become predictions; they are "advisories" which are similar to weather advisories. Such language is, in itself, a forecast of the power that its proponents can unleash.

The president of this organization, John Dinsmore, has stated that his Corporate-Higher Education Forum is not an organization but rather an "interface where business and universities are brought together" (Johnson, 1992, p. 20). For educational change, an advisory is issued; such an advisory is defined as follows: "Like a weather advisory, it sounds an alert that rapidly changing conditions threaten our welfare and require our response. Our advisory draws upon the experience and opinions of advisors who contributed to our understanding. Finally, it offers our advice on appropriate action which we, along with others, should take" (Corporate-Higher Education Forum, 1991, p.3).

Similar to its parallel institution in the United States, the Canadian Forum has been concerned with establishing links with business that are more than merely advisory. The executive secretary, Patricia Roman, has said that the forum "is not involved with partnership but the organization itself is a partnership" (Johnson, 1992, p. 23). One of their first publications shows how guidance is supplied with respect to corporate contributions for universities (Corporate-Higher Education Forum, 1991, pp. 12, 18, 33 & 39). Corporations have gone from simple donations to gifts that are a percentage of the campaign goals of the educational organization. They have shifted to seeking universities which are capable of meeting their predetermined corporate goals. Such activity has increased with declining corporate profits.

Matching government grants for business donations has further enhanced the planning done by these corporate organizations. Corporations should now "monitor" their gifts as part of a continuing program of collaboration. Such monitoring requires cooperation among universities.

Monitoring, like issuing advisories, suggests a program of indirect controls that the French critical theorist Foucault has discussed (Foucault, 1977). Such a program of surveillance unites power and knowledge as a means of control. For Foucault, such controls replace direct rewards and punishment. John Dinsmore, president of the forum, says neither he nor his staff is influenced by, nor has he even read Foucault, even though Dinsmore is aware of the similarity of this philosopher's ideas to their practices (interview, August 10, 1993). Whether by accepting the advice of psychologists, following the results of opinion surveys, or monitoring an endowment program, people are becoming part of their own controls.

However, the Canadian forum has more specific examples of controls with contingent grants (Corporate-Higher Education Forum, 1987, pp. 42–47). "Partners in technology" can include computers, affiliates, visiting professionals, and corporate partners. The development of partnerships with corporations means that, in the computer field, for a fee of $250,000, the corporation will receive benefits justifying the expenditure and that such benefits are available "nowhere else." Consortia partnerships of government with business and universities are being considered. Other consortia are reviewed that involve a number of universities. All consortia are a means of combining "that added value of brainpower," which can lead to calculations in advance of donations, with regard to what will produce the most significant impact.

Any resistance by universities with more humanistic concerns can be undermined (Corporate-Higher Education Forum, 1987, pp. 64, 70–71, 58). Universities which are struggling, are likely to be influenced by "money at the margin" during such difficult times. This more blatant appeal is coupled with recommendations that include peer review by universities, while corporations and universities define their missions. Universities may see the additional value of corporate sponsorship when they compete with other universities. Executives in residence can bring a business perspective to university administration. However, centers and institutes can best respond to "shared values and shared control" by providing organizational flexibility that universities may otherwise lack because of their established structures.

The Canadian Forum has had to accentuate its symbolic power relationships with business. Canadian and international corporations contribute less than a third of the amount that American businesses do to their universities. The Canadian forum lacks the financial clout of its American parallel and cannot begin to match the grant program that allows the American group to obtain publicity and wide support (Business-Higher Education Forum, 1992, p. 3). The American Forum stresses cooperation between public schools and universities and even unions, not just between universities and businesses, which is the focus of the Canadian forum. As a result of its different and more broadly based approach, this American group has been able to make a far larger impact.

The larger financial resources of American companies are also translated into the symbolic models of new schools. The New American Schools Development Corporation (NASDC) is backing nine design teams that are trying to break the model of schools across America. This private organization was founded by business leaders who worked with the federal government program of Goals 2000 (New American Schools Development Corporation, n.d.). Business has been the primary backer of NASDC, whose chief executive officer, Ann McLaughlin, had occupied a similar position with Nabisco, working on another program designed to break the mold of typical schools, Next Century Schools. Reflecting McLaughlin's background as a researcher in education, most of these programs with either Nabisco or NASDC are typical of innovations in education that had taken place before business was even involved. Other programs reflect the effective schools research in education, and the nine components stressed by Business Roundtable (School Management Study Group, 1994). There may be greater emphasis on computers and technology, but the model programs, which are supported by business, are more of a promise for radically new schools than they are for dramatically different accomplishments.

The promise of model schools is, however, a reflection of an important sense of dedication among the business leaders involved with public education. Union Carbide is making a five-year commitment to one school with a donation of $150,000 for each year (School Management Study Group, 1994). Nabisco currently makes a total grant of up to $375,000 over the course of three years for each of forty-two schools in twenty-three states and the District of Columbia (RJR Nabisco Foundation, n.d.). NASDC makes large grants to nine key sites for a five-year period. The emphasis is "commitment for long periods" and it is important that these businesses are not supporting private efforts or voucher plans. Schools, for their part, are, increasingly, taking the names of their business partners in marriage. One of the nine NASDC sites has named the room where it keeps all computers and other equipment the Product Development Center (Bradley, 1994, September). In Alberta, the business plan is full of language imported from the corporate world to control education (Barlow and Robertson, 1994, p. 219).

The bias of business is imposed in a variety of ways other than those suggested by language. In the United States, the national goals are developed by a private group that overwhelmingly represents the executives of business and government, the National Education Goals Panel (Martin Orland, interview, September 23, 1993). The views of students are not considered; indeed, the rationalized thinking that is involved in the business approaches does not even include the people- and event-related knowledge of the young (Everhart, 1983). Panels are designed to set the standard:

model schools are to dramatize the standards as an image of goals developed by executives. "Total Quality Management" tries to show how schools can directly follow the model of corporations, even though such innovations lack the political support of "model schools."

Educational research for a variety of innovations that are welded with the business perspective is, itself, drawn from a military and industrial base with a very rationalized format (Noble, 1993). Through tools such as surveys, planning becomes more global in scope and more limiting for individuals (Foucault, 1977). When the norm for education becomes established, power becomes comprehensive and more limiting than physical coercion has ever been (Foucault, 1980, p. 136). The reform legislation for Chicago, depicted in Chart 3.2, has shown how precise these controls can be; even greater quantitative standards have been used in Kentucky. Business seeks standards that will measure educational achievements and limit expenditures in ways that are similar to profit measures of corporations.

RESISTANCE TO BUSINESS CONTROLS

In spite of the massive increase in the commitment that corporations have made to education through symbolic or organizational relations, it is surprising that there is little evidence that teachers are being transformed. Indeed, there are only a few efforts by business to transform teachers into business leaders. The First Bank of Minneapolis has made one of the few attempts by providing grants to individual teachers who teach rare specialties such as Chinese, where they would have to work for different school boards, join organizations that would require a subsidy, or branch out on their own to teach or tutor for profit (Conference Board, 1988). The Alberta Chamber of Commerce would greatly like to see a change of this sort in teacher culture   (John Ballheim, interview, May 18, 1994). Private partnerships for teachers is the dream of some advocates for charter schools, mentioned in the last chapter. Though teachers may accept business values and are not generally critical of them, few have redefined their role to resemble that of business leaders. When teachers have moved to found their own schools or schools-within-a-school, they are more likely to be motivated by progressive education beliefs than by corporate values (Impact II, 1994).

When businesses are directly involved in controlling educators, there are signs of a boomerang effect, even with school administrators. The Panasonic Foundation, for example, has combined the influence of its parent corporation with the expertise of leading educators, but it has experienced a great deal of difficulty in relating to schools and communities directly. The foundation is cited as one of three leading examples of educational change by the second most influential American business organization for education, the Council for Aid to Education (Rigden, 1991, pp. 28–31). However, a journalist's account shows great resistance to the foundation in one New Mexico community near Santa Fe, as well as signs that other communities have withdrawn from the web of this corporate foundation (Sommerfeld, 1994, June).

What is so remarkable about this foundation is that it has entirely stopped giving grants. Founded by the electronic giant Matsushita, Panasonic started off by giving out a small number of precollegiate grants for Japanese studies. Within three years it had ceased giving any grants and had, instead, begun the process of developing long-term relationships with a few urban districts and state departments of education, where it provides technical assistance. This assistance consists of providing workshops, paying for outside consultants, and sending educators to visit model schools all over the country. One of the three top executives at the MacArthur Foundation, Peter Gerber, has said that Panasonic has "transformed itself into a consulting outfit" (Sommerfeld, 1994, June, p. 26).

The Santa Fe site was the first chosen by Panasonic. At Santa Fe, Panasonic has focused on teachers and students and has, apparently, ignored terrible conflicts between central office and principals and between the principals and teachers. In this city, parents have also become concerned about the lack of discipline and order in the schools. A survey of citizens in the community found that three-quarters believed their school needed a fundamental overhaul (p. 26). In spite of the complaints, an evaluation of Santa Fe and two other communities says the Panasonic projects had developed reflective practitioners, a capacity for change, and some promise of greater student learning.

Perhaps the teachers' ability to change has not been directed by Panasonic. The business foundation has not yet been asked to leave Santa Fe, but seven of its original partnerships are now defunct, including the Seattle board and the Minnesota departments of education. In addition to Santa Fe, active partnerships are holding up in San Diego, Minneapolis, Allentown, Pennsylvania, and the New Mexico education departments. Sensitivity to the community and the federal structure of education are the main problems for Panasonic. In the two other model programs by business foundations which were cited by the influential Council for Aid to Education, the problems at Panasonic were not repeated. At the Champion International Corporation with a middle school and at the Pacific Telesis Foundation with a future project, there is monitoring of programs as they develop and the use of outside consultants as catalysts. But, in the other model programs, there is no such direct involvement as Panasonic has attempted with its long-term partnerships (Rigden, 1991, pp. 19–28).

CONNECTING WITH STUDENTS

Though the attempts at monitoring, consulting, or giving direct aid by business foundations are aimed at the adult professionals in the schools, some significant attempts are made to provide students with meaningful opportunities to be recognized as adult workers in programs developed by government and business. Such opportunities for students, in turn, provide adults with the means to control those students. Many of the testimonials for school-to-work programs demonstrate conversions among students, though there is little systematic evidence of these effects.

Though many of the business partnerships have shown increased positive attitudes, opportunities for job explanation, or development of special opportunities for job identification, only the work-school connections provide extended contacts with employers for young people. The most important of the work transition programs are those that offer two years of an apprenticeship in high schools that connect with two more years of the same program in technical schools.

In Canada, a few youth apprenticeship programs have been developed. In Alberta, the departments of Education and Career Development and Employment have developed the Registered Apprenticeship Program (RAP). This program resulted from the influence of the Conference Board of Canada, which wanted to expand its influence on education and prevent dropouts. Also, the Alberta Apprenticeship Board wanted to reach younger students than are usually enrolled in the established apprenticeship programs (Gerald Regan, class presentation, December 19, 1994). RAP was designed to deal with at-risk students who could benefit from a work experience program and to reach students at a younger age so they could benefit from the new program while still in school. RAP provides an opportunity to begin an apprenticeship at the age of sixteen while students are working toward a high school diploma. In three years there have been only ninety-nine students participating, as a result of limited funds to promote the program and the unavailability of funds to pay the students while they are in the apprenticeship program. A similar program in Ontario, the School Workplace Apprenticeship Program, has been somewhat more successful.

The state of Wisconsin was able to promote an apprenticeship program in 1991 for all its high schools (Olson, 1994, May, pp. 27–28). In Wisconsin, the line between high schools and higher education has been blurred by providing high school juniors and seniors with the option of attending higher educational facilities. New skill standards and certificates are awarded to program graduates. All school districts are required to have school-business partnerships, and participating businesses receive up to $1,000 per student to help finance the program. The University of Wisconsin plans to use a competency-based admissions process so that students who have pursued the apprenticeship route, rather than the college preparation one, can still be admitted to higher education. Three other states have adopted legislation similar to Wisconsin's: Florida, Oregon, and Tennessee.

However, the biggest publicity splash for these programs was that of Bill Clinton's school-to-work law enacted in May 1994 with an initial appropriation of $100 million (Olson, 1994, May 11, p. 21). In 1995, funding was increased to $300 million and was to remain open-ended in subsequent years. The Clinton plan includes career exploration, cooperative efforts, and job counseling; it does more than offer apprenticeships that link public schools with industry or higher education. At the ceremony for the signing of the bill, a student in a program for financial services, Chris Brady, testified that "for the first time ever, I actually like school" and that he hopes that "this legislation helps students across the country understand that school and work are connected, so that they don't have to learn the hard way like myself" (p. 21).

Established programs are full of accounts of students and parents coming to see the light (Jobs for the Future, n.d.). More modest claims to raise the aspirations of vocational students, and to eliminate the general route in high school, have led to improvements in the academic test results of vocational students (Bottoms et al., 1992). However, both the upgraded vocational program and the programs that are more like an apprenticeship have trouble finding students who can testify that the training in work experience and the education in academic programs are closely related (Olson, 1994, January, p. 22).

Many of the youth apprenticeships remain clusters of work training rather than specific routes. The more the work academies are specialized and academic, the more transfers seem to occur. A student in a Geospace Academy, Gindi Lynch, for example, says that she has decided to change her field from engineering to physics (Olson, 1994, February, p. 31). More general programs may lead to jobs that do not have future opportunities. All of the programs could do more than provide status.

For most of the programs, students may respond positively. They must still raise their academic ambitions and, ideally, become more responsible. The lack of such personal responsibility is the major problem that Stephen Hamilton has found in translating his studies of German apprenticeships into American practice (Olson, 1994, March, p. 27). The goal of developing individual responsibility at an early age has led a Chicago group to propose a work partnership in the elementary school (Hively, 1993). Chrysler, with its World of Work project, has been conducting such a program for very young children in Detroit since 1990 (Rigden, 1992, p. 118).

The possibilities of making very young students more realistic and less creative at a very early stage should cause some hesitation. Those who write about school work programs want others to worship these programs. Parents are skeptical that sixteen-year-old students can make a four-year commitment to the youth apprentice programs, while students are concerned that their peers and social life may be upset (Jobs for the Future, 1991, pp. 27, 42 & 44). For the students, good work experiences have occurred outside youth apprenticeship programs that allowed them to learn about people (p. 34).

The students do want courses that will provide practical applications, even if they do not want to give up their other immediate concerns with people and events. Students do not seem to believe they have had enough practical applications! A recent study of Canadian business school students shows, overwhelmingly, that students want more practical applications in their university programs (International Association of Students in Economics and Business, Carleton, 1993). Nursing students are the group most enthusiastic about youth apprenticeships, particularly in rural areas, where they see that such health programs could lead to preventive approaches among youth such as the spread of acquired immune deficiency syndrome (AIDS). Nursing has long been one of the professions with most "hands-on" training and the least theoretical base; the enthusiasm of nursing students may be further grounds for suspecting that academic training and career education are not always being effectively combined in youth apprenticeship programs (Jobs for the Future, 1991, pp. 53, 55).

In the public schools, the program in Alberta, RAP, is a particularly good example of limited expectations. The curriculum for RAP is a brief pamphlet that covered such menial tasks as holding a hammer, hammering a nail, or sweeping a floor (Carol Suddards, personal communication, September 29, 1995). An earlier study reported opening the door for women as a learner expectation of a low-level vocational program (Lind, 1974).

However, it may be that the emphasis on limited practicality, like the use of testimonials, is a fumbling attempt to connect the world of students with business activities. The world of students is people-centered, and the students' interactive knowledge is more affective than rational (Everhart, 1983). The very young students are in a stage of primary socialization where motivation is being developed, while adolescents are just entering the adult stage where power dominates (Brim and Wheeler, 1966). Only in supporting early childhood education does business begin to grasp how different education for children is from the education of managers. The development of students as individuals is ignored by the managerial approach for student responses to school work. Consequently, those involved in youth programs often believe that they must be advocates for students who will otherwise be ignored (Dyckman, 1994).

SUMMARY

The difference between education values and business values has been suggested to be best defined by the difference between instrumental aims and family values. Youth programs should involve social, moral, and developmental concerns. Businesses do not act on the basis of social responsibilities, as shown by laying off employees, ignoring the education of women, or exploiting special education students in the job market. The recognition of youth through programs such as the Boston Compact has occurred more often in disintegrating cities where the survival of business is threatened. Youth may need a more reliable defender than business.

Business has had a lot of trouble getting its own priorities about education in order. It can claim that education has lacked standards, but education's ambiguity hardly accounts for the change in business positions, such as the shift between academic goals and vocational ones that occurred in recent history and the pattern of involvement in school boards and committees, followed by the even more recent withdrawal into civic celibacy. There is no reason to believe that business has been more successful in sorting out its immediate interest in education from its institutional reasons for involvement in it. Business has not seen the value of education for itself, nor has it conveyed the importance of education to others. They have not, for example, attempted to reward higher school marks when hiring school graduates. The fear of controversy is a blinder that can prevent business leaders from seeing the complexity of choices that are inevitably involved in making decisions about education. Education involves moral choices and the opposition of business to the Christian right probably shows that business has not yet come to see the significance of choices that cannot be gathered from instrumental and rational reasoning alone.

There is, unfortunately, no insurance that the inconsistencies and changes in direction shown by business will disappear. Partnerships may be just a fad. If business wants more private schools competing with the public system or even a voucher system, there is little reason for the coalition to be more than a temporary smoke screen for competitive moves. The partnership position has, furthermore, been involved in a great deal of experimentation as to the most appropriate forms of power in education and the most effective strategy to use with public schools. Unless there is expansion of the entrepreneurial role for teachers so they can play the business game, the indirect normative strategy of monitoring education would be more reasonable than the direct participation exemplified by the Panasonic Foundation. The program experimentation with school sponsorship, work cooperation, or policy development could be replaced by programs with broad support; that would be consistent with the coalition strategy as well as the use of more normative controls. The national and regional programs for specifying standards would also fit an approach with much broader support.

The normative strategy, however, must relate to the divergence between teachers and businesspeople. Business, in the position adopted by the Business Roundtable, sees teachers as little more than a part of the production function in education. And teachers, even if influenced by admiration for business, see business as external to the process of education. Business might just have to come to respect educators as people who provide a service different from management education or scientific specialists, for a youth that management would have to go some distance to understand. A common activity that is educational would then be one in which management would aid, rather than lead, teachers and educational administrators. The common activities which business and education can

share would seem to be incidental rather than central. Education might just
have to be recognized as a political, moral, and individual task that is
foreign to the mold of corporate management.

Education may be changed if surrounded by business. It could possibly
come to take business goals and methods for granted though the approaches
are still very different today. Schools for profit may be one part of a larger
set of private businesses in education that includes high technology, test
services, publishing, tutoring, school maintenance and operators of child-care
centers, all of which are private businesses (Walsh, 1996, February). Such
private businesses are companies that have stock traded on the exchanges.
These companies believe that competition between them can generate the
future innovations though there are few signs of creative ideas as yet.

THE CRUX OF THE ARGUMENT

Business brings beliefs and practices, ideology and strategies, to its
current positions on education. The ideology is usually consistent and
includes an immediate interest in profit and institutional interests in stability
and consensus. The strategies of business are more variable and include
either private education that competes with the public system or joint
committees which work to improve the public system. The joint committee
can be either a local or a national effort. The national committees, such as
the Business Roundtable, are very diverse and difficult to comprehend,
particularly in the United States. The national committees are also likely to
seem very remote from the local scene. Local foundations remove the fear
of both a distant group and one that may have a business bias. Such
foundations provide an opportunity for business to develop a shared
perspective with education and provide an arena in which business and
education can experiment with developing bridges between their ideologies.
Ideologies which have no situational supports or that have very few of them,
as in the case of the Panasonic Foundation, are likely to be experienced by
their clients as being very alienating.

In the next chapter we return to the three cases and models, Kentucky,
Alberta, and Chicago. Kentucky, which links the national Business
Roundtable to the local Partnership, can more successfully develop a broad
committee framework. Alberta remains in splendid isolation from national
efforts to join education and business in any more comprehensive way.
Alberta, with its single–track approach, is particularly likely to develop
private education, probably through a system of vouchers. While Chicago,
with its diverse and competing groups, is likely to change course several
times, it will always have more grass-roots support than any of the other
places, unless the rank and file there are exhausted by the many shifts in
organizational restructuring.

REFERENCES

Apple, M. (1982). *Education and power.* Boston: Routledge and Kegan Paul.

Badger, Hanson & Associates (1993, February). Youth perspectives on career education. Paper for Conference Board of Canada conference, Toronto.

Barlow, M. & Robertson H. (1994). *Class Warfare.* Toronto: Key Porter.

Bendix, R. (1956). *Work and authority in industry.* New York: Harper & Row.

Berman, P. & Clugston, R. (1988). A tale of two states: The business community and education reform in California and Minnesota. In Levine, M. & Trachtman, R. (Eds.), *American Business and the Public School* (pp. 121–150). New York: Teachers College.

Bottoms, G., Presson, A. & Johnson, M. (1992). *Making high schools work.* Atlanta: Southern Regional Education Board.

Boudon, R. (1989). *The analysis of ideology.* Chicago: The University of Chicago Press.

Bradley, A. (1994, August 3). Corporate School's plan to merge with Chicago district is "a done deal." *Education Week,* 13(40), 9.

Bradley, A. (1994, September 21). A welcome change. *Education Week,* 14(3), 27–29.

Brennan, G. (1990). *School/business partnerships: Preparing our future workforces.* Fairfax County, Virginia: Fairfax County Public Schools.

Brim, O. & Wheeler S. (1966). *Socialization after childhood.* New York: Wiley.

Business-Higher Education Forum (1988). *Beyond the rhetoric: Evaluating university-industry cooperation in research and technology exchange.* Washington,D.C.: Business-Higher Education Forum.

Business-Higher Education Forum (1990). *Three realities.* Washington, D.C.: Business-Higher Education Forum.

Business-Higher Education Forum (1991). *Putting it all together: Profiling outstanding school-reform alliances.* Washington, D.C.:Business-Higher Education Forum.

Business-Higher Education Forum (1992). *About the business-higher education forum: July, 1992.* Washington, D.C.: Business-Higher Education Forum.

Business-Higher Education Forum (1994). *About the business-higher education forum: September, 1994.* Washington, D.C.: Business-Higher Education Forum.

Calgary Educational Partnership Foundation (n.d.). *Calgary Educational Partnership Foundation.* Calgary: Calgary Educational Partnership Foundation.

Callahan, R. (1962). *Education and the cult of efficiency.* Chicago: The University of Chicago.

Canadian Chamber of Commerce (1990). *Business-education partnerships.* Ottawa: Canadian Chamber of Commerce.

Carnoy, M. & Levin, H. (1985). *Schooling and work in the democratic state.* Stanford, California: Stanford University Press.

Celis, W. (1994, March 19). Private groups to run 15 schools in experiment by Massachusetts. *New York Times,* 1, 8.

Clarke, T. (1992, February 25). "Partners in learning." *Calgary Sun,* 45.

Coalition of Essential Schools, (1993, January). "So now what?" Managing the change process. *Horace,* 9(3), 1–11.

Coalition of Essential Schools. (1993, May). Essential collaborators: Parents, school, and community. *Horace,* 9(5), 1–8.

Cohen, D. (1993, December 1). Streets of despair. *Education Week*, 13(13), 16–21.

Collins, M. & Tamarkin, C. (1992). *Marva Collins' way*. Los Angeles: Jeremy P. Tarcher.

Collins, R. (1979). *The credential society*. New York: Academic Press.

Collins, R. & Dempster, L. (1994, April 2). Education in Alberta, new chapter. *Calgary Herald*, B5.

Conference Board (1988). *Beyond business education partnerships: The Business experience*. New York: Conference Board.

Conference Board (1989). *Business leadership: The third wave of education reform*. New York: Conference Board.

Conference Board of Canada (1993). *Evaluating business-education collaboration*. Ottawa: Conference Board of Canada.

Consulting Network (1994). *Business/education organizations: roles and opportunities to work together*. New York: Council for Aid to Education.

Corporate Community Schools of America (1991). *1991 progress report*. Chicago: Corporate Community Schools of America.

Corporate-Higher Education Forum (1986). *Making the match: Canada's university graduates and corporate employers*. Montreal: Corporate-Higher Education Forum.

Corporate-Higher Education Forum (1987). *From patrons to partners*. Montreal: Corporate-Higher Education Forum.

Corporate-Higher Education Forum (1988). *Going global: Meeting the need for international business expertise in Canada*. Montreal: Corporate-Higher Education Forum.

Corporate-Higher Education Forum (1991a). *To be our best: Learning for the future*. Montreal: Corporate-Higher Education Forum.

Corporate-Higher Education Forum (1991b). *To be our best: Learning for the future* (A symposium on elementary and secondary education, Calgary, March 8, 1991). Two Tapes. Montreal: The Corporate-Higher Education Forum

Council for Aid to Education (1994). *Business/education organizations: roles and opportunities to work together*. New York: Council for Aid to Education.

Cusick, P. (1983). *The equalitarian ideal and the American high school*. New York: Longman.

Daft, R. & Becker, S. (1978). *The innovation organization*. New York: Elseiver.

Danzberger, J. & Uzdam, M. (1989). Partnerships: the Atlanta experience. *Phi Delta Kappan*, 65(6), 393–396.

Day, R. (1993). *A survey of Chicago local school council members*. Evanston, Illinois: Day Associates.

Dempster, L. (1994, February 11). Inner circle redraws classroom. *Calgary Herald*, A14.

Dyckman, A. (1994, March). No four walls could hold this school. *Vocational Education Journal*, 26-27, 46-47.

Eaton, J. (1994). Privatization: What does it mean for American education? *Council Comments*, 1, 1–2.

Edmonton Public School Board Custodial Workers (1994). *Privatizing schools: In the public interest?* Edmonton: Edmonton Public School Board Custodial Workers.

Education Week, (1994, June 22). Education Inc. *Education Week*, 13(39), 41.

Evans, R. (1994). Do motives matter? Unpublished paper.

Everhart, R. (1983). *Reading, writing, and resistance.* Boston: Routledge and Paul.

Farrar, E. & Cipollone, A. (1988). After the signing: The Boston Compact 1982 to 1985. In Levine, M. & Trachtman, R. (Eds.), *American business and the public school*, (pp. 175–237). New York: Teachers College.

Fiske, E.B. (1992). *Smart schools, smart kids.* New York: Touchstone.

Foucault, M. (1977). *Discipline and punish: birth of the prison.* New York: Vintage, Randon House.

Foucault, M. (1980). *The history of sexuality*, Vol. 1. New York: Vintage, Random House.

Frank, C. (1992, May 16). "Students need a real education for the real world." *Calgary Herald*, B5.

Golle, J. (1994, June 22). You must take care of your customer. *Education Week*, 13(39), 44.

Graham, P.A. (1992). *S.O.S. sustain our schools.* New York: Hill and Wang.

Hall, O. & Carlton, R. (1977). *Basic skills at school and work.* Toronto: Ontario Economic Council.

Hamilton, S. (1990). *Apprenticeship for adulthood.* New York: The Free Press.

Hesch, R. (1994). Klein kuts and kontrol in Alberta. Paper presented at the Canadian Learned Societies Conference.

Hess, G. (1991). *School restructuring: Chicago style.* Newbury Park, California: Corwin Press.

Hill, D.M. (1995, May 10). Hire education. *Education Week*, 14(3), 33,35.

Hively, J. (1993, October 25). *A plea for early partnership.* Chicago: Golden Apple Foundation.

Hively, J. (1993, October). *Pass: Pathway to achieving success.* Chicago: Golden Apple Foundation.

Hopchin, B. (1994, November/December). Charter schools: Theory and practice. *ATA Magazine*, 19–22.

Immerwehn, J., Johnson, J., & Kernan-Schloss, A. (1992). *Cross talk: the public, the experts, and competitiveness.* Washington, D.C.: Business-Higher Education Forum.

Impact II (1994). *How teachers are changing schools.* New York: Impact II.

International Association of Students in Economics and Business, Carleton, (1993). *Excellence in education: A student perspective.* Ottawa: Carleton University.

Jobs for the Future (1991). *Voices from school and home: Arkansas parents and students talk about preparing for the world of work and the potential for youth apprenticeship.* Sommerville, Massachusetts: Jobs for the Future.

Jobs for the Future, (n.d.). *Building a state-wide apprenticeship system: #22 conference briefing book.* Cambridge: Jobs for the Future.

Johnson, K. (1992). "Corporate-Higher Education Forum: A case study." Unpublished class paper.

Jones, B.L. & Maloy, R.W. (1988). *Partnerships for improving schools.* Westport, Connecticut: Greenwood Press.

Kenway, J. (1990). Education and the right's discursive politics. In Ball, S. (Ed.), *Foucault and education: Disciplines and knowledge*, (pp. 167–205). London: Routledge.

Klonsky, M. (1994, September). Merger paving way for creation of new schools. *Catalyst*, 6(1), 1, 30–31.

Knight, J., Smith, R., & Sachs, J. (1990). Deconstructing hegemony: Multicultural policy and a populist response. In Ball, S. (Ed.), *Foucault and education: Disciplines and knowledge* (pp.133–152). London: Routledge.

Kyle, C. & Kantowicz, E. (1992). *Kids first-primero los niños.* Springfield: Illinois

Levine, M. (1988) Introduction. In Levine, M. & Trachtman, R. (Eds.), *American Business and the Public School*, (pp. xiii–xxiii). New York: Teachers College.

Levy, C. (1988). Metropolitan Life Insurance and the American educator: partners in leadership. In Levine, M. & Trachtman, R. (Eds.), *American business and the public school*, (pp. 29–43). New York: Teachers College.

Lewis, A. (1989). *Restructuring America's schools.* Arlington, Virginia: American Association of School Administrators.

Lies, V. & Bergholz D. (1988). The public education fund. In Levine, M. & Trachtman, R. (Eds.), *American business and the public school*, pp. 75–88. New York: Teachers College.

Lind, L. (1974). *The learning machine.* Toronto: Anansi Press.

McNeil, L. (1988). *Contradictions of control.* New York: Routledge.

Mitchell, S. (1967). The quest of the beginning teacher. Unpublished paper.

Mitchell, S. (1990 and 1992). *Innovation and reform.* York, Ontario: Captus.

Mitchell, S. (1992). Professionals as partners in innovation - symbolic and concrete models. Proceedings of the 1992 AAACE Post-Conference on Continuing Professional Education. Anaheim, California: American Association for Adult and Continuing Education.

National Alliance of Business (1991). *The Business Roundtable participation guide: A primer for business on education.* New York: Business Roundtable.

New American Schools Development Corporation (n.d.). *NASDC facts.* Arlington, Virginia: New American Schools Development Corporation.

Noble, D. (1993). Insider trading university style. *Our Schools Our Selves*, 4(2), 45–52.

Olson, L. (1994, January 26). Bridging the gap. *Education Week*, 13(18), 20–26.

Olson, L. (1994, February 23). On the career track. *Education Week*, 13(22), 28–31.

Olson, L. (1994, March 23). Putting theory into practice. *Education Week*, 13(26), 25-27.

Olson, L. (1994, April 29). Technically speaking. *Education Week*, 13(30), 29–31.

Olson, L. (1994, May 11). President signs school-to-work transition law. *Education Week*, 13(33), 1, 21.

Olson, L. (1994, May 18). Putting it all together. *Education Week*, 13(34), 26–29.

Ottawa-Carleton Learning Foundation (1993, April). Pushing the boundaries to serve students first and foremost. *The Learning Network*, 2(4), 4.

Ottawa-Carleton Learning Foundation and the Ottawa Carleton Research Institute (n.d.). *Partners.* Kanata, Ontario: Ottawa-Carleton Learning Foundation and the Ottawa Carleton Research Institute.

Public Education Fund Network (1994, February). Community involvement in critical school restructuring: policy update. Washington, D.C.: Public Education Fund Network.

Richardson, J. (1994, February 9). Superintendent for hire. *Education Week*, 13(20), 31–3.

Richardson, J. (1994, August 3). Minneapolis management firm said on track. *Education Week*, 13(40), 18.

Rigden, D. (1991). *Business/school partnerships*. New York: Council for Aid to Education.

Rigden, D. (1992). *Business and the schools*. New York: Council for Aid to Education.

RJR Nabisco Foundation (n.d.). *Next century schools*. Washington, D.C.: RJR Nabisco Foundation.

Roscow, J. and Zager, R. (1989). *Allies in educational reform*. San Francisco: Jossey-Bass.

Rose, B. (1994, July 4). Can this man re-engineer city schools? Reprinted from *Crains Chicago Business Selected Excerpts*. Chicago: Designs for Change.

Rosenbaum, J. (1976). *Making inequality: The hidden curriculum of high school tracking*. New York: John Wiley.

Sarason, S. (1982). *The culture of the school and the problem of change*. New York: Allyn & Bacon.

Sarason, S. (1990). *The predictable failure of education reform*. San Francisco: Jossey-Bass.

Schmidt, P. (1994, August 3). Hartford asks E.A.I. to help run its district. *Education Week*, 13(40), 1, 9.

Schmidt, P. (1994, August 3). E.A.I. faulted on special-ed. compliance in Baltimore schools. *Education Week*, 13(40), 19.

School District No. 80 (1993). Technology 11 and 12 application summary. Kitimat, British Columbia: School District No 80.

School Management Study Group (1994). *Partnership assessment: St. Charles Parish Union Carbide model school reform agreement*. Salt Lake City: Union Carbide.

Seely, D. (1984). Educational partnership and the dilemmas of school reform. *Phi Delta Kappan*, 65(6), 383–388.

Shanker, A. (1994, June 22). There is no free lunch. *Education Week*, 13(39), 43–44.

Shor, Ira (1986). *Culture wars*. New York: Routledge.

Sommerfeld, M. (1994, June 15). Small player, big plans. *Education Week*. 13(38), 25–27.

Timpane, M. (1984). Business has rediscovered the public schools. *Phi Delta Kappan*, 65(6), 389-392.

Timpane, P. & McNeill, L. (1991). *Business impact on education and child development reform*. New York: Committee for Economic Development.

Toch, T. (1991). *In the name of excellence*. New York: Oxford.

Trachtman (1988). Programmatic participation and the policy avenue. In Levine, M. & Trachtman, R. (Eds.), *American business and the public school* (pp. 175–237). New York: Teachers College.

Verma, A. & Irvine, D. (1992). *Investing in people*. Willowdale, Ontario: Information Technology Association of Canada.

Walsh, M. (1994, January 26). Third version reinvigorates pact in Boston. *Education Week*, 13(18), 1, 9.

Walsh, M. (1994, March 2). Details of Edison blueprint emerge in Mass. designs. *Education Week*, 13(23), 1, 13.

Walsh, M. (1994, June 22). Disney holds up school as model for next century. *Education Week*, 13(39), 4.

Walsh, M. (1994, August 3). Question about finances puts Edison project at crossroads. *Education Week*, 13(40), 18, 19.

Walsh, M. (1996, February 21).   Brokers pitch education as hot investment. *Education Week*, 15(22), 1, 15.

Wrigley, J. (1982). *Class policies and public schools*. New Brunswick, New Jersey: Rutgers University Press.

Chapter 6

Creating Coalitions of Partners

> On the most fundamental level, business should become a forceful advocate for education reform in support of children and youths. With the political clout of their parents waning, the nation's young people need a powerful friend and supporter. (Committee on Economic Development, 1990, p. 62)

Though business leaders can grant recognition to students, it is more questionablewhether they can show any understanding of them, and whether there is any necessity for them to replace parents. Business has largely entered into partnerships with schools while maintaining its calculating or bottom-line stance. This calculating model has given way to an interactive model only during extreme conditions. Such conditions in Kentucky and Chicago have modified the usual business approach and will be explored, while events in Alberta have led to an even more restricted corporate position. The type of rational model which is usually employed restricts thinking to solutions that correspond with known solutions; the solutions then can be more easily weighted in terms of benefits to business. Political reality has been the primary blockade that business has had to overcome in pursuing its instrumental approach. Wide-scale allies for political change necessitate pursuing community coalitions rather than supporting the competition of private education. If the coalitions have been so successful that the Committee on Economic Development can seriously think that its executives can dwarf the family and replace it, there are serious consequences to allowing these coalitions to evolve. The family and childhood may be under attack, a very unexpected result of partnerships. The broader coalitions can contain the business interests so long as a racial or educational crisis is present. Alternatively, a financial crisis can lead to a narrow focus which is likely to support private education.

Greater involvement of business can be based on a creative synthesis of the contributions that politicians, parents, and educators can make with business toward the formulation of a new policy for schools, and thus need not be based only on what is perceived as being good for business. A major contribution occurred in Chicago when business was able to develop an advocacy group to transform the educational system with community partners. When political conflict continued, the temptation facing those sponsoring the business advocacy organization was to retreat into supporting a school system that maintained a climate of security and predictability. Aside from stability, business success—the bottom line—can be secured by avoiding controversy that may improve the schools in the long run. In Kentucky, educational quality is claimed to be the bottom line while, in Alberta, even modest relief for schools is always set against provincial debts (Alberta Education, 1995, February).

If business cannot be kept in the orbit of community change, then its many contributions can enrich future educational change. Business can contribute to the financial operation of school organization when the need demands. In Chicago, the desperate condition of schools has led executives, at times, to engage in many controversial efforts for school reform. In Kentucky, business has sought sharp increases in state funds for schools together with creative ways for individuals and corporations to be involved with schools. In Alberta, business has accepted reductions in provincial grants to schools while remaining as external judges of schools (Alberta Education, 1995).

COOPERATION IN CHICAGO

As racial tensions continued to escalate and problems with education were repeatedly demonstrated, business organizations still tried to work with the schools in Chicago. Only when they found themselves unwanted by the top administrators did they join the advocacy groups and community reformers. Two organizations were particularly important: Chicago United and the Civic Committee of the Commercial Club. The Civic Committee is the oldest business club in Chicago and, for the better part of this century, has been far more influential than any other business group including the BRT (Diane Lauber, interview, October 11, 1993). Chicago United is a biracial group of business leaders that formed after the riots which followed the death of the Reverend Martin Luther King, Jr. Initially, Chicago United was a rallying point for businesspeople who became concerned about reforming the schools (Kyle & Kantowicz, 1992, p. 222). The Civic Committee, the elite group of businesses in Chicago since the nineteenth century, had founded Chicago United; the two groups joined to form one advocacy group, Leadership for Quality Education (LQE), that influenced the implementation of the Chicago Reform in 1989 (Shipps, 1995).

In 1981, Chicago United, with its eighty corporate members, formulated hundreds of recommendations to improve the business functions of Chicago schools. The school bureaucracy accepted the recommendations and claimed to have implemented most of them (Kyle & Kantowicz, 1992, p. 221). However, in 1987, when the new policy director of Chicago United asked for a follow-up study, he found that few of the recommendations had been adopted. In the same year, the business leaders in the summit were "flabbergasted" when the superintendent asked them to guarantee jobs for high school graduates, even though he was not prepared to guarantee improvements in test scores (Kyle & Kantowicz, 1992, p. 221). The resentment and alienation of Chicago business leaders had become intense.

Several events brought the business leaders into the orbit of reform. Designs for Change already had a consulting contract with Chicago United. Even before the secretary of education called Chicago's schools the worst in the nation, Chicago United had developed its first plan for decentralizing the school system. Except for wanting an oversight committee to monitor the results, business had plans that were identical with what the community coalition, CURE, was seeking. Finally, during the mayor's second summit, the business and community leaders got past the need for an intermediary. Coretta McFerren, the community activist, came to trust Ken West of the Harris Bank, and the banker came to accept the leader of the welfare group (Kyle & Kantowicz, 1992, pp. 222–224). As these two individuals developed more common ground as a result of reform, they became the confidants I witnessed in 1993 at the meetings of the business advocacy group they both attended as members of LQE's board.

Many company executives became involved in the campaign to bring about school reform. However, few were more flamboyant in their support than Barry Sullivan, CEO, and David Paulus, vicepresident, of the First National Bank of Chicago (John Ayers, interview, October 5, 1993). They flew down in First National's jet and commandeered all sorts of community resources, including the company's telemarketing staff, to support reform. Both Chicago United and the Civic Committee had their offices in the First National Bank's building. First National in Chicago has been identified with the transformation of the Rockefellers' industrial power into financial muscle (Knowles, 1973) and it has now become the base for business to influence education.

When the reform legislation was in its crucial stages, several executives from Chicago United caused a crisis when they went public with their criticism of what they believed to be a watered-down bill. The executives were frustrated by the slow give-and-take process that House Speaker Madigan had instituted as he attempted to get all parties directly involved in the final bargaining. Because the business leaders wanted the oversight board, the community leaders feared a pullout by that group. The authoritarian speaker, Madigan, reproached the executives about airing their concerns publicly and told them, "Just don't let it happen again" (Kyle & Kantowicz, 1992, pp. 276–278).

The oversight issues led to attacks on business by Blacks. During the process of developing legislation for Chicago reform, community leaders representing the poor showed great distrust of business leaders. Because of the racial issues involved, business leaders found that they were taking a position against the education bureaucracy similar to that of the poor and Black groups (Kyle & Kantowicz, 1992, pp. 222–224). One Black leader claimed the supervision of an oversight commission would be like that of "a plantation overseer under slavery" (Kyle & Kantowicz 1992, p. 295). Business creates power problems because of fears of its dominance even when it is close to cooperating with other social groups. The oversight issue would be resolved at the time by using an existing board, the Chicago School Finance Authority, which had been established when the school system was bankrupt. The inflated egos of the executives were a bit restrained by such confrontations with political and community power. Still, business contributed to the mix of money, people, and expertise that led to the success of reforms in Chicago (O'Connell, 1991, pp. 19–30).

After the passage of the legislation, business groups in Chicago attempted to institutionalize an advocacy role for business in education. With their substantial budget, Chicago United and the Civic Committee were able to secure Joe Reed, the vicepresident for external affairs with AT&T, to head the new Leadership for Quality Education (LQE). Reed and other business executives were shown to be as naive as members of the interim school board and were held responsible for the many problems of this interim board; Reed was probably replaced at LQE because of those problems. Reed and his replacement, a former Republican legislature member, Diana Nelson, developed an extensive plan to implement education reform. The new program tried to train parents and community leaders for service on school councils, to coordinate various reform groups, to counter misuse of school funds, and to change the school system, including the school board.

Various corporate groups developed other programs. The First National Bank awarded $1,000 to any council to which one of its employees was elected. Illinois Bell trained its employees to run for council elections and developed an award program for councils with innovative ideas (Illinois Bell, 1991). Though now discontinued by Illinois Bell itself, similar programs have been developed by other companies and foundations. However, it is probable that the most significant change was the formation of LQE. The development of this business advocacy group moved educational involvement out of its former marginal status. Typically, most companies had added educational reform to the duties of an existing officer, such as public affairs, community relations, or personnel (Timpane & McNeill, 1991, p. 33). Here, for the first time in a local community, was a specialized agency sponsored by business and devoted to reform.

THE RETREAT

In Chicago, there have always been tensions between business and the other reform groups. Executives sought and gained a superagency above the schools. The same leader who compared the oversight commission to a plantation overseer later claimed that, in reorganizing its advocacy group, Leadership for Quality Education, business was walking away from reform in Chicago (James Deanes, interview, April 8, 1994). Deanes had his appointment to coordinate the inclusion of the Corporate/Community School into the public system temporarily suspended (Klonsky, 1994, September). In that metropolitan area, there are substantial tensions between business interests and the aims of community action groups. As a result of the changes in LQE, community groups could remember only that business did not support an amendment making education a right; they had forgotten how much they had deferred to business expertise in the past (Diana Lauber, interview, April 11, 1993).

The distrust between the reformers and business increased when the Civic Committee President, Lawrence Howe, in late 1993 decided to absorb LQE into the parent Civic Committee. The president of LQE, Diana Nelson, resigned in protest, although she had earlier accepted new legislation which other reform groups continued to oppose. The acceptance of the legislative package was truly remarkable, since only one day earlier, on November 11, 1993, LQE, under Diana Nelson, had orchestrated a coordinated position of opposition. In fact, on the very day she would sign on to the legislative settlement, Nelson issued her statement of opposition. Her claim, that Howe had told her to end the opposition to the proposal that resulted from a collective bargaining agreement between the school board and the teachers' union, could hardly be questioned (Diana Nelson, interview, November 23, 1993). As the letter from Joan Slater indicates, Designs for Change continued to oppose the legislation (Joan Slater, letter to Bob Kustra, November 12, 1994). With the "hostile takeover" of LQE by the parent Civic Committee, Mrs. Nelson reported that Don Moore of Designs for Change felt that they would have to carry on the fight for reform without a business ally.

The actual issues raised by this retreat from reform are relatively limited. Teachers laid off from one position continued to be employed, sometimes in clerical positions, and still had to be considered for new jobs. These teachers, the supernumerary ones, have been declining drastically in numbers (Charles Kyle, interview, November 10, 1993). The principals have always had to battle with janitors and their supervisors for authority. Because of drastic financial limitations, state funds for poor children (labeled Chapter 1 funds) would be divided between the school system and the local councils; before reform, the school bureaucracy had regularly used the funds for their general operations. The reformers had fought against this practice and had all state Chapter 1 funds given to local school councils to use for poor children. Now half of the state funds, though not federal funds for a similar program, have been lost. It was a galling defeat, but it hardly spelled the death of reform.

In 1995, two years after the takeover of LQE by its mother organization, the Civic Committee, legislation was enacted that went much further, giving control of education in Chicago to the mayor. Supernumerary positions were eliminated. The board appointed by Mayor Daley was given control of finances and the new board superseded the School Finances Authority. Chapter 1 funds were reduced but would not be reduced further. No new funds were found for Chicago schools. The newest legislation had the blessing of the reorganized LQE (John Ayers, interview, May 15, 1995); there were regrets that the reorganization plan that business had worked to develop with the school superintendent had not been implemented.

Though the takeover of LQE would later pale in comparison to the elimination of the school board, the reorganization of LQE led, at the time, to a significant challenge to business influence on the reform movement. The bias of business in education has been revealed. Usually, business influences on education are denied as conspiracy theories. Among the six women who worked at LQE, there was no doubt; all of the staff were denied severance pay if they rejected alternative positions with the Civic Committee (Diana Lauber, interview, November 23, 1993). At no time was the reorganization of LQE defined as a gender or racial issue even though two White men were making the decisions about the futures of six White women on staff who were in limbo and the one Black woman assistant who was laid off. Three of the former staff with LQE were, a year later, working for the Cross City Campaign. The former president of LQE, Diana Nelson, worked temporarily with Designs for Change and has since secured a permanent executive position with an elite center for business and professional people, the Union Club. The new executive of LQE, John Ayers, became, temporarily, a key person in the plan to reorganize the central administration of the Chicago school board (Ken Rolling, letter, July 1, 1994). Peter Martinez of the MacArthur Foundation initiated the counterrevolution, which is focused on reorganizing schools and which came to include redirecting LQE, but Martinez is known to withdraw after he has others involved in any activity (Diana Nelson, interview, September 8, 1994). The former and present members of LQE tried to work together in developing a reorganization plan for central office under the new executives while raising business funds for the Annenberg grant.

Since the reorganization plan had called for a refocused research division, the consortium of university researchers became a key component of the business-led reorganization in Chicago. The university researchers have provided the legitimacy for reform; whether or not it is actually changing the education of students is another matter. Their initial proposal for research stated: "Area universities can and must serve a variety of functions if Chicago school reform is to succeed. . . . The Consortium provides a vehicle for school officials to execute this responsibility . . . the 'Chicago Experiment' still stands as the boldest effort to date by a major urban school system to renew itself" (Consortium of Chicago School Research, 1991, pp. 7–8). The research consortium has been described by one local critic as a selfserving group whose research probably would not help education (Jan Hively, interview, October 25, 1993). However, as a part of a restructuring plan which is influenced by business, the interests of researchers was substantially altered in appearance. A proposal was top secret for most of a year and a gag order on principals and administrators, supposedly, was issued to prevent public discussion (Diana Nelson, interview, September 8, 1994). The researchers and their business supporters may have painted themselves into a corner, though the new political control of the system seemed to change this.

The reorganization plan was developed as a cost saving approach by another organization of the Civic Committee which parallels LQE, the Financial Research and Advisory Committee (Janet Froetscher, presentation to Chicago School Turnaround Commission, April 27, 1994). The study of roles, responsibilities, and relationships was expected to cost $9 million over two years. Foundations would provide $1.5 million; business consultants who were sought included McKinsey, Gemini, and Arthur Anderson. CSC Index was picked to lead the charge of consultants. Supposedly, CSC was donating services worth $200,000 per month. All this time the Catholic board in Chicago has been providing an example of a community and religious organization that administers a very large system with barely forty employees, while the Chicago public system still has over 3,000 administrators (Kyle & Kantowitz, 1992, pp. 168–169). However, business organizations seem unwilling to look toward religious institutions for serious direction even when the Catholic schools have a much lower per pupil cost. Business ideology is too different from religious ideology for this to happen.

Aside from the reorganization plan in Chicago, there are other signs of an increasingly conservative power that is influencing the reform movement there and to which business is contributing. In the spring legislation of 1994, the sponsors of legislation sought by the reform group withdrew until the school board would also support the changes advocated (Diana Nelson, interview, May 23, 1994). The consensus reforms, including standards and staff training, have been mentioned previously. It is becoming questionable whether Peter Martinez, with his foundation working with business consultants, has any continuing tie to the Alinsky heritage and whether John Ayers, with his business advocacy group, has any link to the original aim of Chicago reform.

As the conservative direction in Chicago is asserted so strongly, the Chicago Teachers' Union, together with the Chicago School Board, has developed the usual business approach to standards mentioned in Chapter 3; the teachers' union has also welcomed the corporate/community school and plans to work with it in the public system. The union, long ago, lost its socialist and broader foci of changing society (Herrick, 1971). Speculation that the teachers' union can be an alternative to corporate power seems absurd, particularly since it has been stripped of its bargaining rights (Shipps, 1995). In any event, the mayor's appointment of his former executives to operate the school system has eclipsed the direct business plans.

Many of the positions mentioned are common in other conservative or business groups. The business advocacy group in Chicago has long wanted to avoid any controversy, and the reorganization of LQE was engineered because the advocacy organization was too critical of the school's budget (Diana Lauber, interview, April 8, 1994). School-based decision making has been supported in Chicago together with choice among different schools within one building (John Ayers, interview, April 25, 1994). Kentucky, with its Council of Education Technology, school-based management, new assessments, and incentives seems to have the innovations that business seeks from the schools aside from sane and sober assumptions (National Alliance of Business, 1991, p. 63). In Canada, raising the academic level of achievement, increasing science courses with added technological applications, and transferring site-based management to schools is the heart of an important position paper (Corporate-Higher Education Forum, 1991). In Canada, no one has developed so specific a plan for business as that of BRT. Kentucky had to improve since the court decision which established its inferiority also required that a plan be submitted for change. Kentucky's businesses have become so sensitive to school needs that they have developed classroom teaching units (Nickerson et al., n.d.). Ashland Oil of Kentucky claims, in an advertisement, that America's bottom line is educational excellence.

THE CAN-DO REACTION

Kentucky's legislation is a response to an educational crisis and the people guiding business in Kentucky are determined to overcome that crisis. A series of shocking facts are used by business and its allies to get public attention on educational reform.

Did you know. . . ?
- Kentucky trails every other state except West Virginia in the percentage of adults who finish high school.
- For every 100 children entering elementary schools in Kentucky today, only 63 will complete high school.
- Kentucky has the least educated adult work force in the nation....

Did you know. . . ?
- Kentucky's youth population dropped dramatically between 1980 and 1990.
- Fewer children mean fewer workers in the years ahead.

- We historically have had one of the highest unemployment rates and lowest income rates in the nation. (Partnership for Kentucky School Reform, 1994)

The business people in Kentucky have no doubt that "image and the reality of a weak education system has slowed Kentucky's economic growth" (Partnership for Kentucky School Reform, n.d., p. 1). But where else have the problems of an entire area been as defined in educational terms as in Kentucky? Certainly not in Chicago or in Alberta. As has been shown previously, Chicago's racial, political, and financial problems led to its educational legislation. The decisions in Illinois led to the most recent law, which created the new superboard; the Republican governor has been able to turn the problems of the city over to the Democratic mayor (Harp, 1995, June). In Alberta, the educational reforms have been repeatedly argued to be subordinated to the problems of the government's debt; the educational system is assumed to have high standards, at least higher than those of American schools.

While Chicago represents political reform of education with static financing and Alberta stands for administrative changes together with declining expenditures, Kentucky symbolizes progressive innovations together with a substantial increase in funding. Funding in Kentucky for elementary and secondary education went from $1.53 billion in 1989/90 to $2.05 billion for 1991/92 and has maintained that increase since (Partnership for Kentucky School Reform, n.d.). Far greater equality of funding has also been achieved; the poorest one-fifth of the school districts have had an increase in basic per pupil grants of 86 percent from 1989 to 1994. As shown in Chapter 4, the financial revolution in Kentucky has been accompanied by a mushrooming in the number of program innovations. In Alberta, equity in funding among districts appears to divert attention from declining total support for education.

Key support for the Kentucky program, including the financial changes, has come from business leaders who are linked to the efforts of the Business Roundtable nationally. In 1991, three chief executive officers, who were dedicated to the national effort and whose companies had their home offices in Kentucky, joined to form a broad partnership in Kentucky. John Hall, Ashland Oil, David Jones, Humana, and Kent (Oz) Nelson, United Parcel Service, organized the Partnership for Kentucky School Reform. The current fifty members are extremely diverse and include government leaders and officials as well as lawyers and social activists. A minority of the members are corporate leaders. The AFL-CIO in Kentucky has endorsed the partnership though it is not actively involved with it (Robert Sexton, interview, May 4, 1995).

While linking a variety of organizations and interests, the partnership has helped maintain the sense of commitment among business leaders in Kentucky even when it has wavered elsewhere (Cross, 1995, June). The partnership has connected education to organizations for the arts, science and technology, and religion. It has also attempted to include students in its speakers' bureau, coordinate an association of school councils, reduce the resistance of school trustees to school councils, and work together with the teachers' association. Most of all, the partnership shares offices with the Prichard Committee and is so interwoven with the committee that it is impossible to tell where one organization ends and the other begins.

Within the partnership, individual entrepreneurs and corporate executives have provided public models of what dedication to education can mean for business. For example, Billy Harper, who runs a series of construction companies, has used posters and check stuffers to get his employees involved with him in support of educational reform. Harper found that middle school students are particularly interested in his avocation, drag racing. With his Red Line Racing crew and his 1968 Plymouth Barracuda, Harper captures student interest in order to show them the importance of basic mathematics and science. With an on-board computer, he teaches them how new gear ratios can be calculated for better performance. Though Harper provides rewards to students with perfect attendance, his message for adults is "Look at what you enjoy doing and think about how that activity can be incorporated in a school" (Partnership for Kentucky School Reform, 1994).

A number of companies go beyond sightseeing tours and superficial partnerships to actively engaging students with an educational objective. The National City Bank does an evaluation of its tour but also gives the students a problem in encoding deposits. When the deposits do not balance, they must determine why, how to make corrections, and what the impact of the mistake on the customer would be. Ashland Oil has developed a fair on educational reform where an entire class with all the children and all the furniture is moved to their office, a brown-bag lunch discussion about education among employees occurs, and an evening dinner is provided simultaneously with recruitment for specific jobs in assisting education. In 1991, Ashland, one of the founders of the partnerships, developed a videodisc, "The Adventures of Jasper Woodbury," to present fifth grade students with realistic word problems in mathematics. An employee with Ashland spent half of her time showing two teachers how to implement the program with a computer and customized software. Evaluation was made of students who had experienced the Jasper program and those who had not done so (Partnership for Kentucky School Reform, 1994). Ashland Oil was in the educational research business!

Another member of the partnership, United Parcel Service (UPS), has worked with teachers in Fayette County to produce a unit for elementary students that includes their shipping and receiving operations in order to show the knowledge that is required (Nickerson et al., n.d.). Using UPS symbols and lesson plans and Bloom's taxonomy, a variety of problems from handling hazardous materials, lifting and storing packages, and mapping and delivering packages are covered. Chart 6.1 shows how the elementary curriculum is then related to this approach. The demonstration for the class is then combined with a tour of their plant. United Parcel has also developed units on communication, world culture, and Appalachian life. It has had two teachers on temporary assignment with the company for these curriculum projects. UPS is also working on math and science units for middle and high schools, developing a leadership training program for principals with the academy of a public school board, and is considering future involvement of principals in their management training program. Some of the companies are almost becoming fellow educators in Kentucky.

THE PUBLIC RELATIONS PLOY

Before one accepts the colleagues from the corporate world too completely, a more critical stance is needed so that the public relations policies are understood, the instrumental thinking of business is again recognized and, indeed, the ideology of these companies that are so supportive of education is grasped. In an opening letter for the partnership guide, Oz Nelson, chairman and CEO of Ashland Oil, states that his current advertising campaign stresses educational quality. However, Mr. Hall also notes that two of the company's previous campaigns were given to nonprofit associations for use as public service announcements after the company had ended its association with them. The previous campaigns stressed dropout prevention and teacher appreciation. In Chapter 7 we will see that the impressive sponsorship of integrated services by the Continental Bank occurs in a context in which no other companies are seen to be contributing. Even when company interest is most enlightened, as in Kentucky, it is still a case of company paternalism.

Indeed, the Partnership and the Prichard Committee constantly advertise the benefits of education. One advertisement claims that "People Without Children in School Make Education Their Business;" another says, "Retired Workers Make Education Their Business." The famous yellow bus with computer displays tours the state showing how the reform works. Still other publicity efforts stress that the basics are being learned under reform and that professional development days help improve the quality of education. The partnership has a task force on the professional development of teachers (McDiarmid, 1994). At no time are the campaign interests of the sponsors revealed nor the reasons for beginning or terminating this particular publicity effort stated. The readers are not shown how they can change reform or how they can get campaign sponsors to listen to them.

The instrumental process of having readers move toward known goals is still typical of these most benign of corporate sponsors. Chapter 4 has shown some of the resistance to educational reform in Kentucky, especially among teachers; Chapter 7 will show, more specifically, the lack of support revealed by parents to reforms, though they find some aspects of them personally useful. Unlike in Chicago, there are few grass-roots advocates for

Chart 6.1
The Curriculum Use of a Company Program

UNITED PARCEL DELIVERY

Introduction
What does UPS mean?
Who uses it? Why?
Who owns UPS?
Where is it located?

Problem Solving
Overtime: holiday
and weekends
Scheduling:
interdependence
Order and sort packages
Load/Unload package cars

Guest Speakers
Safety on loading/unloading
Hazardous Materials
Delivery person

Math
Scales: weight of
packages—grams, ounces
pounds
Mileages/gas
Measurement: different
length of package car
Measurement: length

Language Arts
"Exceptions"
Goals: rewards for
efficiency
Research and role
play careers
Read and interpret
delivery schedules
Story starters
Write own route

Art
Build class UPS
package car:
paint, make shelves
Build portable package car
Design your own package car

Field Trips
UPS—send package
Safety City

Health
Safety in lifting
Stress control
On the job safety

Economics
Service/Product
Cost/Profit: Time saved equals money saved
Supply/Demand: Christmas packages
Assembly Line: Preload, box line

Science
Study hazardous materials
Computer scheduling
DIADS
Transportation safety: road signs and
how to drive UPS
Driving Test

Social Studies
Past/Present/Future:
UPS
Transportation
DIAD boards
Mail delivery
Mapping: maps and globes of Lexington,
Kentucky, U.S., World
Careers at UPS
Diagraming in package cars

Source: The UPS *Thematic Lesson Plan.*

reform in Kentucky. Again, unlike Chicago in its early years, Kentucky has never needed public relations assistance (Robert Sexton, interview, May 4, 1995). The Prichard Committee in Kentucky is one continuous public relations effort.

One further educational specific in the large unnumbered, but indexed, handbook for businesspeople reveals clearly the bias of this thinking. As a success story, the Benton Bank is shown establishing a bank in a school because "students don't really understand interest rates and late charges." Unlike similar efforts elsewhere, particularly in Alberta, this project is not primarily self-serving since the bank donates $5,000 to start the accounts (Partnership for Kentucky School Reform, 1994). However, like the businesses involved in youth apprenticeship programs which were reviewed in Chapter 5, the bank does not appear to see that childhood is built on more than concern for interest rates and late charges.

If ideology is seen to involve a different way of thinking, then those responsible for the Benton Bank program are ideological (Boudon, 1986). Bankers may be as taken up with fashionable reform ideas as intellectuals are, contrary to claims by an economist (Boudon, 1986, p. 121). However, bankers and intellectuals think differently and have different values; that difference is like the one between believers in magic and those who have always rejected anything magical. When the scientist or geologist must employ a waterwitch to find water for his home in a remote area, he or she is aware of these differences, which involve more than money or the feelings of the parties (Spindler, 1963). Similarly, religion, family, and politics all differ from business in their ideologies.

The examples of business interest in the curriculum are more in the rational and less in the mysterious, more oriented to mathematics than to poetry. Business leaders take for granted the values of planning, evaluation, and publicity. To seek involvement in existing plans seems reasonable. However, what seems most reasonable to businesspeople can be totally repugnant to others. Speaker Madigan, it might be recalled, did not understand or accept the business leaders' desire for rapid action. In Kentucky, probably more than anywhere else, the focus of education is on planning, which is based on annual improvements. Annual improvements do not reveal that even businesspeople will sustain their own interest annually, as the discussion of BRT in Chapter 5 has shown. However, the focus of teachers on the stages of growth, control, and autonomy is not easily reconciled with attention to annual improvements or increments of changes. Whether it is changes in the Boston Compact, the plans for Chicago councils, or the elaborate rewards and measurements in Kentucky, it is the annual improvement that is the dominant concern, a bottom line for managers but not for most other people.

THE DEBATE IN ALBERTA

On March 16, 1995, a debate was arranged between John Ballheim, president of the Alberta Chamber of Commerce, and Heather-Jane Robertson, director of professional development services for the Canadian Teachers' Federation. John Ballheim is also president of DeVry Institute of Technology and an adviser to the Alberta government (John Ballheim, interview, May 17, 1994). Heather-Jane Robertson is the coauthor of *Class Warfare*, whose attack on control of education by business was cited in the last chapter.

The debate between these two opponents was very ideological, reflecting opposite values, sources, and conceptions of truth. Ms. Robertson argued that schools were an essential part of a democracy and must serve children and their families as citizens, while the opposition advocated competition among schools, which would treat people as clients. Robertson felt that inequalities would occur because some parents could spend more time and effort, if not money, than others. In contrast, Ballheim claimed that he wanted only new alternatives for the public schools on which both debaters could agree. However, he asserted that bureaucracy prevents meaningful change and that the system is incapable of reforming itself. Schools, he claimed, still followed an agricultural calendar and had all the limitations of monopolies, which are the same as bureaucracies.

While speaking past each other in their arguments, both speakers used different evidence for different purposes. Robertson reinterpreted facts that are often accepted; according to her, higher expenditures on education in Canada result from combining funds spent on higher and basic education while, in other countries, higher education has a larger private component. Mr. Ballheim cited authorities that supported his position, including the work of *Reinventing Government*, and ignored those who did not seem to do so, including some studies of the effects of expenditures on educational achievements.

In order to reach an audience that was largely composed of classroom teachers, Ballheim referred to his experience in working with schools in Chicago for ten years. Some of the teachers charged that he was trying to impose a model from Chicago on them. However, when he argued that the Catholic schools achieved greater results with far less money, resources, and administrators than the public schools, Ms. Robertson scored against him. In a style often associated with the Jesuits, she turned his words against him and suggested that the silver bullet for educational reform must be Catholicism. She had defended truth against the infidel.

THE ALBERTA ASYLUM

Though outsiders may score occasional victories against the self-proclaimed advantage of life and education in Alberta, a system of instrumental, seemingly objective thinking is being erected by its supporters. The curriculum direction is stated in a business plan for education which starts with the issue of "building a strong social and economic future for Alberta" and moves to "focus education on what students need to know," which can be done better by various increases in "efficiencies and effectiveness in education" (Alberta Education, n.d., p. 5). Education is not considered a contributor to democracy nor an end in itself. One must never ask what students ought to know or whether they should be interested in becoming better people.

Rather, results are specified and strategies are suggested. Higher scores are to be achieved, greater satisfaction is to be provided, and too much government is eliminated by curtailing opposition groups, such as school boards. From its initial meetings, the government reported, "Groups described measurement as a diagnostic tool capable of identifying strengths and weaknesses and providing the direction for change" (Alberta Education, 1993, p. 14). With conceptual and measurement tools, one can sit back and evaluate the contribution of education to the economy; the evaluators and administrators believe that they are not part of the process which they are trying to change.

Students are a particularly interesting case since they are, apparently, taught writing and critical skills only to have their voices heard through satisfaction surveys (Alberta Education, 1995, p. 1). Teachers, unlike some models, such as Socrates, are not to make students unhappy with their lot. Students, unlike those student teachers in change situations, such as those at New College at Columbia University during the 1930s, are not to start a change process themselves (Mitchell, 1992, p. 130). Students are to be measured by the extent to which the system satisfies them and they, in turn, are trained to work (Vivone, 1994, p. 15).

Parents fare somewhat better in the attempt to produce the system that is to reduce costs and make Alberta more competitive. Enhanced communication with parents is intended "to increase their involvement in their child's progress" (Alberta Education, 1993b, p. 18). But what are they to do after they are involved? The government only says that parents should be very interested in progress toward careers or higher education. Should parents travel with them, read and write with them, or what? Parent involvement in school councils also appears to lack an active educational purpose, as we will discuss shortly.

Parents, as well as other participants in planning Alberta Education, are not guaranteed that their views will even be registered by the system. Views of such people that international comparisons "would not be valuable" (Alberta Education, 1993b, p. 18) are ignored in subsequent guides (Alberta Education, n.d., p. 19). It might be noted that the government had a computer-aided content analysis program to develop its results, nevertheless some replies were ignored. Similarly, Chapter 7 will show that the objections of participants to regional authorities for integrated services were ignored. Perhaps the government should fill in the boxes on their surveys in advance.

In contrast to the views of parents or most participants, which, on occasion, may be ignored, the views of businesspeople are repeatedly and uncritically accepted. From an initial inquiry about the "perceived effectiveness of partnerships with business" and other groups, government reports jump to conclusions about the ways business can be more involved in providing education (Alberta Education, 1993a, p. 27 and Alberta Education, 1993b, p. 35). Teaching results are required, but no evidence about the effectiveness of business partnerships is needed. Links between business and technology continue to be made (Alberta Education, 1993b, p. 24 and Alberta Education, n.d., p. 14). Interestingly, in a prototype for evaluation, a business is discussed as the organization which will be conducting the satisfaction surveys (Alberta Education, 1995).

Aside from business, the government's other main support is from the religious Right. There is no obvious appeal to this group in the writing of educational plans and evaluations. Several commentators have claimed that charter schools were a reward for the religious supporters (Taylor, 1994 and Vivone, 1994). However, if we compare the reforms in Alberta with those in Kentucky, a number of omissions are revealed. In every statement of educational aims, the phrase "self-reliant, responsible, caring and active participants in society" is used (Alberta Education, 1993a, p. 6). There is none of the social sensitivity which was seemingly unrelated to academic results and which got the Kentucky reforms in trouble with the religious Right there. If business wants its employees to be able to work in teams, it can certainly evaluate Alberta's system against this criterion. But the system will not be set up to be attacked for having team goals.

In fact, no progressive approach of grading, organization, or curriculum planning that might aggravate the religious Right is used in this province. Discussion of performance-based tests has not led to the spread of exhibitions or portfolios. Nor have percentage grades been abandoned for the fivefold classification from novice to expert used in Kentucky. Mandatory early childhood education for all disabled students from age three or all poor children from age four, as in Kentucky, would cost money as well as risk the label "Nazi child snatchers." The preoccupation with the system prevents any issues of substance from being considered, just as the same government tried to prevent a debate on abortion.

A STEP TOWARD COLLABORATION

In all three cases, school councils are a procedure being adopted as a part of a system for reform. The councils provide the opportunity to achieve a new consensus from the grass roots when associations of the school councils are developed. If the councils are to provide no more than a limited or false sense of participation in decisions already made by central government, then the promise of councils for coordinating reform will never be realized.

The more business dominates a reform movement, the less likely it is that councils will ever develop an association that will play a significant role in governing a school system. When thinking stresses system, consistency, conflict avoidance, and incremental improvements, as does business ideology, there is little recognition of the world of conflict, confrontation, and compromise that is a part of political reality.

The association of councils can eventually be a part of the governmental scene even if many of them are now light-years away. The transition from concern about one's own child to involvement with an entire school is enormous (Mitchell, 1992, p. 162). Ideological convictions, including religion as well as pay for part-time jobs, are often a part of the reason for parents taking this big initial step (Bonito Street, interview, May 12, 1995). Experience in leadership positions, including going beyond "having a voice to being heard," must precede moving further in developing representation for councils (Fine, 1993).

In order to become more active, councils are given support in each of the situations that have been examined. In Chicago, before it was changed into a more conservative group, the business advocacy organization Leadership for Quality Education provided such support. LQE developed a video series for training council members as well as encouraging participation in larger reform groups that it helped to initiate. The MacArthur Foundation supplied a grant for the formation of the Chicago Association of Local School Councils. A first convention was held by all the councils on January 7 and 8, 1995, focusing on school leadership, "creating nurturing classrooms" and "positive" schools, developing "planning, monitoring and evaluation schedules," and becoming advocates by defining problems, finding the right person to hear these problems, and continuing to motivate supporters (Chicago Association of Local School Councils, n.d.).

The consensus and position developed in Kentucky stress the integration of principals, teachers, and parents. The Kentucky Association of School Councils was formed in 1991 when David Allen of the Kentucky Education Association (the teachers' union) and Jean Arrowwood of the Kentucky Congress of Parents and Teachers convened a meeting of the three constituencies. Training, legal services, publications, and an annual convention are provided by this association of councils. In Kentucky, a lawyer, writer on reform and former associate with the U.S. Department of Education, Susan Weston, was hired as the first executive director. In Chicago, the executive is Sheila Castillo, a Latino parent, former city of Chicago employee, and active council member.

Without even the general links of the Partnership in Kentucky to the business community, no business support for the councils in Alberta has as yet developed. An announcement for training council members, teachers, and principals for school-based decision making notes that the Alberta

Home and School Association and the Alberta Teachers' Association are jointly developing an orientation manual for school councils (Dempster, June 28, 1995). At the start of its revolution, Alberta used roundtables of largely preselected supporters as a public relations device—a secret committee of three planned alternatives for higher education. The secret committee reportedly included business educator, management guru, Stephen Murgatroyd, and treasurer, Jim Dinning (Lisac, 1995, p. 151). Perhaps the influence of business is now so established that it is no longer needed in the system directly; it is the unseen hand in Alberta. The major cities in Alberta have a Key Communicator program in public schools which appears to function somewhat like an association of councils when important decisions are given to it.

A REVIEW

The attempts of business to form broader coalitions have been limited by the ideology of business. The development of people, parents, or students is not a high priority. Chicago has been an exception with the common front that was formed by business with social activists, but a more conventional position of restructuring the system has now been taken. Kentucky has developed even more of a bridge between the ideologies of business and education. The Alberta advantage is achieved by isolating the two camps. A litmus test of how dominant ideology has become is whether or not business sees itself as engaged with families so they better understand reform as in Chicago, directing families so they better understand reform which happens in Kentucky, or claiming to represent families as in Alberta or replacing them as described by the Committee on Economic Development (1990, p.62).

The association of councils is important insofar as businesses respect families, rather than trying to speak for them. The association of councils allows one to see whether business and its partners are prepared to invest in an infrastructure that may help realize the democratic dream in the future. The structure of reform movements needs to be rethought. Chicago, with its many competing groups, has never been able to sustain more than temporary alliances or occasional retreats. Kentucky has the centralized and overlapping Partnership and Prichard Committee. Alberta has its informal alliance that includes business and the impersonal system that appears to exclude no one. Federated structures can emerge from competing relationships; this is the goal of integrated services (discussed in the next chapter). A federation of councils can develop collaboration so that a joint staff, combined training, and shared resources are, increasingly, employed to integrate health, education, and social services (Melaville & Blank, 1993). Associations of councils are one area of the reform movement where collaboration, rather than competition, appears to be emerging.

REFERENCES

Alberta Education (1993a). *Meeting the challenge: An education roundtable workbook.* Edmonton: Alberta Education.

Alberta Education (1993b). *Meeting the challenge: What we heard.* Edmonton: Alberta Education.

Alberta Education (1994). *Meeting the challenge: Three-year business plan.* Edmonton: Alberta Education.

Alberta Education (n.d.). *Meeting the challenge 11: Three-year business plan for education 1995/96—1997/98.* Edmonton: Alberta Education.

Alberta Education (1995). *Accountability in education discussion paper.* Edmonton: Alberta Education.

Alberta Education (1995, February 1). *1995/96 Education funding announced.* Edmonton: Alberta Education.

Boudon, R. (1986). *The analysis of ideology.* Chicago: The University of Chicago Press.

Chicago Association of Local School Councils (1995). *Construction ahead... LSC at work.* Chicago: Chicago Association of Local School Councils.

Committee for Economic Development (1990). *An America that works: The life-cycle approach to a competitive work force.* New York: Committee for Economic Development.

Consortium of Chicago School Research (1991). *Achieving school reform in Chicago.* Chicago: Consortium of Chicago School Research.

Corporate-Higher Education Forum (1991). *To be our best: Learning for the future.* Montreal: Corporate-Higher Education Forum.

Cross, C. (1995, June 7). The downsizing of corporate philanthropy. *Education Week,* 14(37), 44.

Dempster, L. (1995, June 28). $1.9 million earmarked to train school councils. *Calgary Herald,* A18.

Fine, M. (1993). [Ap]parent involvement: Reflections on parents, power and urban public schools. *Teachers College Record,* 94(4), 682–710.

Harp, L. (1995, June 7). Governor signs bill putting mayor in control of Chicago schools. *Education Week,* 14(37), 11.

Herrick, M. (1971). *The Chicago Schools.* Beverly Hills, California: Sage Publications.

Illinois Bell (1991). *Local school councils ideas and successes.* Chicago: Illinois Bell.

Kentucky Association of School Councils (1992, November). *A few words about KASC.* Lexington: Kentucky Association of School Councils.

Klonsky, M. (1994, September). Merger paving way for creation of new schools. *Catalyst,* 6(1), 1, 30–31.

Knowles, J. (1973) *The Rockefeller financial group.* Andover, Massachusetts: Warner Modular.

Kyle, C. & Kantowicz, E. (1992). *Kids first-primero los niños .* Springfield: Illinois Issues.

Leadership for Quality Education, (1993). *Leadership for quality education.* Chicago: The Leadership for Quality Education.

Lisac, M. (1995). *The Klein revolution.* Edmonton: NeWest Press.

McDiarmid, G. (1994). *Realizing new learning for all students: A framework for the professional development of Kentucky teachers*. East Lansing: National Center for Research on Teacher Learning, Michigan State University.

McKersie, W. (1993). Chicago's paradox, Chicago School reform. *Education evaluation and policy analysis*, 15(2), 109–128.

Melaville, T. & Blank, M. (1993). *Together we can: A guide for crafting a profamily system of education and human services*. Washington, D. C.: U.S. Department of Education and U.S. Department of Health and Human Services.

Mitchell, S. (1992). *Innovation and reform*. York, Ontario: Captus Press.

National Alliance of Business (1991). *Business Roundtable participation guide: A primer for business on education*. New York: Business Roundtable.

Nickerson, J., Lenox, M. & Mielcarek, G. (n.d.). United Parcel Service ungraded primary schools thematic unit program guide. Unpublished paper.

O'Connell, M. (1991). *School reform Chicago style*. Chicago: Center for Neighborhood Technology.

Partnership for Kentucky School Reform (n.d.). *Education we make it our business: A Partnership for Kentucky School Reform*. Lexington: Partnership for Kentucky School Reform.

Partnership for Kentucky School Reform (1994). *Education we make it our business; A planning and resource guide*. Lexington: Partnership for Kentucky School Reform.

Shipps, D. (1995). Big business and school reform: The case of Chicago, 1988. Ph.D. Dissertation, Stanford University.

Spindler, G. (1963). *Education and Culture*. New York: Holt, Rinehart & Winston.

Taylor, A. (1994). "How do they get away with this stuff?" The context of educational restructuring in Alberta. Paper presented at the Canadian Learned Societies Conference.

Timpane, P. & McNeill L. (1991). *Business impact on education and child development reform*. New York: Committee for Economic Development.

Vivone, R. (1994, November/December). The government flexes its muscle. *The ATA Magazine*, 15–17.

Wrigley, J. (1982). *Class, politics and public schools; Chicago 1900–1950*. New Brunswick, New Jersey: Rutgers University Press.

Chapter 7

Professional Services
for Families

Confused and upset, LaJoe walked silently out of the room, slamming the door behind her. She would later apologize to her inquisitors for her impoliteness, but she wouldn't offer much defense against the department's charges. She didn't deny that Paul occasionally stayed over. She didn't ask whether she was entitled to legal counsel. She didn't ask for a caseworker to come out and look at their home. Now, as she made her way through the labyrinth of desks, she wondered how to break the news to the kids.

Lafeyette knew his mother had gone for a hearing and that the department was considering cutting her benefits, so when she came home that afternoon he was by the door to greet her. As she walked into the apartment, his eyes locked with hers. His long fingers cupped her face.

"What'd they say?" he asked.

"Off," LaJoe replied in a voice that barely approached a whisper. Lafeyette's shoulders sank. LaJoe hugged him.

She chose not to tell Pharoah, at least not yet; she was protective of him. Because he had lately responded to nearly every instance of violence and family trouble with the same refrain—"I'm too little to understand"—she feared that the problems, when he was at last ready to confront them, would be too deeply buried for him.

"The reason I don't go to Pharoah is because I like Pharoah just being a kid," she explained. "I better enjoy it now, because I don't know how long it's going to last."

She wished, in fact, that she hadn't told Lafeyette, but he was the only person she felt she could talk to about it. It was as if he were as much a husband as he was a son. He was her confidant. (Kotlowitz, 1991, p. 97)

La Joe; her children, Lafeyette and Pharoah; and her husband, Paul, are a poor family who are the focus of integrated services. One organization, social services, denies family assistance when the husband, Paul, is found to be in the home and becomes a possible source of support. The problems of LaJoe and her children could also involve their health, conflicts with the police, or a host of other agencies to which high-risk families are exposed.

Such interrelated problems are the context in which high-risk parents attempt to educate their children.

The organizations to which high-risk families often turn are fragmented and unrelated to the problems of the poor. In Chapter 3, the example of two sisters, Shawn and Tish, was drawn out in order to show how school demands for a vaccination and their mother's presence, when the girls were being looked after by their grandmother, meant that they were kept out of school even after they had the certificates. Criteria for eligibility, funding differences, areas served, and problems of confidentiality prevent the emergence of common goals among organizations (Melville and Blank, 1991). In the last chapter, the possible development of collaboration among councils was seen as a major benefit of joint planning. The development of collaboration between organizations who serve high-risk families is an even more important goal.

Though educational and social organizations often function from limited visions, the businesses and the political right wing, discussed in Chapters 4 and 5, have even more limited perspectives for helping those in poverty. Businesses frequently look at high-risk students from the standpoint of their potential as employees or, at least, as like those in an employee status when jobs, as supplements to education, are only developed in the last years of high school. As a result, the students for whom businesses try to find employment and related education are not the ones in most need; the business programs often do not begin until grades eleven and twelve, when many students are already seriously handicapped or have left school (McMullan & Snyder, 1987, pp. 64–65). Also, businesses often ignore the relationships among education, work and family. A program offering jobs to young men in suburban areas ignored the fact that many had lost their driver's licenses and were less important than the women in the families; the young men were arrested for driving without licenses and conflicts and fights within the families intensified (Padfield & Williams, 1973). Proposals for welfare reform by the right wing ignore the extent to which women on welfare, unlike LaJoe, are abused by their men and need strength in order to overcome these experiences before they can be gainfully employed (Bowen & Sellers, 1994, p. 48 and Jouzaitis, 1995, February). Integrated services require a change in policies which business and all political groups could help bring about.

In spite of the support by the BRT, businesses are only occasionally involved in sponsoring integrated services while the right wing consistently opposes them (Dryfoos, 1994). In Minnesota, one company sponsors a school for unwed mothers, but, elsewhere in the country, it is difficult to find examples of companies that do more than provide furniture for resource centers. In Chicago, a series of projects has tried to assist families in high-risk areas. In Chapter 5, the Corporate Community School, which includes a comprehensive program of service and health care under the leadership of Joe Kellman, was discussed. A larger project in Chicago centered around one high school and its feeder elementary and middle schools, the Orr Network; this project was sponsored by the Continental Bank, which has merged with the Bank of America. However, even in Chicago, involvement of business in the integration of services is very rare.

Without serious support from business, community agencies have developed programs to assist people in an area; such an effort was made in the Orr Network and in similar efforts in other parts of Chicago by Sokoni Karanja and Ben Kenrick (mentioned in Chapter 2). Though based on the Razin Orr High School and its feeder schools, the Orr Network actually involves a whole series of networks that overlap. An education network based at DePaul University supplements the program, as does a school board program for training staff to work in such areas. Social agencies, including the famous Hull House, and health programs from several sponsors are a part of a still only partially coordinated set of networks. The Orr Network has itself expanded into community development, where it meets with the efforts of other community organizers in Chicago. The community efforts and school programs are further linked through family resource centers, such as those which Kentucky has developed more extensively than any other state or province.

Both the Orr project and the Kentucky program have been stimulated by a private organization, Cities in Schools, a pioneer in coordinating social and health programs for the education of high-risk students. While providing training for professionals in Kentucky and Chicago, Cities in Schools has increasingly stressed the use of volunteers and paraprofessionals in providing integrated services. The model for nonprofessionals is the Atlanta Project, and Cities in Schools is again involved through its Georgia affiliate.

The Georgia Cities in Schools has been a supporter for the Atlanta Project which has had over seventeen thousand volunteers work on its various campaigns of immunization, literacy, and housing (Atlanta Project, 1995). The Atlanta Project plans to become Project America and expand across the country. The cluster project in Chicago was a rather unsuccessful attempt to copy it. In spite of its extensive program, Kentucky has not followed the call from Atlanta and pushed the involvement of volunteers; it has rather relied on the efforts of its creative coordinators to bring together resources and clients.

Other governments, such as those in Alberta, have developed integrated services as a way of redefining professional services and increasing community involvement with these services; such aims could lead to the greater use of volunteers and paralegals. Alberta has probably not developed volunteer efforts with a sense of social purpose because integrated services was seen, primarily, as a way of attempting to reduce the costs of various services (Alberta Commissioner of Services for Children, 1994). The Alberta government's initiatives often copy American plans in San Diego or Canadian efforts from more dominant centers of ideas. The government's programs attempt to empower community groups, but there are only rudimentary groups available in the communities who can initiate any actions. In Chicago and Kentucky, there are often sizable volunteer efforts for educational reform that have not always been directed toward integrated services. The ultimate aim might be to get high-risk families to the point where they can help other high-risk groups; this aim is met only by the more dazzling Atlanta Project, which Jimmy Carter heads.

The experience of volunteers and professionals working together can be a resource for an increasing range of programs in community development and school reform. A number of special programs can be developed for high-risk families: health clinics, dental services, teen parenting, and programs that focus on AIDS. It appears from the Kentucky evidence that family resource centers can lead to the development of more specialized programs as coordinators tap resources and develop abilities of families to use them (Cannon et al., 1994). From Chicago it is clear that community involvement has been built on the assistance that lawyers, accountants, and retired executives gave the school councils (Iris Krieg & Associates, 1992); these efforts at coordinating professionals have not been developed for educational reform in general, but there have been some attempts to extend the pattern to integrated services.

Programs that proceed without volunteers and professionals developing a common set of goals may make the problems of the poor in dealing with bureaucracies worse. In Kentucky, with the separation of the top-down Prichard Committee from poor people, there is already a substantial distance between the ideas of experts and the opinions of parents and ordinary people in the community. The value of family resource centers has been recognized by parents and community members, but the family centers have not become a serious link in developing the ideas of such people. Support for right-wing groups is a continuing symptom of the alienation of innovations and citizens.

A broader understanding of the process of integrating education with health and social services for more than professionals is a critical aim when integrated services are being developed. Integrated services involve changes in the way services are provided to clients, the way organizations are related, and the development of public policy to help clients (Kagan, 1993). Joint planning with clients, involvement of parents and community members in setting policies for agencies, and redefinition of the relationships of professionals, professional aids, volunteers, and clients are also necessary.

THE ORR NETWORK

A good example of an attempt to realize the promise of integrated services is the Orr Network. The anchor for this network of thirteen schools is the Rezin Orr Academy High School on the northwestern side of Chicago. This high school has been engaged in an extensive search for an educational approach to a community that has become characterized by Black poverty, young people who themselves have very young children, and little hope for either. Seventy-five percent of the community is below the poverty line, and the average age is twenty-five (Bill Duffie, interview, May 11, 1995). The elementary and middle schools in the same geographical area have a similar constituency of poor people; several of the feeder schools are more dominantly Latino than Black. The high school joined the network to get more students to attend the high school, while the feeder schools sought services that could be supplied through the high school. (Martin, 1993, p. 10). Activists from outside the schools, including several from the Continental Bank, were probably the reason the network was founded; the schools had their own reasons why they joined the effort.

The Orr Network may not be representative of attempts to develop policies for students in high-risk areas. The programs for other communities have been developed with an eye to serving a small number of high-risk individuals in a largely affluent community. The Orr project represents areas with extreme poverty where only the church, school, and liquor store are left (Coretta McFerren, interview, May 5, 1994). In areas with such extreme poverty, drastic educational and social changes which in wealthier regions are not needed are obviously required; with less poverty a more limited focus on a few individuals is sufficient.

For the Orr High School and many of its feeder schools, the Orr Network is one of a host of attempts to deal with race and poverty. Staff training for teachers to deal with such community problems is provided through a systemwide initiative, Creating A New Approach to Learning (CANAL). CANAL was a part of a settlement with the federal government over the treatment of Blacks by the school system; it involves learning school-based management within a conflict situation (Chicago Public School, n.d.). Orr has also tried to raise academic aspirations by involvement in the variation of the Great Books program, Paideia. Community services are brought to the network schools through Cities in School as a part of its national program, which will be described shortly. Only the high school, with the help of Hull House, provides a nursery, teaches parenting skills, and provides a clinic with a nurse. Only the high school, the Ounce of Prevention, operates a school health clinic, which has not been incorporated into the Orr Network (Bill Staughton, interview, May 11, 1995). Some of the high school's programs have not been shared with the feeder schools because they were established before the network, and the feeder schools and related community organizations have not yet been able to negotiate changes.

The Orr project, which grew out of the sponsorship of the school by the Continental Bank, is the most unique effort made in this depressed community. However, the Orr Network has involved an increasing number of partnerships. For the parents, the first priority was to create a safe community so that their children would not be attacked on the way to and from school. The safety program was called Broader Urban Involvement and Leadership Development (BUILD). BUILD organizes parent patrols to protect students from gangs and drugs. However, for parents and staff, the curriculum quickly became a focus for improving the work of the school.

Art and science programs for the schools have been developed through other partnerships. The Golden Apple Foundation has been brought in to develop science materials for schools in the network as well as to give awards to teachers, usually its major activity. "Hands-on" science is emphasized in the programs sponsored by the Golden Apple Foundation as well as other partners. Similarly, active art programs are developed in the network schools through the help of the Chicago Arts Partnership in Education. The art program has tried to bring about the integration of arts with other curriculum areas, such as English; one elementary school, Noble, has become a model of arts-centered teaching for all subjects (Benshoff, 1994).

There are many partners with both the science and arts programs. Other contributors to the science program include the Shedd Aquarium, which provides staff training, special nights for all Orr parents, and programs at the aquarium for students. On-line technical assistance is available from the Teachers' Academy for Mathematics and Science, which was founded by the famous Leon Lederman of the Enrico Fermi Institute; this program is directed by the former principal, Lourdes Monteagudo, who was introduced in Chapter 2. The Children's Museum provides a family science program, while the Max McGraw Wildlife Foundation offers staff development on animals and conservation. The Orr High School helps elementary schools establish after-school science programs and operates a store for teachers to buy science materials (Bank of America, 1995 and Nancy Brandt, interviews, November 2, 1993 and May 11, 1995).

The arts program involves almost as many partners as those in the science area. Art Resources in Teaching offers six-to-twelve week-long programs in schools; this hundred-year-old organization, which promotes arts in schools, provides artists for three classroom visits with each of the network elementary schools. Teachers in each school plan the visits and, in the classrooms, artists and teachers become team teachers. In the summer of 1995, students who participate in another program run by the Marwen gallery were preparing a large mural for the Orr High School. The Marwen Foundation and its gallery provide studio training to students who show artistic aptitude. For the Marwen program, students are bused from elementary schools to the studios by high school buses. The high school was the scene of two special performances of *Die Fliedermaus*, by the Lyric Opera. Dance companies have also presented programs for the schools as a part of regular classes. There does not seem to be the same emphasis on family participation in the arts programs and teacher training is not as direct as it is with the science partners.

However, another important partner further supplements both art and science training for schools in the Orr project as well as elsewhere in

Chicago. For the Orr project, the DePaul University Center for Urban Education provides a resource coordinator who works both with the arts and science curriculums. DePaul, for several years, has worked with Art Resources in Teaching, which is the leading organization to secure grants for more than the program of neighborhood artists for network schools; DePaul has, recently, obtained funds for a writing specialist to work with ten schools. It has also developed materials that are particularly relevant to the local Chicago scene, such as problems in contextual mathematics. DePaul's director, Barbara Radner, always provides examples from her own practice when she is teaching teachers through visual cues and symbols (Barbara Radner, interview, November 11, 1993). Barbara Radner, Nancy Brandt from the bank sponsor, and women from each of the other main partners provide coordination and continuity for the Orr project (Nancy Brandt, interview, November, 1993).

Both DePaul and the Orr Network have developed parent and teacher volunteers for the school curriculum, while the Orr project has moved out beyond the school to providing an employment center and a base for community development. Former Peace Corps members, as well as newer student volunteers, work as teaching assistants for the network of forty-seven schools that DePaul runs, which includes the Orr schools. Training programs for parents are increasingly centered on the basic curriculum areas that their students study. A parent involvement coordinator works with a school community representative from each of the schools in the Orr Network. Parent resource areas or rooms have been established in each of the schools, and the high school is developing plans for a complete family resource center. For one of the elementary schools in the network, the Nia Family Center provides early childhood education together with health services. The health clinic at the Ryerson Elementary School, unlike the one at the Orr High School, is open to the community. The Nia Family Center is run by the Chicago Commons at the University of Chicago, which also runs an employment center for the area. The Nia Family Center was developed by the West Humboldt Park Family and Community Development Council. This council has further extended the Orr project into planning libraries, parks and prospective businesses (Martin, 1993). The two-pronged expansion of the Orr project does not yet mean that facilities are always coordinated in the school and community. There are now two health centers; one in the high school which was never included in the Orr Network, and one in the community. There are also two family centers, the Nia Family Center in the community, and one which is being planned for the high school which is evolving from the family room and other activities for parents.

Perhaps because it is part of so many overlapping networks, the Orr Network is still not seen by many of those involved as cohesive; however, it is probably better coordinated than many similar projects. The Cluster Initiative that seemed so promising (discussed in Chapter 2) has lost all but one of its participating schools. The Orr Network is, apparently, most meaningful for those involved in its planning and parent groups. For teachers and students, the project is seen as fragmented and is only important when, for example, a math teacher uses its math program as a resource (Bill Duffie, interview, May 11, 1995). The separation by double-locked doors of the nursery from the rest of the high schools must convey a message to teen parents, as do staff doubts about the number of nonacademic tasks they want to take on. The limitations of the Orr project probably cannot be hidden from students (Bill Slaughton, interview, May 11, 1995).

COMMUNITY ACTION AND EDUCATIONAL REFORM

The Orr project, with its many partners, led to formation of the Development Council as a result of the numerous meetings directed at the school; the focus on education yielded to a concern for change in the community. Community concerns include local employment, libraries, and health clinics (Martin, 1993). Though there had been an employment center in the community for over twenty years, there was no planning agency to relate the diverse areas of policing gangs, health services, affordable housing, and business opportunities to the needs of people until 1992 (Bank of America, 1995). Opportunities for young people to find jobs and establish families with the support of basic and adult education were crucial for this project. Ironically, in the view of teachers in the school, the Bank of America, which supports the Development Council, no longer provides job opportunities for high school graduates, as it did in its early years (Bill Duffie & Bill Staughton, interviews, May 11, 1995).

In the Orr Network, as well as other areas of Chicago reform, there are problems with keeping together those involved in the movement. This network is only an exception in that the bank is involved. The Bank of America claims an exclusive franchise on community programs and the educational activity, with its complex array of interacting partners; its activities led to the development of community planning. In other parts of Chicago, a number of community action groups were involved in initiating educational reform and community development. The People's Coalition, with Coretta McFerren, Tomas Sanabria, and Sokoni Karanja (discussed in Chapter 3), was a key player in organizing a people's chain of resistance to the teachers' strike as well as alternative schools. Though the People's Coalition did not survive and Tomas Sanabria is no longer active in the reform movement, the other founders of the coalition are still very important. Besides Coretta McFerren and Sokoni Karanja, there has always been one other very significant player, Ben Kenrick.

Ben Kenrick is executive director of the Marcy-Newberry Association. This association includes the Newberry Center, one of the original Chicago settlement houses which were contemporary with Hull House. Aside from its original center on Maxwell Street, the association consists of thirteen centers in different parts of Chicago, including the base which Coretta McFerren now has, the West Side Schools & Communities Organizing for Restructuring & Planning Progress (WSCORP). Kendrick has sponsored Coretta McFerren even though, in his view, she is limited by her strong positions (Ben Kenrick, interview, April 28, 1994). Sokoni Karanja is the founder of Centers for New Horizons, which is currently involved with two large development planning projects on the south side of Chicago. Mr. Karanja seeks advice from Mr. Kenrick so often that the references in an interview were frequently to "Ben and me" (Sokoni Karanja, interview, April 5, 1994).

For Karanja and Kenrick, community survival and planning are the key considerations rather than educational reform in itself. Ben Kenrick is personally concerned with the survival of the area around the Newberry Center where he grew up and which is currently threatened by the expansion of the University of Illinois campus, which earlier engulfed Hull House. Sokoni Karanja is involved with two adjoining areas on the south side of Chicago that are both supported by the MacArthur Foundation as part of its Collaboration Project. The projects on the south side attempt to build on the historic ties of the community, including its contribution to Jazz and Black history, while expanding opportunities for youth and business investments. Mr. Karanja says he would be happy to have a Wal-Mart in communities with many abandoned stores (Sakoni Karanja, interview, April 5, 1994). Aside from plans for community development, these community associations carry on programs of early childhood education, daycare, and support for seniors. Their main activities involve youth counseling and employment; family support and parent education are also important program areas at the center. As in the Orr effort, the focus is on very young people, who often have very young children.

Unlike in the Orr Network, there are signs of alienation from educational reform in these community development efforts. Ben Kenrick is particularly disappointed in councils, such as those across the street from the Newberry Center, where very uneducated people are expected to make decisions for children (Ben Kenrick, interview, April 28, 1994). Sokoni Karanja is still heavily involved with reform organizations, including serving as a community representative on the board of Leadership for Quality Education. Tensions with the educational establishment are revealed by criticisms of Don Moore and Designs for Change and an unpublished report on the community project, Mid-South, that states: "One of Black Metropolis' goals is to repopulate the schools with new, non-union teachers and administrators" (MacArthur Foundation, n.d.).

A CATALYST FOR FAMILY RESOURCE CENTERS

   For social activists, family resource centers are one of the most promising
links between educational reform and community development.   Such
activists are developing these programs themselves as well as watching
similar developments in schools (Center for New Horizons, n.d.).   In
Chicago, Kentucky, and, in its initial organizing stages, Canada, Cities in
Schools (CIS) is a crucial organization involved with social agencies in
general and family resource centers in particular. The coordinated program
of health, education, and social services with families that Cities in Schools
developed has become the focus of a complex set of activities for dropout
prevention among adolescents in poverty.   Cities in Schools is a major
partner of the Orr Network (Janet Hudolin, interview, May 15, 1995). It has
always been an informal partner with Kentucky in developing family and
youth centers (Marsha Morganti, interview, May, 5, 1995). CIS has several
projects in the Toronto area and Yorkton, Saskatchewan; it has appointed
a national coordinator for Canada, Janet Longmore (Cities In Schools, 1995,
p. 8).
   Since 1972, Cities In Schools has constantly developed a variety of
organizations that are very much in tune with publicized demands for
change. CIS has grown in spite of a number of evaluations of its programs,
none of which has been very positive (*Center for the Future of Children*, 1992,
p. 136).   The dynamic director for its entire history has been Bill Milliken,
who began street academies by working with students who had dropped out
of regular schools in tutoring programs or alternative schools.   Later, social
and health services were provided through postal academies with the
sponsorship of the U.S. Postal Service.   Academies currently are mostly
within schools and are sponsored by the U.S. Department of Justice, Burger
King, and an investment banking firm, Goldman Sachs (Cities In Schools,
1994).   Each year leading musical artists come together to record a song and
video, while other entertainers have donated twenty-five cents of the price
of concert tickets to support CIS.   Entertainers involved include Garth
Brooks, Barbara Mandrell, and Charlie Daniels for the 1992 video, and
those providing support through their concert prices include Madonna, Janet
Jackson, and Prince. After each Super Bowl, the National Football League
establishes a new academy, run by CIS.
   With its high profile, CIS has probably not had much to worry about in
terms of its specific programs of integrating services within schools.
Commentators on these evaluations have stressed that the early efforts were
"plagued by problems of communications, administration, professional turf
protection, and inconsistencies"; and the programs were "only peripherally
integrated into the ongoing curricula, culture and operating procedures of
their host schools" (Crowson & Boyd, 1993, pp.153–154).   A statewide
evaluation of CIS in Texas for 1985–87 was more positive (The Future of
Children, 1992, p. 136).   Texas is one of the largest states involved in CIS

with a current budget of $38 million (Janet Hudolin, interview, January 18, 1995). Current evaluation by the Urban Institute of the ninety-eight local programs reaching 117, 000 students annually has been completed, but its release has been delayed for over six months.

In Kentucky, CIS has now become an official partner for integrated services after having been an informal partner in developing the family centers from the beginning (Marsha Morganti, interview, May 5, l995). As the CIS is increasingly recognized in Kentucky as well as elsewhere, it seems important to ask what it brings to the experiments in integrated services. The picture is incomplete. CIS has trained the coordinators for the family centers in Kentucky and has operated a national training program for any interested group. The president, Bill Milliken, has stressed that, aside from bringing resources to the schools, student interns and volunteer mentors and tutors are primary groups for the integration effort. A further specific is the training of teachers in the case method of social work when these other professionals are not available in schools. The ability to deal with the immediate problems of families has probably been a part of the learned experience of CIS. CIS has brought this general approach to personal difficulties to Kentucky (Marsha Morganti, interview, May 5, 1995). CIS is currently in tune with the appeal to volunteer efforts that has been related to the aspirations of idealistic university graduates who cannot now find jobs. The continuing search for evaluation reports by CIS may be more of an attempt to make news than a concern for acceptance. CIS always seems to be successful in getting publicity.

THE JEWEL IN THE CROWN

Unlike CIS, the family resource centers in the elementary schools and youth centers in the high schools have, unquestionably, been successful in Kentucky. Studies of legislators and the public show that in the opinion of both groups these school integration efforts have been the most widely accepted parts of the Kentucky reforms (Interagency Task Force on Family Resource and Youth Service Centers, 1994, p. 12 and Roberts & Kay, 1993, p. 6). Both quantitative and qualitative studies commissioned by the Cabinet on Human Resources have produced laudatory reports on the efforts (Illback & Kalafat, 1993 and Cannon et al., 1994). A study by an independent advocacy group of seventeen centers in the Louisville area produced a positive sense that staff and clients were involved in the innovation (Kentucky Youth Advocates, 1994). Two reports to the Prichard Committee are generally positive, though finding problems, such as increasing frustration and disappointment among unsuccessful applicants for centers (Roeder, 1992 and Roeder, 1993, p. 56). The Kentucky centers have been cited as a successful example of developing reform on a large scale (Cohen, 1994, March).

As for CIS, the question raised by these and other studies is, What services do the Kentucky centers provide? One study questions the effectiveness of linking teachers into the process while showing that parent education tended to be neglected (Smrekar, 1994, p. 429). Other studies, though previously listed as generally supportive, find that neither parents nor volunteers are strongly involved in the activities of the centers aside from their own immediate demands for service or occasional appointments on advisory committees (Kentucky Family Resource and Youth Service Centers, 1991 and Roeder, 1993). My own visits found that coordinators were frequently preoccupied with immediate parental problems, such as paying utility bills during the winter, and involved few outside volunteers (Susan Schweder, interview, May 8, 1995). The desire to deal with an immediate problem has been a goal of those who developed the program as well as those administrators who looked forward to the program as a way of dealing with immediate pressure from parents (Judy Carter, interview, May 1, 1995 and Center for the Study of Social Policy, 1991). General writing about family centers, furthermore, stresses the charismatic character of center organizers who can find ways to deal with perceived needs (Bowen & Sellers, 1994, p. 29).

Center directors have been criticized for directing an inordinate amount of their time to a few cases as well as other signs of a failure to plan (Office of Accountability, 1994, p. 156). The concern of directors with immediate problems is compounded by limited resources in rural areas even when they can find very imaginative leaders (Judith Toomey, interview, May 5, 1995). Criticism of centers that provide too many field trips for the benefits yielded by them has also been made (Office of Accountability, 1994, p. 161).

The success of centers for integrated services and the limitations of the same programs are both probably related to the way the centers were introduced. Planning was left to the experts and competition for centers between schools increased anxiety and made planning by center coordinators, already preoccupied with immediate client concerns, much more unlikely. Just as the success of schools was financially rewarded in Kentucky through the planning of experts, the centers were introduced through a process of competition between proposals as a part of an expert's plan. In the first year, 1992, 133 centers were successful; in 1993, the numbers increased to 223 centers; the number grew to 373 in 1994; and there was a total of 455 centers in 1995. Most of the centers serve more than one school so that, in 1994, there were 752 schools with a center of the approximately 1,030 schools that could submit proposals (Interagency Task Force on Family Resource and Youth Services Centers, Cabinet for Human Resources, 1994). No school could even submit an application unless 20 percent of its students qualified for a federally supported free lunch program.

In the first year, bonus points were awarded to schools with a greater percentage of students eligible for the free lunch program as a part of an elaborate scoring procedure (Kentucky Family Resource and Youth Services Centers, 1991). As Chart 7.1 shows, thirty-two criteria are used in the most recent form for reviewing grants; this is an increase from the twenty-three standards used in 1991 (The Family Resource and Youth Services Centers Branch, Kentucky Cabinet for Human Resources, 1994, November, pp.17–20). Neither outside volunteers nor organizations are listed as criteria. As in previous years, each proposal is evaluated on a rating scheme which includes (1) fair, (2) satisfactory, (3) good, and (4) excellent, and, since some of the criteria are believed to be more important than others, a weight (1–3) is also assigned. In this very objective-looking procedure, a total score of 180 is now possible. In the first year, the highest possible score was 168, though, at that time, bonus points were added. Through the contests, any reviewer who gave a score of plus or minus 15 percent or more variance from the median score must have the application returned to another reviewer with another team.

This procedure, in addition to subsequent reports, seems to ensure that the official program is more a catechism than a function to which day-to-day activities will connect. Even more importantly, there is little opportunity to develop links between long-term programs and immediate problems. Perhaps another way in which the competitive process has locked the Kentucky program into a limited and local situation is seen by studying a report by the Center for the Study of Social Policy of financing options for family resource centers that was ignored at the same time that virtually all of the recommendations were accepted from the Family Resource Coalition. Though this report was ignored, it could have brought Kentucky more than $16 million annually from the federal government by obtaining payments through Medicare, employment and special education programs (Center for the Study of Social Policy, 1991).

The use of federal financing was, apparently, rejected because of additional forms, procedures, and relationships that would be required (Marcia Morganti, interview, May 5, 1995). The integration of state agencies that is so striking in Kentucky has not been extended beyond the state though it may be, if the easier block grants come from the federal government in the future. Both the departments of education and human resources are involved in cosponsoring the centers. A large number of other state agencies and nongovernmental organizations are members of the task force that directs the experiment. At the local level, grants from businesses and cooperating social agencies are required (Interagency Task Force, 1991). Foundations, such as the Annie B. Casey, have been involved, along with national experts, in designing the integration experiment, but the federal government was too much to include!

The limits on the integration among organizations are related to the restricted nature of governance for the centers. Judy Carter's original plan did not clearly state a procedure for electing members to run the centers;

Chart 7.1
Grant Application Review Form

Scoring

1 — Fair (Below Average)	3 — Good (Above Average)
2 — Satisfactory (Average)	4 — Excellent (Outstanding)

---

1. The application's abstract provides a brief overview which summarizes the major elements of the proposal, the needs identified and the primary goals and objectives for the center (1).

2. The application describes the needs assessment process including the development of the instrument used, the people surveyed, the types of questions asked and the results (2).

3. Existing in-school resources are identified in which linkage is shown for addressing programs, services and activities offered through the center (1).

4. Existing community resources are identified in which linkage is shown for addressing programs, services and activities offered through the center (1).

5. Any barriers or gaps in services for students and/or families which need to be addressed by the center are described (1).

6. The rationale for the center indicates a mission and purpose related to the needs identified (2).

7. The needs assessment results and the gaps and barriers to services identified are linked to programs, services and activities which are addressed by the center's core and optional components (2).

8. It is clearly evident that school staff, community representatives, parents and students have been actively involved in the needs assessment process (2).

9. The description of the demographics of the community or neighborhood, and other at-risk factors associated with the children and families to be served (including % of students eligible for free school meals) clearly establishes a need for the center (3).

10. It is clearly evident that the local advisory council has been actively involved in the grant application and the needs assessment process (2).

Chart 7.1 (Continued)

11. The applicant describes the process for developing collaborative relationships with and commitments from other agencies to provide services, activities and programs with the center (1).

12. The grant application describes strategies to encourage parental involvement in center operations and activities (1).

13. Local interagency agreements and/or letters of commitment relate to identified services to be offered and indicate collaborative support to address the needs of students and families (1).

14. The site for the center appears to be easily accessible to students and families and also provides a friendly, non-threatening atmosphere (1).

15. The site for the center appears to be adequate to conduct center operations and makes provisions for privacy (1).

16. The grant application describes a plan for how those students and families identified as being the most in need will be given priority for services (1).

17. Strategies to minimize stigma that might be associated with the center are described and appear appropriate (1).

18. Strategies to provide awareness of the center, its activities, programs and services are described (1).

19. Procedures for obtaining parent/guardian consent for services, programs and activities are described appropriately (1).

20. Procedures for maintaining confidentiality of records and for sharing information with others are described (1).

21. The description of how the center will evaluate its effectiveness and impact in the school(s) and community appears appropriate (1).

22. The workplans address the core components in ways that strive to meet the identified needs (1).

23. The workplans for optional components that have been developed are related and reflective of the needs identified for students and families in the needs assessment (2).

24. The workplans for each of the core and optional components appear to be doable and realistic with regard to the goals, proposed objectives/outcomes, activities and timelines established (2).

Chart 7.1 (Continued)

25.   The proposed objectives and outcomes for each of the core and optional components are feasible, quantitative and measurable (1).

26.   The staffing pattern developed for the center appears appropriate in comparison to the budget and workplans (2).

27.   Training and professional development opportunities for the center coordinator, center staff, advisory council members and volunteers are described (1).

28.   The job description/position description for the center coordinator appears appropriate with regard to carrying out the duties and responsibilities necessary to operate the center (2).

29.   The job description(s)/position description(s) for other center staff appear(s) appropriate with regard to the responsibilities for carrying out center programs, services and activities (1).

30.   The budget line/item analysis breakdown reflects appropriate understanding of the fiscal responsibilities of the center (2).

31.   The line items included on the FRYSC Grant Funds form and the amount of funds allocated to each appear appropriate with regard to the center's overall operation (2).

32.   The projected in-kind contributions from the school board and the community indicate their support for the center (1).

TOTAL APPLICATION SCORE _____

representative appointments were made (Family Resource Coalition, 1992, pp. 32–34). There is no consideration of interest groups in the plan. The opposition of right-wing religious groups to the centers was intense in the first years (Marcia Morganti, interview, May 5, 1995). The right-wing groups have curtailed their extremism and focused more on issues with which the general public is also concerned, such as assessment exams. However, no basis for involving the right wing or any interest groups has been established. Nor are the family centers, unlike school councils, responsible to parent and community constituents. Official criticism is still made that the advisory committees for the centers have not been related to the membership of school councils (Office of Accountability, 1994, p. 156). Judy Carter originally proposed overlapping memberships of family centers and school councils (Family Resource Coalition, 1992, p. 340).

Aside from the political and organizational issues, the knowledge claims for the current resource centers are usually not examined. The emphasis on "sympathy and support" leads to the selection of staff in terms of "proven capacity" for building strong relationships, "experience with the low income families and children," and "high energy, high enthusiasm and a willingness to go the extra mile" (Family Resource Coalition, 1992, pp. 23–24). These three quotes hardly show the professional knowledge or understanding of the relationships between learning in different professions that is required. The current personnel who are, usually, trained as teachers, social workers, or, less frequently, nurses, command a large percentage of the center's budget. Official critics ask whether individuals with less training cannot be employed (Office of Accountability, 1994, p. 155).

Several interviews suggest that family development may itself be a knowledge base that could be expected of those directing family resource centers (Susan Schweder, interview, May 8, 1995 and Judith Toomey, interview, May 5, 1995). An impressive review of the literature, based on historical approach and organizational studies, suggests that such a knowledge base is being systematized (Kagan, 1993). Curriculum materials for training were reportedly developed by Bala Cynwyd for the Family Resource Center (Cohen, 1994, June, p. 9). However, there is a further reason for seeking a knowledge qualification in the field. Is there only one kind of family resource center? One of the quantified studies in Kentucky suggests that the more specialized, medical centers may develop from the more generalized ones that now operate in Kentucky (Cannon et al., 1994). Alongside the family centers, there are now a variety of medical centers in schools, dental programs for schools, programs on the dangers of AIDS, and schools for teen parents (The School-Based Adolescent Health Care Program, n.d. and Hill, 1994). The justification for locating centers in schools seems to hinge on the availability for students of these specialists' services (Dryfoos, 1994). Confronting professional knowledge and the differences among professionals is a necessity for the further development of integrated services. Family centers can move away from general counseling or counseling for family emergencies to provide more specialized services.

PROFESSIONAL VOLUNTEERS

While professionals have been involved in the health clinics and family centers, a different group of professionals has been involved in educational reform. Landscape architects assisted the students in the Cluster Initiative in developing a plan for their school grounds (discussed in Chapter 2). The Kentucky reforms, it might be recalled, had lawyers as their initial leaders. In Kentucky, business organizations and educational experts became the basis for expanding reform, though it had been hoped that family resource centers would lead to the further involvement of parents. In Alberta, reforms have remained a more informal agreement of those in the pew with similar economic interests, though these same people are, at times, assembled in roundtable forums.

Only in Chicago has there been an outpouring of professionals who have tried to improve their schools. Drawing on its experience as a public-interest law firm, the Business and Professional People for the Public Interest (BPI) joined the Chicago Lawyers' Committee for Civil Rights under the Law (CLC) to form the Lawyers' School Reform Advisory Project shortly after the Reform Act passed in 1988 (Iris Krieg & Associates, 1992). The leading groups of accountants used their existing organization to provide advice on school budgets and planning (CPAs for the Public Interest, 1993). Both lawyers and accountants provide free advice to the school councils as well as training programs for council members with funding from the MacArthur Foundation. Initially, the association of public relations personnel provided free assistance, but they withdrew and the advocacy organizations, as well as the *Catalyst* newspaper, provided publicity for the reform efforts. Over time, the association of retired executives has become actively involved with reform and the councils (Executive Service Corps of Chicago, 1992).

Each of these programs, with the help of foundations, has become extremely active in parts of Chicago, but none has been able to cooperate in ways that improve the lives of children. Most of the professionals are identified with a star performer and, in the case of the lawyers, that is the only way that most people can remember the too-complicated names of the organization, that is Alex's group. The BPI is led by Alex Polikoff, whose organization provides space for the lawyers' advisory group, led originally by Peggy Gordon and presently by Zarina O'Hagin. Alex Polikoff is a prominent lawyer who is credited with stopping the construction of an airport in Lake Michigan with bumper stickers stating "Don't Do It in the Lake." He also fought for locating public housing in better neighborhoods, including his own, and welcomed his new neighbors when that dream was achieved. Alex generally supports reform and is an active member of the Small School Workshop, which attempts to create schools in larger school plants (Lyon, 1994, April). When council members were asked what would happen if they did not have the lawyers' advisory group, several said they would have to go directly to Alex for help.

Like Alex, Roz Lieb was originally active and got the law society involved in helping reform. CLC continues to act as a financial agent for the lawyers' advisory group, but Roz Lieb is no longer involved in any defined way with educational reform. The executive director of the lawyers' groups was Peggy Gordon, who was widely accepted; she retired in 1993 (Iris Krieg & Associates, 1992). Zarina O'Hagin, Peggy Gordon's replacement, has been commended for her impartiality (Zarina O'Hagin, interview, November 9, 1993). In the first four years, over forty-five hundred telephone requests were handled. Over a hundred lawyers were trained to serve the school councils; such training included a short account of the principles of education so that they would understand the program. The staff served on numerous commissions, prepared legislation, advised advocacy groups, and issued a number of publications. The publications included advice on hiring a principal, ways the councils should use Chapter 1 funds, and guidelines for monitoring internal accounts.

The accountants have an even larger group of volunteers than the lawyers and have, on several occasions, tried to get the lawyers to work cooperatively with them. When Leadership for Quality Education was founded, such cooperation was attempted (Diana Lauber, interview, February 8, 1995). In 1993, the accountants developed a plan to work together with the lawyers and the retired executives which would allow them to concentrate their volunteers on the south central part of Chicago. The lawyers felt they did not have a sufficient number of people for this task and the leader of the retired executives for education, Layette Ford, retired. Earlier, the lawyers had tried to assign a lawyer to work with Ford on the west side of Chicago. Without the other professionals, the accountants have had to concentrate their resources for training on their own. They are, furthermore, likely to work with accountants who do not have the highest credentials, as well as reform activists, in providing educational programs for school councils. The lawyers have not accepted paralegals and the lack of certification for paralegals in Illinois is a, perhaps welcomed, barrier to participation with a greater variety of groups. Integration of professionals is often attractive to those on the fringe: new professionals, paraprofessionals, or those with practical experience (Kane, 1975).

The accountants are more likely to play a supportive role than the lawyers. They are recruited from one church and may be more influenced by their commitment to assist school councils, but they do not attempt to change educational policies. They do not take a position on controversial subjects or enter into the political spotlight as much as the lawyers do (Gordon Sterns and Leslie Anderson, interview, November 8, 1993). Working extensively with other organizations, such as Designs for Change and PURE, the accountants, in one year, have assisted councils for ninety-one schools (CPAs for the Public Interest, 1992). The training programs have focused on reading computer printouts of budget information from the school board, budgeting, and the development of school improvement plans.

Like the lawyers, the Executive Service Corps of Chicago (ESC) has been dependent on exceptional people to provide leadership. The former chairman of Inland Steel, Joseph Block, was particularly influential in starting the organization and Lafayette Ford has been important in establishing a substantial educational program. The loss of both men may make it more difficult for the program to continue. The ESC provides an extensive program of job placement for high-risk youth throughout Chicago but, for schools and council members, its executives have concentrated on a model program on Chicago's Near West Side. With the support of foundations, eighty consultants have contributed over sixteen hundred hours to improve thirty-five elementary and secondary schools (Executive Service Corps of Chicago, 1992, p. 4–6). Other organizations, such as CNA Insurance, with programs such a Math Works, have been a part of this model project. ESC, in this and other areas, has worked with the interrelations of employment, education, medical, and even banking services. For example, it has helped by broadening the financial base of the Westside Holistic Family Service, a minority owned enterprise in a Black area. The consultants with ESC may have come closer than the lawyers or accountants to concrete and interrelated problems of high-risk families. Like the lawyers, and, unlike the accountants, ESC has been active in the meetings of educational reformers which I observed during 1993 and 1994. Currently, the ESC program has been changed and its policy will no longer focus on such a close relationship to schools and communities (Diana Lauber, interview, August 16, 1995).

The effort of professional volunteers in Chicago is not duplicated in any other setting. In Canada, a recent report on schools in Chicago, which Canadians might consider, failed to mention the assistance that professionals provide to the councils (Lewington, 1995, May, pp. 1 & 6). In Canada, obtaining professional advice for education through foundations is still not imagined. After visiting Chicago, the Prichard Committee decided to recruit lawyers to provide advice to their councils but only after they had screened the calls for assistance (Robert Sexton, interview, May 4, 1995). Of 119 calls received by the Prichard Committee from council members, only 13 were referred to attorneys by the staff of the committee (Prichard Committee for Academic Excellence, 1993). This program was only in its first year, but the access and support for Kentucky council members, that has seemed so important to council members in Chicago, would be hard to establish with such controls. The Prichard Committee is very clear that it "will not litigate on behalf of councils" (Prichard Committee for Academic Excellence, n.d.). Though the Chicago lawyers have tried to maintain an impartial position, they have come very close to litigation through referrals in cases involving the removal of principals and where they were involved with the challenge brought by the principals' association to the constitutionality of the Reform Act. The lawyers in Chicago are more clearly in an advocate's position and are worried when the Chicago Board of Education asks them for legal advice (Zarina O'Hagin, interview, November 9, 1993).

SEARCHING FOR THE PATTERN

Without the support of professionals, only very modest steps are made toward political involvement of parents. The Comer schools, where parents have become a part of the governance systems, are the best known example of policy setting by parents in individual schools (Comer, 1993). However, it is Comer's colleague at Yale Edward Zigler who appears to have had the greatest current impact (Zigler & Finn-Stevenson, 1989). Zigler, whose current work is with the Schools of the Twenty-First Century, is one of the founders of Head Start. Zigler's ideas about changing service to young children and their families do not involve any serious change in school governance.

The Zigler effort includes programs within schools as well as outreach services from schools. The new program of child care within schools includes all-day, year-round care for children ages three to five from early in the morning to early evening, and child care before and after school and during vacations for school children, ages five to twelve, often, as well, for extended hours. The outreach services include home visits from the third trimester of pregnancy until the children are three years old, a network of advice and resources for babysitters (family day care providers), and a referral service for all families in the community so that they can find quality child care. Particularly with new efforts for developing nutrition and health knowledge, the Zigler program provides an even more complete approach to family centers than those found in Kentucky.

Other than an emphasis on community healing within the First Nations communities, a major experiment in Ontario, *Better Beginnings Better Futures*, largely repeats the Zigler program or that of similar American efforts, though the parallels are never mentioned. Along with avoiding any links to the Americans, the Ontario effort does not learn from its own mistakes over an eighteen-year history of pursuing integration of services. Managers within the Ontario government say that the biggest problem in achieving integration has been the barriers between separate programs and funding accounts (Alberta Commissioner of Services for Children, 1994, p. 33). However, *Better Beginnings Better Futures* did not even include organization and funding changes as a part of its research program; change is something that local communities are expected to achieve. *Better Beginnings Better Futures*, with its accompanying video of the same name, has been widely distributed throughout English Canada.

Most significantly, the Ontario program does not start with an association of groups involved with integrated services in Ontario or across Canada. The original eleven communities in the program are very loosely linked, with no affiliation to the leagues supporting Zigler or Comer schools. The difference in advocacy organizations in the two countries, discussed in Chapter 3, may explain the isolation of efforts in most of Canada. The possibilities for any organization between communities acting as a basis for parent power and change has not been considered in Canada. Even in the United States, the empowerment of communities and policy roles for parents has not been strongly pursued since the 1960s (Kagan, 1993).

As American ideas spread to Canada, political empowerment beyond separate communities and individuals has not been pursued. On the west coast, the province of British Columbia has had a history of problems in trying to develop integrated services at the local level without changing the larger political organization (Advisory Committee on Children's Services,

1990, p. 113). In 1990, as a result of a critical report by the provincial ombudsman, this province started a Child and Youth Secretariat. But, in 1993, an external evaluation of the secretariat found separate managers with separate budgets were again preventing meaningful integration of services. Perhaps because of its greater sense of political direction, only Quebec has implemented its own initiative of integrated services (Alberta Commissioner of Services for Children, 1994a, p. 34).

The search for a service change without a corresponding political change is, ironically, exemplified in Alberta with its program of wholesale changes in the scale of government. Though there are occasional references to reinventing government as a related idea to integrated service, Alberta has based its program primarily on this idea (Kagan, 1993, p. 86; Osborne & Gaebler, 1992; and Alberta Commissioner of Services for Children, 1994a, p. 4). Borrowing ideas from the American book, the Alberta report, *Finding A Better Way*, states that services must be customer-focused, outcome based, decentralized, and must use budgets based on known benefits. The research for *Finding A Better Way* showed that people did not want regional government agencies in–between the province and local government, but there are seventeen regional agencies anyway (Alberta Commissioner of Services for Children, 1994b, p. 18). The Alberta plan currently includes the political appointment of boards in these seventeen districts, which opens up large opportunities for patronage. The regional boards were also included in the health boards; this, even as a temporary measure, raises questions about the organization's integration, just as the initial appointment procedure leaves the development of citizen participation unresolved.

Local programs, as much as the provincial programs, can reveal a preoccupation with control over people rather than empowerment of people. Calgary and three other Alberta cities have developed experimental programs (Government of Alberta, 1993). The Calgary program in the community of Huntington Hills has been preoccupied with coordination of professionals, but the principal with the local school is no longer involved and parents are excluded from the meetings of professionals who work for the province (Fowler, 1994). These exclusions of significant people occurred in the Calgary program, which was modeled on the American program in San Diego. In San Diego, the parents were involved and the school was the center of the program. In a second Alberta program, which was primarily for natives in Wabasca/Demarais, there was little parental involvement and no native organizations were represented in the program that, supposedly, separated natives from nonnatives, but, in fact, had a majority of cases from natives in both groups (McVey, 1994). Of the two other programs in Alberta, the one in Edmonton was also based on the San Diego experience, and one in Lethbridge tried to focus on research and needs assessment; both seemed to be searching for a formula.

In Saskatchewan, the local programs are the basis of provincial efforts and the people involved with the local programs seem to have more political influence than those in Alberta (Saskatchewan Education, Training and Employment, 1994). Saskatchewan has built its integrated services around a concern for prevention of problems and has used a foundation of previous efforts at community schools and community development (Roseanne Glass, interview, August 1, 1995). In order to save money, Alberta eliminated its community schools and has not related its current efforts for integrative services to previous work in community development. The Family First program in North Dakota was a model for Saskatchewan in its early years.

There is no fixed answer that can be used for the expansion of these services into Canada. In the United States, the marginality, as mentioned previously, was reinforced by the withdrawal of the Pew Charitable Trust from its ten-year plan to spend over $55 million on integrated services (Sommerfeld, 1994, April, p. 9). The possible future importance of integrated services is the replacement of the Department of Education in Minnesota by a Department of Learning (Richardson, 1995, June, p. 11). The Carnegie Foundation has made a similar proposal for all the states. Political coalitions among the usual suspects, who can be rounded up for integrated services, is not enough. There is a long history of attempts to integrate services which were started in the 1930s and then abandoned because the foundations that were sponsoring these attempts decided they wanted to support more scientific work (Sedlak, 1980). To modify separate services, the integration of these many varied experiences needs to be combined with a renewed attempt at democratic control of integrated services.

BRIDGING THE GAP

The challenge is to link the world of these varied professional experts to the lives of parents and their children. Integrated services has been defined to include integration of services for clients, integration of programs, and policy integrations. Policy integrations reflect a philosophy of government and organizational change (Kagan, 1993). Most of the efforts at integration, including in Kentucky, have focused on the more indirect forms of integration. Group casework and a common location of services for people have been among the few efforts directed at clients. Parental decision making about any of the different kinds of integration which are to be undertaken has been minimal (Dryfoos, 1994 and Kagan, 1993).

Our exploration of links with lawyers, accountants, and executives is also intended to suggest the question of which of the groups are integrated. Professionals as well as the services they provide for high-risk clients need to develop a plan for integration. The emphasis on social agencies has not been tied with involvement of businesses or the higher professions. The Orr project is exceptional in its focus on art education and the contribution that practicing artists have made; arts and crafts is a more typical addition to a family center. The original profession, religion, which has some claims to linking people before family resource centers were developed, has been neglected. In several situations, including the parent room program at the Orr High School and the rural site in Bracken County, Kentucky, religious leaders, as speakers, were the most important part of the educational program (Bonita Street, interview, May 11, 1995 and Judith Toomey, interview, May 5, 1995). In these cases, as well as others, there was an apparent contradiction in that there was a hesitancy to make a professional referral to ministers even for comfort at the time of a death. The limits on the involvement of ministers appeared to be organizational and professional rather than based on consultations with parents or children.

Significantly, right-wing religious leaders have shown that they would not be ignored (Kannapel, Moore, Coe & Aagaard, 1995). Involving the right wing raises the more general issues of casting a wide net so that both controversial leaders and alienated people are involved in integrated services. Councils of churches provided a basis for churches being involved in the Calgary program as well as the one in Bracken County, Kentucky, so that competition among them was prevented. Similar links can be provided with other groups. The actual fears of the lonely and isolated people should be a basis for new programs rather than the trickery of toy exchanges or baby showers at the centers as a cover for parent education and networking (Susan Schweder, interview, May 8, 1995).

The family resource centers have many possibilities for creative ties between education and families. Though, in Chapter 4, the Kentucky program was shown not to link with parent involvement in politicking for school councils, it is best to see the current programs as just establishing an initial step between parents and schools. Some parents confused school councils with school counselors (Kay & Roberts, 1994, p. 16). Parents have not often found access to schools controlled by educators; in Kentucky, the family resource centers have welcomed parents where they have not been accepted before (Kay & Roberts, 1994, p. 11). Parents have not been individual constituents of the schools rather than members of a community which exists alongside schools (Roberts & Kay, 1994, p. 8). Parents welcome the opportunity to discuss discipline of their own children with one another though not in formal parenting programs (Kay & Roberts, 1994, p. 8).

Unfortunately, discipline is one of the major areas where parents differ from schools and the experts who advise the schools on discipline seem foreign to most parents (Johnson & Immerwahr, 1994, p. 12). The moralistic orientation of Americans means they are particularly likely to blame the schools for a lack of discipline and character development of students; the necessity for student achievements in science and mathematics for a more competitive environment that is valued by experts and business people is questioned by most parents (Immerwahr, Johnson & Kernan-Schloss, 1991). Since, among parents and community members, moral development is weighed as being more important than expertise, educators might begin to learn to justify reforms in moral rather than instrumental terms. Parents and experts can also work together to establish safety for students in schools, as the Orr network showed, because safety is even more important for parents and students than is order and discipline.

For parents and educators to develop a better understanding, parents must be involved in the educational process as exemplars of education for students. The greater contribution of the family to education than of schools has been, increasingly, focused on training parents as teachers, early childhood activities, and the traditional practice of parents reading to students (U.S. Department of Education, 1994). However, parent involvement is best expressed through activities such as the Algebra Project discussed in Chapter 3, so that parents will actively understand the approach. Similar to the Algebra Project, a program of teaching writing for parents in Milwaukee leads the parents to see how the process of writing occurs. Parents tend to see knowledge, the basics, as fixed and something which students must do (Johnson & Immerwahr, 1994, p. 17 and Kay & Roberts, 1994, p. 17).

After learning that knowledge is an important process for them and their children, parents might find the practicality of educational innovations a more important consideration. Parents are, increasingly, involved in computer classes so that they can learn job skills or ways of improving their education (U.S. Department of Education, 1994, p. 20). However, if the computer classes were based on an understanding of change, it might be more possible for technology to be appreciated. At present, secure jobs are what parents want for their children whether or not the students' future jobs are part of a growing economy based on technological change (Immerwahr et al., 1991, pp. 16–17). The lack of concern for government debt has been replaced with a preoccupation with it; other parts of traditional views on education that make any education beyond the basics a frill can also be altered (Immerwahr et al., 1991, p. 8).

Traditional values about discipline, the basics, and even ability grouping have been altered when parents were welcomed into schools, became involved in education, and became supporters of reform initiatives (Kay & Roberts, 1994, p. 30). The number of people who are involved in such schools is very small. In Kentucky, about 60 percent of the public and 40 percent of parents did not understand reform after four years of publicity (Holland, 1995, p 5) Their numbers could be enormously increased by the involvement of volunteers who would reach those who remained entrenched conservatives. There are a large number of volunteers assisting schools (parents, students, and seniors), but they are not, as yet, committed to understanding the purpose and promise of education (U.S. Department of Education, 1994, p. 27).

If volunteers can join businesspeople in supporting education, the significance of education will be more generally understood. As suggested in Chapters 5 and 6, employers must prove to students that education is important by using grades and activities in school when hiring students and by supporting parent education and student monitoring of jobs on company time. Parents must, similarly, show the signs of their dedication by practicing education and by changing their ideas about education. Students learn moralism and blaming others for their own decisions from their parents; they need to accept the consequences of their own actions, while seeking new visions (Roberts & Kay, 1993, p. 7). Students must want to be better, but adults, themselves, need to change if educational reform is to succeed. A school which is a communitiy and which knows it is a community can be a potent force for all of its constituents.

In spite of the potential for involving volunteers and developing a greater sense of community, our examination of integrated services shows that thinking which is similar to that of business still affects those who plan these services. In Kentucky, the form required to receive a grant for family resource centers is like the business bottom line. In Alberta, the emphasis on reinventing government as a basis for integrated services involves the application to government of business guides. In Chicago, only exceptional individuals have been able to transcend the boundaries of professionals and organizations; the lawyers' failure to accept paralegals is an important example. Use of paralegals could not only help school councils but provide jobs for people in the communities that the councils serve. Protection of professional spheres acts as a barrier to integrated services while an instrumental approach offers some wrong directions to this movement.

REFERENCES

Advisory Committee on Children's Services (1990). *Children first*. Toronto: Queen's Printer for Ontario.

Alberta Commissioner of Services for Children (1994a, November). *Finding a Better Way*. Edmonton: Alberta Commissioner of Services for Children.

Alberta Commissioner of Services for Children (1994b, November). *Focus on children*. Edmonton: Alberta Commissioner of Services for Children.

Atlanta Project (1995, April). *Because there is hope*. Atlanta: Atlanta Project.

Bank of America (1995, April 1). *The Orr school network a community-based educational partnership 1989–1995*. Chicago: Bank of America.

Benshoff, A. (1994, October). How an inner-city school became a model for all. *Catalyst*, 6(2), 18-22.

Bowen, L. & Sellers, S. (1994). *Family support & socially vulnerable communities*. Chicago: Family Resource Coalition.

Cannon, G., Kalafat, J., & Illback, R. (1994, June). *Implementation evaluation of the Kentucky Family Resource and Youth Services Center program: Qualitative analyses*. Louisville: Reach of Louisville, Inc.

Center for New Horizons (n.d.). *Agency profile and summary of programs*. Chicago: Center for New Horizons.

Center for the Future of Children (1992). *School linked services: The future of children*, 2(1), 1–144.

Center for the Study of Social Policy (1991, January). *Refinancing in Kentucky: Expanding the base for Family Resource & Youth Service Centers*. Washington, D.C.: Center for the Study of Social Policy.

Chicago Public School (n.d.). *Creating a new approach to learning--Executive summary*. Chicago: Chicago Public School.

Cities In Schools, (1993). *Agile responses in a time of change annual report*. Alexandra, Virginia: Cities in Schools.

Cities In Schools (1994, December). *Cities In Schools turning kids around*. Alexandria, Virginia: Cities In Schools.

Cities In Schools (1995, Winter). *Networks News*. Alexandra, Virginia: Cities In Schools.

Cohen, D. (1994, March 29). Going the extra mile is hallmark of Family Resource Centers in Ky. *Education Week*, (27), 6–7.

Cohen, D. (1994, June 1). Demise of Pew project offers lessons to funders. *Education Week*, 13(36), 1, 9.

Comer, J. (1993). *School power*. New York: The Free Press.

CPAs for the Public Interest (1992). *CPAs for the public interest 1992 annual report*. Chicago: CPAs for the Public Interest.

CPAs for the Public Interest (1993, November 8). *School Reform Project District 6 Initiative*. Chicago: CPAs for the Public Interest.

Crowson, R. & Boyd, W. (1993, February). Coordinated services for children: Designing arks for storms and seas unknown. *American Journal of Education*, 101, 140–179.

Dryfoos, J. (1994). *Full-service schools*. San Francisco: Jossey-Bass.

Edelman, P. & Radin, B. (1991). *Serving children and families effectively*. Washington, D.C.: Education and Human Services Consortium.

Executive Service Corps of Chicago (1992). Executive Service Corps of Chicago Annual Report 1992. Chicago: Executive Service Corps of Chicago.

Family Resource and Youth Services Centers Branch, Kentucky Cabinet for Human Resources (1994, November 23). *FY 96 FRYSC grant application instructions and reference guide*. Frankfort: Family Resource and Youth Services Centers Branch.

Family Resource Coalition (1992). *Kentucky Family Resource and Youth Services Centers guide for planning and implementation*. Chicago: Family Resource Coalition.

Fowler, C. (1994). Opening doors. Class paper, the University of Calgary.

Government of Alberta (1993, August). *Briefing coordination of services for children*. Edmonton: Government of Alberta.

Hill, D. (1994, February). The doctor is in. *Teacher Magazine*, 5(50), 18–23.

Holland, H. (1995, January-March). Focus: Kentucky's educational reforms show successes & pitfalls. *Perspectives*, 6(1), 5.

Illback, R. & Kalafat, J. (1993). *Initial evaluation of a school-based integrated service program*. Kentucky Family Resource and Youth Services Centers. Louisville: Reach of Louisville.

Immerwahr, J., Johnson, J., & Kernan-Schloss, A. (1991). *Cross talk*. Washington, D.C.: Business-Higher Education Forum.

Interagency Task Force (1991, January). *State implementation plan*. Frankfort: Interagency Task Force.

Interagency Task Force on Family Resource and Youth Services Centers, Cabinet for Human Resource (1994). *Annual implementation status report.* Frankfort: Interagency Task Force.

Iris Krieg & Associates (1992, December). *Lawyers' School Reform Advisory Project recommendation for the future.* Lexington: Iris Krieg & Associates.

Johnson, J. & Immerwahr, J. (1994). *First things first.* New York: Public Agenda.

Jouzaitis, C. (1995, February 19). Abuse traps women in welfare. *Chicago Tribune.*

Kagan, S. (1993). *Integrating services for children and families.* New Haven, Connecticut: Yale University Press.

Kagan, S. & Weissbound, B. (1994). *Putting families first.* San Francisco: Jossey-Bass.

Kane, R. (1975). *Interprofessional teamwork.* Syracuse, New York: Syracuse University School of Social Work.

Kannapel, P., Moore, B., Coe, P., & Aagaard, L. (1995). Opposition to outcome-based education in Kentucky. Paper presented to the Annual Meeting of the American Educational Research Association.

Kay, S. & Roberts, R. (1994). *Parent involvement: New challenges.* Lexington: Roberts and Kay.

Kentucky Family Resource and Youth Services Centers (1991, February). *Grant application package.* Frankfort: Kentucky Family Resource and Youth Services Centers.

Kentucky Institute for Education Research (1994, December). *A review of research on the Kentucky Education Reform Act.* Frankfort: Kentucky Institute for Education Research.

Kentucky Youth Advocates (1994). *Family focused.* Louisville: Kentucky Youth Advocates.

Kotlowitz, A. (1991). *There are no children here.* New York: Doubleday Anchor.

Levin, R.A. (Ed.) (1994). *Greater than the sum.* Washington, D.C.: ERIC Clearinghouse on Teacher Education.

Lewington, J. (1995, May 20). Parent power shakes up schools. *The Globe and Mail*, A1 & 6.

Lyon, J. (1994, April 17). The good guys. *Chicago Tribune Magazine*, 10–18.

MacArthur Foundation (n.d.). Update on the collaboration project. Chicago: MacArthur Foundation.

Martin, M. (1993, September). Orr network keeps expanding while Orr turns inward. *Catalyst*, 5(1), 9-11.

McMullan, B. & Snyder, P. (1987). *Allies in education.* Philadelphia: Public/Private Ventures.

McVey, M. (1994). Power or process in innovating. Course paper, the University of Calgary.

Melville, A. & Blank, M. (1991). *What it takes.* Washington, D.C.: Education and Human Services Consortium.

Melville, A. & Blank, M. (1993). *Together we can.* Washington, D.C.: U.S. Department of Education.

National Governors' Association (1994). *Communicating with the public about education reform.* Washington, D.C.: National Governors' Association.

Office of Educational Accountability, Kentucky General Assembly (1994). *Annual report.* Frankfort: Kentucky General Assembly.

Osborne, D. & Gaebler, T. (1992). *Reinventing government.* Reading, Massachusetts: Addison-Wesley.

Padfield, H & Williams, R. (1973). *Stay where you were.* New York: J. B. Lippincott.

Peters, R. & Russell, C. (1994). *Better beginnings, better futures project.* Toronto: Queen's Printer for Ontario.

Prichard Committee for Academic Excellence (1993, July). *Lawyers for school reform annual report 1933.* Lexington: Prichard Committee for Academic Excellence.

Prichard Committee for Academic Excellence (n.d.) *Lawyers for school reform.* Lexington: Prichard Committee for Academic Excellence.

Richardson, J. (1995, June 7). Minn. abolishes Education Department, merges state services in new agency. *Education Week,* 14(37), 11.

Roberts & Kay, Inc. (1993). *Kentuckians' expectations of children's learning: The significance for reform.* Lexington: Roberts & Kay.

Roeder, P.W. (1992). Assessment of family resource and youth services centers: A first-year report to the Prichard Committee. In *First Year Reports of the Prichard Committee.* Lexington: Prichard Committee for Academic Excellence.

Roeder, P.W. (1992). Family centers in Kentucky schools: Politics and policy in education and welfare service delivery. Lexington: Prichard Committee for Academic Excellence.

Roeder, P.W. (1993). Assessment of family resource and youth services centers. In *Second Year Report of the Prichard Committee.* Lexington: The Prichard Committee for Academic Excellence.

Saskatchewan Education, Training and Employment (1994). *Working together to address barriers to learning.* Regina: Saskatchewan Education.

School-Based Adolescent Health-Care Program (n.d.). *The answer is at school: Bringing health care to our students.* Washington, D.C.: School-Based Adolescent Helth-Care Program.

Schorr, L. (1988). *Within our reach.* New York: Doubleday Anchor.

Sedlak, M. (1980). Welfare professional and American youth, 1930-1965. Paper presented at the annual meeting of History of Education Society.

Smrekar, C. (1994). The missing link in school-linked social service programs. *Educational Evaluation and Policy Analysis,* 16(4), 422–433.

Sommerfeld, M. (1994, April 6). Pew abandons its ambitious 10-year "children's initiative." *Education Week,* 13(28), 9.

U.S. Department of Education (1994). *Strong families, strong schools.* Washington, D.C.: U.S. Department of Education.

Wehlage, G., Smith, G., & Lipman, P. (1992). Restructuring urban schools: The new futures experience. *American Educational Research Journal,* 29(1), 51–93.

Wotherspoon, E. (1992). *Opening Doors.* Calgary: School-Agency Collaboration Project Steering Committee.

Zigler, E. & Finn-Stevenson, M. (1989). Child care in America. *Educational Policy,* 3(4), 313–329.

Chapter 8

Voices of Reform

Student writing is reduced to filling in the blanks, darkening (with number two pencils) the circles or squares on the op-scan sheets (Eastman, 1981)

Student voices are the missing link in school reform.... The most important reason to give kids authority in the classroom is so they acquire the habit of reasoning out for themselves the intellectual problems we all face—Ted Sizer (Cushman, 1994, pp. 1 & 5)

Students in the National Writing Project (NWP) are expected to become articulate and strong leaders rather than conforming soldiers who stay in the trenches. In Chicago, the local version of the writing program is considered one of the best new practices for schools that have resulted from reform (National-Louis University, 1993). Unfortunately, a survey of students in Chicago which tries to measure their reaction to reform has the students back to filling in the spaces (Consortium on Chicago School Research, 1995). In Kentucky, students are completing more open-ended and authentic assessments, while process views of writing have been made a part of the curriculum. Though Kentucky has long had NWP centers, particularly in Louisville, separate teacher networks have not been considered a part of the state's reforms until recently. In Alberta, the focus is deliberately on standardized exams, though Calgary has, for a long time, been one of the more isolated parts of the NWP realm.

While students have some access to publications for their writing, there are extensive independent publications on educational reform in the United States and a large number of governmental publications in Canada. The voices of official publications and advocacy groups that try to include students in reform activities have been particularly limited. Students have often been expected to respond to the requests of reformers, but there are some publications where students can express themselves. Chicago has several publications and groups competing for students, while Kentucky has given them recognized roles as scholars and speakers for reform. One student advocate for reform in Kentucky started a student publication (Mills, 1993). There are also several teacher-inspired collections of student writing in Kentucky as in the other sites. Alberta has the usual collections of student writing and newspapers.

The inconsistency between the aims of the writing programs and the opportunities for students to write is not recognized. Supporters of major campaigns for reform are all trying to promote writing efforts. The campaign to promote the engagement of students with active learning through writing is interpreted differently in each reform site. Chicago, with its competing groups, recognizes the writing program as one of its best new initiatives although the school board, previously, prevented the introduction of such programs by groups outside the system (Fred Hess, interview, October 8, 1993). Kentucky, with its tradition of compromise, stresses the general reforms that include many of the process ideas from NWP (Robert Sexton, interview, May 4, 1995). In Calgary, the NWP local project has been a separate activity from reform; certainly no NWP consultant-teacher has become an active supporter of reform in Alberta as some have in Chicago. Though the reform efforts in Alberta are very recent, there does not appear to be any expectation that any group, including students, will do more than complete a consumer survey on education.

THE WRITING CRISIS

Over twenty years ago, many universities in the United States and Canada experienced a crisis when it appeared that their entering students could not write well enough (Cronk, 1977). Similar to the current crises that have been discussed, ideas involving people and processes were developed with regard to this objective problem of achievements. The process view of writing was developed at the University of California by James Gray. Mr. Gray, a teacher without tenure, a Ph.D., or research experience, developed the view that all teachers from elementary school to university could relate to a common view of writing (Goldberg, 1989).

In this unorthodox position, Professor Gray argued that practicing teachers were the people who knew the problems and some of the answers to the problems. Experts were not to be trusted because they were distant from teachers and usually believed there was only one answer to writing improvement. The actual writing process in Gray's plan includes brainstorming, execution, peer review, revision, and evaluation. In order to take the learner's perspective, all teachers in NWP training sessions go through the writing process (Krendl & Dodd, 1987). However, outstanding or master teachers were identified in order to ensure that an initial presentation of a successful practice occurs and later development of papers would lead to awarding the title of consultant. Early identification of teachers was made so that they would be more reliable resources than the transient experts. The teachers would increase their competency by follow-up training and by work as consultants to other teachers. Identification of participants is currently not as rigid as when the program began in Berkeley in 1974 (Batiuk, 1993).

Today the National Writing Project is the most successful teacher-oriented innovation ever developed. In the United States, it has 158 sites in forty-eight states. NWP has also spread to six Commonwealth countries (Pritchard, 1989). In Canada, there are NWP sites in Calgary, Vancouver, Regina, Yellowknife, and Halifax (Washburn, 1991). NWP claims to have trained 1,318,264 teachers and administrators between 1982 and 1993 in the United States alone (National Writing Project, 1995). In 1991, federal support was enacted in order to spread the innovation to as many as 250 cites; at that time, the appropriation was $3,211,000. NWP claims that it is an extremely cost-effective program since its courses serve teachers for $22 each and generate $4 for every federal dollar received.

Aside from the money, numbers served, and numerous endorsements by prominent observers, such as by the former secretary of education, William Bennett, overwhelming numbers of teachers have expressed their support for the program. NWP allows participants to overcome social isolation, develop personally, and, perhaps, undergo a conversion as they frequently become advocates for NWP (Gomes, 1988). One entire Calgary class reported similar positive evaluations by all participants (Calgary Writing Project, 1986). Unexpectedly, a study which employed the more structured approach of levels of use for innovations, found similar changes in social and personal orientations (March et al., 1987, pp. 19-20). Monthly follow-ups were always provided and now specialized courses and networks make NWP a social movement that continues to gain momentum. It should be added that Jim Gray got a permanent job and a great deal of recognition for his efforts and has now retired as executive director of NWP (Gray & Sterling, n.d.).

In spite of the many signs of success, the NWP still confronts a number of dilemmas. Because of problems in getting the supportive environment for teachers that Gray wanted, it has not been possible to expand the program to the 250 sites that federal legislation called for. The project has never attempted to change the structure of schools and universities, but both types of organizations are involved in providing the joint writing programs. The major question has been whether students are changed. Students have not been involved in the decision to undertake or to continue with the programs. However, student leaders, who are discussed later, do mention the support of leaders in NWP for their own writing efforts. In general, it is only clear that students write more and have more school time for their writing after NWP is adopted (Purves, 1992 and Putka, 1992). Do students write better and do they want to become even better at writing?

At least a broad evaluation of the program can be made by considering the extent of involvement for both parents and students. Beginning in the Milwaukee area, parents are increasingly involved in the writing program, thus setting a strong example for students (Vopat, 1993). However, in all locations, parents have been involved as monitors of students' work. Though the original program was meant for all subject areas, separate courses have been developed in a number of specialties, including science. In the original home of the NWP, California, the success of the program has led to six additional subject matters developing similar programs; science, mathematics, history, foreign languages, literature, and the arts (Rigden, 1991, p. 71). Project Zero at Harvard is using similar ideas about process, and criticism to develop programs in art, music, and literature, as illustrated by a video (Harvard Graduate School of Education, n.d.). Though much smaller than NWP, a mathematics network seems to have a similar effect on those involved in Memphis, San Francisco, St. Louis, and other cities (Little & McLaughlin, 1991). Students are, presumably, influenced by the curriculum parallels to the writing program.

COMPETING FOR TURF IN CHICAGO

The leaders in Chicago worked as a part of a network to promote a variety of curriculum reforms when the structure of the school system changed. A number of the consultants and administrators with the writing program in Chicago have written about reform and, in some cases, became involved in the meetings for reform. There are competing programs in Chicago: the Chicago Writing Project, which follows the original format set by Gray, and the Illinois Writing Project, which split from the other organization so that the project organizers could experiment with teacher-writers on approaches as well as time arrangements (Steve Zemelman, interview, October 9, 1993). For four years, a large annual newspaper appeared that carried the writing of leaders about all curriculum areas; this paper, *Best Practice*, is used in the training of lawyers as well as Chicago school council members (discussed in Chapter 7).

Other leaders of the Chicago reform movement praise the efforts of the writing projects as a model for curriculum reform that is expected to follow from the change in governance of the system (Fred Hess, interview, October 8, 1993 and John Ayers, interview, October 11, 1993). In 1992, the local educational television station, WTTW, produced a film, *Teach Me*, which features the leaders of the Illinois Writing Project. *Teach Me* was distributed by the business reform organization Leadership for Quality Education. The film is also being sold together with the book, *Best Practice*, written by the leaders of the Illinois Writing Project, Steve Zemelman and Harvey Daniels, and a leading reformer for mathematical education, Art Hyde (1993).

CALGARY, A QUIET PLACE FOR WRITING

While the Klein revolution causes debate because of major changes in the educational system, the once-active Calgary Writing Project (CWP) has become subdued. The summer of 1995 was the first time that its two courses were not offered. The immediate reason for the limited activity by CWP is the retirement of its longtime director, William Washburn. Also, budget cuts have eliminated school board funding, beginning in 1992 (Batiuk, 1993). The Calgary Writing Foundation was formed to raise money for the extended program, particularly for the network of teacher-consultants. However, in the current situation, a catalyst is needed to relate the writing program to business needs in the increasingly competitive environment.

In the past, the CWP has been best known for its publication of children's writing and for student contests that resulted in submissions for these publications. Since the start of CWP in 1981, two collections have been published every year: *Ubzab* for elementary students and *Rebound* for secondary ones. The work of teachers in the courses offered at the University of Calgary was regularly published by the Calgary Board of Education until the current period of fiscal restraint. An informal newsletter, *The Write Stuff*, was also published several times a year since the start of CWP. However, there was very little general publicity and many people were not aware of the program at all. The former director, Dr. William Washburn, opted for more theoretical work to supplement the writing by the teacher-students; names like Vygotsky, Chomsky, and Gardiner were supposedly familiar to his students (Washburn, 1991).

THE FORCED MARCH IN KENTUCKY

Abstract views of learning do not appear to be major concerns of the Kentucky teachers as they feel the pressures toward the collective goals of comprehensive reform. Indeed, the official view, that students must participate in and construct their own learning, runs counter to the perspective which teachers hold of themselves as being the direct agents of education (Appalachia Educational Laboratory, 1994, p. 9). Writing is currently heavily emphasized in the state's transitional test that mixes multiple-choice and open-ended response questions with performance events focused on problems. Performance events are expected to become more important in the overall plan but such unorthodox tests have recently been attacked (Hambleton et al., 1995). Most teachers are pressured to teach writing as a result of the exams; one complained that having essay answers on all tests amounted to "programming students"! The legislature responded to pressure on teachers by separating the years when mathematics and writing portfolios must be prepared in early elementary grades; both had been required in grade four before 1994.

In spite of the demands on them, the number of teachers in one study who complained about the increased emphasis on writing was equaled by the number who believed that the greatest improvement from KERA had been in writing and related thinking activities (Appalachia Educational Laboratory, 1994, p. 6). Most of the elements of NWP are included in the Kentucky program, including writing as a process, peer editing, and a constructivist view of learning (Kentucky Department of Education, 1993). However, the writing program's components are all part of a general set of reforms. Cluster leaders, for example, are all trained by the state in using portfolios and are expected to pass the information on to their colleagues (Appalachia Educational Laboratory, 1994, pp. 6-7).

In the summer of 1994, the NWP affiliate, the Kentucky Writing Project, became the official trainer of elementary teachers, awarding the title of KERA Fellow to graduates of this program. The statewide publication for the writing program is now published by the Kentucky Department of Education, *Kentucky Writing Teacher*. Kentucky is one of nineteen states that provide state support in addition to the federal funds for the NWP. State support in Kentucky for the writing program began in 1986, before the more general reform of the state, and had grown to $4 million in support for the 1988–1990 biennium (Walker, 1988). As the NWP becomes welded to the state program in Kentucky, there is a threat to the autonomy of the program which seems to be a necessary condition for its effectiveness for teachers.

Before the NWP becomes linked to the establishment in an arrangement similar to a state religion, it would have to control the growing list of competitors. In eastern Kentucky, teachers are working with students in producing publications such as *Mountain Voices* and *Foxfire* (Robert Sexton, interview, May 4, 1994). A rival of NWP, Writing to Learn, operates in the state's one large city, Louisville. Writing to Learn involves more on-site coaching than does NWP, but the programs appear otherwise similar. Writing to Learn is administered throughout the United States by the Council for Basic Education (Association for Supervision and Curriculum Development, 1993). Writing instruction is also provided by the Kentucky teachers' union, where teachers with successful KERA records are given release time to help other teachers in their classrooms (Kentucky Education Association, 1994). Interestingly, the location and operations of the NWP in Kentucky are not known by the leaders of the Prichard Committee (Robert Sexton, interview, August 25, 1995). The general reforms in Kentucky have clearly not even included the NWP in Kentucky; the writing activities, generally, require greater attention by the Prichard Committee in order to relate the general reforms to the interests of teachers.

There is other evidence that teachers feel very separated from the KERA reforms. In one study of thirteen schools, only one had the active involvement of people on the site (Appalachia Educational Laboratory, 1994, pp. 8–9). In the majority of schools in the same study, teachers were unsure what the comprehensive school plan was that they were, supposedly, implementing for their school councils. This situation is similar to past innovations developed by administrators in which school board members were not aware of the innovations (Fullan, 1982). KERA may be just too perfect a set of innovations for either individuals or groups to live with and strive for. The recommended and specified approaches may not leave groups enough room to develop their own reactions to reform.

AN AUTHORITATIVE VOICE ON BEHALF OF STUDENTS

As described in Chapter 3, the Coalition of Essential Schools is active in each of the three sites. It was a force in Kentucky even before KERA and continues to have a number of prominent affiliated schools, particularly in Louisville. CES has twenty schools in Illinois, though it has been limited by the politics involved; it faces no such limits in Kentucky. Illinois and Kentucky are both Re-Learning states and CES is one of the most influential networks in either place. Only in Alberta is CES impotent, with only a single site; that site, Bishop Carroll in Calgary, is actually a product of an earlier American network with a long-forgotten set of reforms.

CES and its founder, Ted Sizer, have recently become extremely important as a result of the gifts by the Annenberg Foundation. After seeing CES receive the largest share of the Annenberg bounty, Sizer became the key adviser for the distribution of gifts to American urban areas that included $50 million for Chicago. Kentucky may qualify for a rural areas grant if not for those involving urban cities. In the two years before the establishment of the Annenberg Foundation, a national network of students in CES was established. Forums in Hartford and St. Louis in 1993 led to conferences in New Hampshire and Chicago in 1994. Students rewrote Sizer's principles to put greater focus on helping students. These student meetings led to tentative calls for freeing students (Cushman, 1994, pp. 3&7). CES and Ted Sizer are sounding as if they might defend student rights.

As yet, the steps by the students and CES have both been quite tentative. Students are similar to other subordinated groups in the past with an initial tentative vocabulary: "Talk to the others. Ask permission. If they will let us" (Cushman, 1994, p. 7). Sizer has always argued that students should acquire the habit of reasoning for themselves; exhibitions are valued as a way of displaying such student autonomy (Sizer, 1992). In CES schools in Racine, Wisconsin, and Columbia, South Carolina, students are members of each graduation committee, which can decide upon requirements for their assessments. Furthermore, a number of coalition schools have student-faculty legislatures with constitutions and judges. Five schools in New York state are said to be examples of "just communities," for which Lawrence Kohlberg has developed a model. According to Sizer and his planners, students are following a path previously taken by teachers in developing active classes, networks, newsletters, and responses to assessment approaches. Students will, they believe, become involved in the governance of schools (Cushman, 1994, p. 7).

CURRENT PRACTICES

Few reformers have championed student issues generally or attempted to establish contact with the emerging student organizations. In Chicago, a student survey of reactions to reform was undertaken after studies of principals, teachers and parents had been made. This event is cause for concern because it provides students with very few opportunities to exercise their new–found writing abilities and students' organizations or newspapers which promote student writing were not consulted.

Surprisingly, the reformers who had opposed the dictatorial school board in Chicago present a very authoritarian approach to students, one that completely violates the teaching principles of the writing projects. Some of the instructions and questions from a survey which was supported by the reform consortium are reproduced in Chart 8.1. The one survey item that allows for any writing involves the reasons for changing schools. Students might tell their inquisitors that the school had closed or burned down; these reasons for changing schools would not be due to the characteristics of students. Active, thoughtful plans that students might make as a result of moves made by the school itself are probably not considered. The students are seen as the problem.

Students in the survey are expected to respond in terms of their reactions to schools rather than their thoughts about their education. Student results are to be reported together with teacher replies (Consortium on Chicago School Research, 1995). The division between questions asked of students and those asked of teachers is similar to the ideology that once separated women from men. Teachers are asked about school leadership (influence of councils, principal, teachers, school plans, and recent changes) and professional development activities (staff collegiality, reflective dialogue, classroom practice, orientation to innovation, in-service training, and professional development by outsiders). Students are not asked about any of these, presumably because they do not understand leadership or professional thinking.

Excluded from the areas where the "big people" do the planning, students in grades six, eight, and ten were asked about the involvement of people (parents' involvement in students' learning) and, most of all, the school climate (safety, classroom, teacher personal treatment of students, and support for learning). Students, similar to women in the past, are expected to know about their reactions to other people and the personal treatment of students in schools. In the areas of student questions, teachers are asked for similar information, but teachers alone are asked about leadership in schools and professional development of teachers, areas of which students

Chart 8.1
Survey of Grade 8 Students: Selected Items

▼ Marking Instructions

- Please use a No. 2 pencil only

- Darken the circles completely   Incorrect Marks
                                          ⊘ ⊗ ◐ ⊙ ◕
- Erase marks completely

                                          Correct Mark
- Make no stray marks   ●

▼ Fill in one circle for each question, unless the question asks you to do something else. Choose the answer that is most true for you.

▼ The next questions are about yourself and your friends.

1. I am good at...	Strongly Disagree	Disagree	Agree	Strongly Agree
Asking teachers for help when I get stuck on schoolwork	○	○	○	○
Working in a group with other students	○	○	○	○
Taking part in class discussions	○	○	○	○
Remembering things taught in class and school books	○	○	○	○
Understanding what I read	○	○	○	○
Finishing my homework on time	○	○	○	○
Writing papers or stories	○	○	○	○
Learning math	○	○	○	○

2. How many of your friends in this school...	All	Most	About Half	A Few	None
Feel it is important to attend all of their classes?	○	○	○	○	○
Feel it is important to pay attention in class?	○	○	○	○	○
Think doing homework is important?	○	○	○	○	○
Try hard to get good grades?	○	○	○	○	○
Follow school rules?	○	○	○	○	○

▼ This section is about SOCIAL STUDIES. Answer these questions if your birthday falls between January and June.

13. In your social studies class, how often do these things happen?	Never	Once In A While	Once A Week	Almost Every Day	Every Day
The teacher lectures for most of the period	○	○	○	○	○
Students work together in small groups	○	○	○	○	○
The class has a discussion where lots of students participate	○	○	○	○	○
Students work by themselves in class on worksheets or questions in the textbook	○	○	○	○	○
The teacher assigns homework	○	○	○	○	○

15. About how often do you have assignments for social studies class that require you to...	Never	Once In A While	Once A Week	Almost Every Day	Every Day
Fill in blanks or answer multiple choice questions?	○	○	○	○	○
Answer in complete sentences?	○	○	○	○	○
Write about a paragraph?	○	○	○	○	○
Write 1 page or more?	○	○	○	○	○

16. Did you write a research paper of 5 or more pages for this class?
   ○ Yes
   ○ No

Chart 8.1 (Continued)

▼ This section is about LANGUAGE ARTS. Please answer these questions if your birthday falls between
July and December.

24. In your <u>language arts</u> class, how often do students...

	Never	Once In A While	Once A Week	Almost Every Day	Every Day
Take spelling or vocabulary tests?	○	○	○	○	○
Do grammar exercises?	○	○	○	○	○
Write an essay about what they are studying?	○	○	○	○	○
Write in a journal?	○	○	○	○	○
Write a story or poem?	○	○	○	○	○
Give a report in front of the class?	○	○	○	○	○
Use the library to work on an assignment?	○	○	○	○	○
Listen to music or look at art?	○	○	○	○	○

25. About how often do you have assignments for <u>language arts</u> class
that require you to...

	Never	Once In A While	Once A Week	Almost Every Day	Every Day
Fill in blanks or answer multiple choice questions?	○	○	○	○	○
Answer in complete sentences?	○	○	○	○	○
Write about a paragraph?	○	○	○	○	○
Write 1 page or more?	○	○	○	○	○
Write a paper or story of at least 5 pages?	○	○	○	○	○

26. How often does your teacher have you rewrite papers after giving you comments?
○ Never
○ A few times
○ Several times
○ Most of the time
○ All of the time

▼ The next several questions are about changing schools.

66. The last time you changed schools, what were the main reasons? (Mark all that apply)
○ My family moved
○ My old school was not safe
○ I wasn't doing well at my old school
○ I was having trouble with other students at my old school
○ I was having problems with the teachers at my old school
○ My new school has a better academic program
○ My new school has a better sports program
○ More of my friends went to the new school
○ I changed for another reason (please write in) _____

Source: Charting Reform: The Student Speaks, Grade 8 Survey, Spring, 1994.

are assumed to be ignorant.

   This segregated study of students is a result of a power relationship which excludes students. The committee that is responsible for the study mainly includes academics; there are also two representatives of the school board, a minister from the Chicago Urban League, and one person from the regional educational laboratory (Consortium on Chicago School Research, 1995). There are no students on the committee, nor any representatives of student organizations, student representatives from school councils, or the student member who attends the school board consulted. I was told that students were involved in focus groups, but they had no time to meet with student representatives nor the editors of the student publications (Kay Kirpatrick, interview, May 1, 1995). In previous surveys of principals and teachers, there had been time to meet with their representatives. Results of the student survey were not available ten months after they were collected; however, some of the selected findings were published in the official organ of reform, *Catalyst* (Forte, 1994). Because of the distance between student leaders and reformers, none of them had known about the availability of results in order to ask for them. To reflect on the power relationship involved, a few words should be added to the title of the student survey, which is called *Charting Reform: The Student Speaks* (Consortium on Chicago School Research, 1994). "When spoken to" should be added to the title.

STUDENT CIRCLES

Students are not at all sure that they want to be involved in the actions of the reformers. Susan Herr, the editor of *New Expression*, stated that she wanted to be at arms length in her relationship with reformers because they, like others inside schools, do not support freedom of expression (interview, May 2, 1995). The organization that is a rival of *New Expression*, the Student Alliance, reports that, in spite of their repeated attempts, reform groups have not been willing to cooperate with them on this survey or many other matters (Philip Bleicher, interview, May 2, 1995). The Student Alliance is more concerned with issues than is *New Expression*. *New Expression* is a well-established student newspaper that, since 1976, has been publishing for students. Its earlier issues seemed to contain more intellectual pieces with more complicated styles and formats. In more recent years, it has presented striking graphics, simple sentences, and subjects chosen for their appeal to students.

The Student Alliance, started in 1991 by a small group of students, still reflects a greater concern for issues and ideas. It began as a citywide coalition of students in Chicago and, in 1992, began to hold national meetings of student representatives on school boards; it is only now beginning a regular publication. The Student Alliance is focused on educational rights and educational policy toward students. Its leader, Philip Bleicher, has plans to communicate directly with students through community television.

These two organizations are as critical of each other as they are of reformers. A representative of *New Expression* said that its staff would cover the Student Alliance as a news item but the alliance was a minor player in school reform (Dennis Sykes, interview, May 2, 1995). The leader of the alliance cites many specific problems with *New Expression*; in seventeen of seventy-three schools, the publication is not distributed by the school office; there have been delays in their opening a bureau on the south side of Chicago, and their role with one of the mayor's summer programs for youth is questioned (Philip Bleicher, interview, May 2, 1995).

Both of these organizations are very exceptional since student publications in the United States or Canada tend to be controlled by schools (Walsh, 1995, June). Both of the Chicago efforts are beyond the control of the school administrators and faculty advisers who have been able to curtail student expression in most local publications since the U. S. court

Hazelwood decision (Click, 1990). *New Expression* allows students to make the transition from volunteer writer to full-time staff. Over twelve full-time staff, who are largely in their twenties, produce the publication, which not only has an office in the center of the city with facilities comparable to those of a small town paper, but has two bureau offices on the north and south sides of the city, though these bureaus are located in schools. The Student Alliance has two paid staff with donated office space and equipment in the area just north of the central business district near a rapid transit stop so students can easily reach them. Though now a student at Columbia College, the leader of the Student Alliance is even younger than those at *New Expression*. Philip Bleicher served as the first student representative on the Chicago Board of Education while helping to start the Student Alliance.

The two student organizations are attempting to establish new alternatives for students. The Student Alliance is trying to get teachers and educators to consider the views of their customers, students. They believe teachers should listen to students and local school councils should respect their student representatives. In thirty-five high schools that Mr. Bleicher visited, the student representative was frequently not involved and, in one case, the student council member had to sit in the audience (Philip Bleicher, interview, May 2, 1995). National policies, according to the same leader, should be based on an awareness of the position of students; this was the reason for the national conferences which began in 1992.

New Expression is an alternative to the staff-controlled publications that, in most schools, provide opportunities for a few accepted students to publish their writing. One Calgary student paper ran the story of the promotion of the assistant principal to principal as the main story on page 1 (Lundy, 1995, June). *New Expression*, in contrast, features the prom: where to eat, what to wear, and how to act, together with a great many advertisements, which, aside from grants, are needed to pay for the paper, which is free to students. A review of all Calgary high school publications and all *New Expression* issues since 1985 found that this difference is typical and that contrast has, apparently, increased over time. Several individual high school publications in Chicago showed that they were influenced by the format of *New Expression*.

Unlike the individual high school newspapers, *New Expression* is supported by a nonprofit organization, Youth Communication. Youth Communication was responsible for a study of Chicago schools conducted by eight students including two dropouts. The writers at *New Expression* are still very proud of their role in publishing this student study (Adolf Mendez, interview, May 2, 1995 and *New Expression*, 1985, September, pp.1–12). The student report, Project InSIDER, had twenty recommendations that stressed a greater sense of community that was needed between students in many different streams and between staff and students. One of the eight students, Robin LaSota, has since become a program coordinator at the North Central Regional Educational Laboratory.

Aside from the study of students, the Youth Commission has undertaken a number of important activities to support students in Chicago and other communities. With funding from the Woods Foundation, a program, College Bound, works with local universities to train high school students as college counselors. Another program, Students United for Participation and Representation, led to the training of fifty students in decision making; the discussion of this report led to Philip Bleicher's becoming the first student representative on the board, and the attempt to further the implementation of their recommendations resulted in the formation of the Student Alliance.

As well as unexpectedly founding a rival organization, the greatest significance of the Youth Commission and *New Expression* is the increasing opportunities for students to express themselves in writing and in the arts. Almost every issue of this paper has writing contests to get response from an estimated 160,000 students who read the 80,000 copies printed ten times a year. Financial rewards are offered in all of the contests. Chart 8.2 shows a survey about art for which students are also offered a reward; the saliency of this survey stands in contrast to the meaningless nature of the earlier one by academic researchers shown in Chart 8.1. The survey in *New Expression* is relevant to students since it attempts to develop the kinds of programs that teens want in art, music, dance, theater, and literature. Both students and teachers receive rewards.

However, the significance of the contests for students is particularly accentuated in the annual art contest. First-place winners in a large number of categories, including videos, painting, poetry, and photography, win $1,000, while their teachers win $100. The publication of a special supplement to the paper is made possible by a leading department store, Marshall Field's. The art contest in Chart 8.2 is part of one such supplement. Furthermore, the occasion of the contest and its many winners is taken as an opportunity to publicize the building of an arts program in any high school; a special phone number, 1-8OO-8O8-ARTS, is established for this purpose by the Chicago Center of Youth Communications (*New Expression*, 1994, April).

Youth Communications is attempting to develop similar programs and publications in a number of other cities. A network of papers exists in New York, Los Angeles, Washington, Atlanta, Boston, and San Francisco with an estimated readership of almost 1 million teens (*New Expression*, 1994, April). With regular student newspapers declining, particularly in poorer urban areas, the alternative provided by Youth Communications appears to be very important (Arnold, 1993). Though concern is increasingly expressed about the independence and autonomy of student publications and their advisers, there seems to be little awareness, outside Chicago, of the alternatives that *New Expression* and the Student Alliance provide (Walsh, 1995, June and Lain, 1992).

STUDENTS AS A CENTERFOLD

A number of programs recognize the contributions of students to Kentucky's reform efforts. Distinguished scholars have lobbied against efforts by the right wing to repeal significant sections of KERA (Harp, 1994, May, p. 25). Every summer, seven hundred Governor's Scholars come together on college campuses for five weeks of motivational experiences to get them involved as citizens. In 1993, the Partnership for Kentucky School Reform worked with the Governor's Scholars Program Alumni Association to create the Education Ambassadors Program. The Education Ambassadors give talks to civic, political, and business leaders in which they "stress the importance of supporting the implementation of the Kentucky Education Reform Act" (Holmes and Mielcarek, 1993). The Ambassadors are a part of an increasing number of new programs, including focus group meetings with parents, which have appeared as a result of failure by a growing number of Kentuckians to support KERA (Holland, 1995, pp. 4–5 and Berger et al., n.d.). A new compact is to be made between teachers and parents, particularly since teachers are telling parents that they, as the key professionals, do not understand school plans or the new testing; the teachers' statements undermine the support of parents for all of KERA (Davis, 1994, pp. 1, 4). Specific efforts include meetings between parents and teachers all over the state, community support for family-school partnerships in two pilot schools, and a communitywide program in one town to promote the importance of parents and families and their need for community. There is no program for the partnership or the Prichard Committee to show how they can change their ideas so that families would find them more acceptable. The recent challenge by experts to the new assessments will probably be more difficult to deflect than just the discontent of parents (Harp, 1995, July).

The efforts by students to support KERA should be seen as a part of the wide-scale publicity efforts by the partnership and the Prichard Committee to sell KERA in the same way that products and political candidates are sold. The music and visual effects for videos that the partnership has developed, together with the advertisement campaigns, in particular, show the publicity campaign tactics (Partnership for Kentucky School Reform, 1995). The quarterly paper, *Perspectives*, is comparatively bland in comparison to its videos and advertisements. *Perspectives* reproduces articles from other sources, reports on staff activities to support reform, and publishes occasional articles by parents and students that are intended to be models for other clients of reform. One article by a high school student compares work for reform to *The Little Engine That Could* (Jones, 1994, p. 8). The Ambassadors program produces a more dramatic impact since the paper is handicapped by the lack of reporters. Though several attractive female students have received attention in the Ambassador campaign, the star was a handsome young man, Eric Mills (Holmes & Mielcarek, 1993).

Chart 8.2
Art Survey Questions

COMPLETE THIS ARTS SURVEY AND YOU MAY WIN $50
1. Which of the following arts-related activities have you ever done?
___Visited an arts museum
___Attended a music concert or performance
___Attended a play or dramatic performance
___Attended a dance performance
___Had one of your artworks exhibited in public
___Sang or played a musical instrument for an audience
___Danced for an audience
___Wrote a play, poem or short story

2. Please indicate whether you agree or disagree with the following statements.
    If you aren't sure whether you agree or disagree, or the statement does not
    apply to you check "don't know."

___I am artistic
___I feel lost in museums
___My family members encourage me to be creative
___The arts can make learning other subjects more fun and interesting
___My friends are not the "artsy" type
___There are opportunities in my neighborhood for me to get involved in the arts
___The arts seem to be for other people, not me
___My teachers encourage me to be creative
___I would like to go see a play or concert, but I wouldn't know enough about
what's going on to appreciate it
___Art helps me express myself
___The arts in schools are not nearly as important as other subjects like math,
English and science

3. For the next few questions, choose the one activity out of the four listed that you
    would most like to do. Place a check next to the one activity you chose.

A. Would you most like to (check one):
    [ ]   sing or play a duet with a professional musician you admire
    [ ]   go to a music concert with someone who could explain the music to you
          and answer your questions about it
    [ ]   sing or play in a musical group with teens of your age either in school or
          outside school
    [ ]   learn about the music of your own or other cultural or ethnic groups

B. Would you most like to (check one):
    [ ]   visit an arts museum with a guide
    [ ]   talk to a professional artist about how and why he/she made a particular
          work of art
    [ ]   paint a mural with a group of people, take an art class, either in school or
          outside of school

Chart 8.2 (Continued)

C. Would you most like to (check one):
  [ ]   learn about traditional dances of your own or other cultural or ethnic
        groups
  [ ]   take a dance class with a professional dancer
  [ ]   go to a dance performance with someone who can explain the dance to you
        and answer your questions about it
  [ ]   perform a dance in public with a group of people

D. Would you most like to (check one):
  [ ]   learn the basics of how to write a play, poem or short story
  [ ]   join a group of kids your age who write plays, poems or short stories so you
        can talk about each others' writing
  [ ]   talk to a famous writer you admire about the things he or she has written
  [ ]   go to a play with someone who can explain the play to you and answer your
        questions about it

E. Of all the activities listed above in A,B,C and D--which ONE would you
    most like to do?
    Write the activity on the line below.

_____

4. On a scale of 1 to 6, with 6 being the best rating and 1 being the worst rating,
    how would you rate the art classes and programs at your school?

              WORST 1 2 3 4 5 6   BEST

5. Please describe below the BEST arts experience you have ever had. It could
    have been at school or outside of school. It could have been visual arts (like
    painting or sculpting), performing arts (like theater or dance), musical arts (like
    singing or playing an instrument) or literary arts (like writing a play, poem or
    short story). Please describe the experience and explain why you enjoyed it.

    _____
    _____
    _____

Source: "Discovering the Arts" in *New Expressions* 18, no. 3 (April 1994).

After attending the Governor's Scholars program, Eric worked with the
council in his school to develop a council of students to promote KERA.
Further, while other ambassadors wrote articles about KERA in their school
newspapers, Eric developed a whole new student newspaper to show the
success of educational reform in his county. The paper, *The Road to
Success*, opens with the blessing of the school's superintendent, recounts the
exam successes and changes in subject areas, and shows student attempts to
help other students before it moves to any more conventional areas, such as

sports and group photographs. In the large page paper, accounts of outstanding students are interwoven to include Eric and another attractive Governor's Scholar, Amanda Six. Amanda studied science in her five weeks in the Governor's Scholars Program while Eric participated in a leadership program. Amanda did not become an ambassador, but Eric did and, in this role, applied his subject of study.

THE MEDIA AND REFORM

Though Alberta has not yet made students a part of its program for education reform, it has developed a sophisticated program of government blitzing of the media as part of an effort to influence the public. Invited guests for roundtable discussions, touring task forces by members of Parliament, and multiple news releases with new programs all announced on the same day are some of the techniques that have been employed by a government that is led by a former television reporter, Ralph Klein. These techniques avoid criticism of government as a distant force, and students who speak out against the government have been condemned.

In Chicago, a former writer for the *Chicago Sun Times*, Linda Lenz, edits the voice of Chicago school reform, *Catalyst*. Ms. Lenz makes it clear that she decides what will be known about Chicago school reform. For example, she decided not to report on a program of students questioning the school superintendent which was arranged by ACORN. In her view, any publicity about the event would promote ACORN (interview, April 28, 1994). However, regular columns are written in *Catalyst* by the leaders of the teachers' union and the school superintendent until the latter position was abolished. Presumably, for Ms. Lenz, such institutional interests should be promoted!

Catalyst has made weak, but repeated attempts to include students in its coverage of Chicago education or reform. For many years, it paid students to write personal diary accounts along with similar ones by teachers (Mitchell, 1995). For the past two years, *Catalyst* has occasionally carried stories on student activities. Neither the personal diaries nor student activities had much to do with Chicago reform. Ms. Lenz told Philip Bleicher to write a story on the Student Alliance for an upcoming issue (Philip Bleicher, interview, July 28, 1995).

In Chicago, Kentucky, and Alberta, educational television has connected the specialized educational stories with reports of a more general nature in newspaper and television stations. In Chicago, for example, WTTW has done far more than the series on reform that culminated in *Teach Me*. Paralleling the meeting with experts that Bill Clinton used to start his presidency, WTTW aired over seven hours of expert discussion of Chicago reform. WTTW has also worked with other stations and educational laboratories to produce a course on reform for teachers (North Central Regional Educational Laboratory, 1990). It is not the course, but the more spectacular accounts that general news sources tend to accentuate, such as conflicts between Catholics and Premier Klein in Alberta. Resistance to control of the media's interpretation of reform by the government is particularly crucial in Alberta because of the absence of many voluntary organizations or significant involvement of students in education.

THE MIX BETWEEN THE MEDIA AND STUDENT ACTIVITY

Though the government's influence is very dominant in Alberta, there has been an attempt by one of the local newspapers to promote student writing. For over three years, the *Calgary Herald* has assisted students with the production of a paper, *Herald High*, which stands in contrast to the usual student publications (Poole, 1995, p. 2). *Herald High* carried stories about the effects of cuts in government spending or ways in which the opportunities for disabled students in higher education will change as a result of the government's program (Hood, 1994, p.1 and Jensen, 1995, p.2). The political coverage of *Herald High* also included the only reports of student attempts to form a provincewide organization. Beginning with the announcement of cuts in 1993 and for the next two years, representatives of six Calgary schools tried to get the other nineteen Calgary high schools, as well as those throughout Alberta, to form the Alberta Secondary Students Council (Hood, 1994, p.1).

The usual student newspapers reported on neither this attempt at organization among students nor any other events involving controversy. The student newspaper in Calgary which avoids issues most relevant to students as much as, if not more than, others is the award winning *Scarlett Fever*. This paper has twice won first place in the contest conducted by the American Scholastic Press Association, a contest based largely on technical qualities, such as layout, rather than relevant content (Dempster, 1995, October, p. B7). In 1994 and 1995, most of the stories involved school staff, sports, entertainment, and student activities; one story on the educational innovation of charter schools did appear (Raath, 1994, December, p. 25). At the other extreme, *Scarlett Fever* has proclaimed its unquestioning loyalty to the school and the status quo in education; the school, E. P. Scarlett, is the "best place to be," and "the greatest thing that high school gives to an individual is a sense of home and friends" (Lamers, 1995, January, p. 3).

Student publications have a difficult time surviving and political controversy makes that survival much more difficult (Arnold, 1993). In Calgary, the most pointed position found in a student publication was a rather satirical report on the then education minister, Jim Dinning, in a paper that has ceased publication (Dawoud, 1991). Aside from politics, school support and advertising revenue are critical for the survival of the student newspaper. Interestingly, the *Calgary Herald*'s support of a high school paper is carried on without any advertising other than for the *Calgary Herald*; perhaps it is viewed as a future investment as with the literacy campaigns of magazines.

The motivations of students to get involved with newspapers are equally complicated, though career advancement is certainly involved (Bond, 1995, October, p. B7). The most successful student newspapers are, apparently, produced by journalism classes in high schools. The newspaper which Eric Mills started in Kentucky was produced by such a class, as is *Scarlett Fever* in Calgary. The more typical motivations are social contact and fun (Dempster, 1995, October, p. B7). Though the improvement of writing for English is asserted as an advantage of writing for the student publications, social criticism or political debate is not cited as a reason why students should be involved (Ius, 1994, April, p. 2). Democracy among adults with freedom of the press and freedom of speech must not have to be practiced among students in order to be achieved later.

The attempt of a general newspaper to provide political news has not gone well in Alberta. The Catholic schools in Calgary chose not to "participate in this program because of the potentially controversial articles which might appear" (Poole, 1995, p. 2). The Catholic decision was made before their confrontations with the Klein government, but the significance of student political involvement does not appear to be appreciated even now. The difficulties of student organization are also shown by the limited participation in *Herald High*. Only six or seven high schools were involved in the production and distribution of this publication. In Alberta, student publications and voluntary organizations have been as difficult to achieve among students as among adults.

NOBLE LIES

Unlike the student groups, the reform groups advocate a position even to the point of distorting or ignoring alternative views. The Prichard Committee was, perhaps, the most innocent of the advocates who would be overzealous in promoting their idea of truth. Even with the Prichard Committee, I was told that one survey of public attitudes would probably never be released (Beth Mitchell, interview, May 2, 1995). In several instances, reports of reform studies which were funded by the MacArthur Foundation could only be obtained with the help of selected individuals, including the unpublished report on the Chicago community, Mid-South, which was cited in the last chapter and which included the proposed removal of White teachers (MacArthur Foundation, n.d.). Garth Norris, the public relations person for Alberta Education, has stated that research studies commissioned by the department must meet their expectations before they would be released. Advocates who are totally committed, such as Don Moore, claim that critical academic reports can be ignored since they would not be read widely enough to harm the movement (Diana Lauber, interview, May 1, 1995).

However, the most extreme position in limiting the free flow of ideas is taken by the Pew Forum. Elite reformers from all over the country join this exclusive and secret society that is supported by the Pew Foundation, as mentioned in Chapter 2. According to Dorothy Shipps who worked with him, Marshall Smith, who was dean of education at Stanford and is currently undersecretary of education in the Clinton administration, was a key figure in organizing this club. Several reports indicate that this elite group of educators and government leaders created great social distance between them and local reformers in Chicago. In his meeting with them, John Ayers felt that quasi-judicial decisions were being made by this self-selected jury concerning the success of Chicago reform (interview, November 5, 1993). In appearing before them to describe his work with the cluster of schools, Greg Darnieder felt very uneasy and "totally out of his element" (interview, October 17, 1993). From the information that is available, the Pew Forum appears to be similar to an administrative agency I have described elsewhere, which, though it had very little real power, virtually saw itself as a Supreme Court and created great distance from its clients (Mitchell, 1995, pp. 63–75).

AN UNCOMMON VISION

People need to see the significance of the monumental changes in educational systems which have been involved in each of the three patterns of cases. Community influences have been dominant in each of these dramatic transformations; in contrast, early innovations within the educational system seem subdued. Advocacy groups, legislative efforts by governments, business partnerships, collaboration between professional groups, and publicity efforts by reformers have driven educational reform in each of the sites. Students have not been a very active group in any of the sites, and they often felt very distant from the reformers.

Any benefits for students or their families have often been an indirect result of other changes made in the systems of education. For example, the main effort of the NWP has been to improve the writing of teachers; the network of related programs, including those for parents, has led students to write more and to relate their writing to different subjects in school and a variety of concerns outside school. The efforts of *New Expression* to sell newspapers and involve students have provided opportunities to create in the arts as well as in writing. The efforts of reformers with fixed-answer surveys provide even fewer opportunities for these students.

The split between the interests of reformers and the needs of students results from the priority that is given to reforms and organizations over people that occurs in each case. Noble lies result from this preoccupation. Critical issues are often ignored. Chapter 2 reveals most of the important problems of education: gangs and discipline, achievement results, and financial needs. But reform efforts have led to much more discussion of school councils, charters, school-based management, business partnership, and integrated services. There are, however, few discussions of how such tools are to be related to the more basic problems.

At most, our study has shown that each site has focused more on one of these problems while ignoring the others. Alberta has been preoccupied with financial issues and has only begun to plan for measures of accountability and for rewards for successful schools (Mitchell, 1995, January, pp. 1, 2). Kentucky has increased its relative academic position on most measures. Chicago attempts to deal with student fights through community efforts; a recent attempt to use parent patrols, role playing by students, jobs for students, and mentoring of students by other students is typical (Vazquez, 1994, p. 9). However, the issues of general financial support for education or higher achievement by students are not related to a coherent program for reform in Chicago. Students need more than a focus on one issue at a time.

Students can be most easily provided with opportunities for growth through their involvement with community coalitions. Ted Sizer has recognized the importance of this step. Students can remove the brake in their efforts for academic achievement, become responsible for their own community, and demonstrate, over time, the dividends to the larger community of an investment in education. Currently, students are not taken seriously by reformers; no one from Designs for Change, for example, would even return phone calls to the Student Alliance when they were attempting to get a grade eight student as a representative on school councils (Philip Bleicher, interview, July 28, 1995). The desire of students for involvement can disappear more rapidly than it appears unless support is provided by those who claim to be interested in reforming their education.

If they are left with any decisions to make, the involvement of students may make it possible to increase the varieties among reforms for schools. Though the greater variability of families compared to that of schools has long been known to be the main reason that parents influence academic achievement more than teachers do, alternatives in education have not often been seen as a way station to the goal of the best reforms for education (Mitchell, 1992, p. 154). The current coalitions among schools, including the NWP and CES, do not develop different strategies for the sharp differences among Kentucky, Chicago, and Alberta. Many cities have far more different programs than we have discussed. For example, Montreal has trilingual programs and integrated arts efforts, such as FACE (Mitchell, 1992 and Oddleifson, 1995, p. 15). Differences among students and their families could be a basis for increasing the differences among schools and reform approaches as valid alternatives.

A closer relationship between students and reformers is probably one of the better ways of developing creativity in education. Because of the instrumental thinking of business, students are seen as objects that can be linked to the organization through work experience programs. School councils have modestly changed the views of parents on schools.

Professionals have great difficulty in overcoming their singular perspectives toward integrated services. Government, in its turn, has seen reforms as an opportunity to give citizens a sense of ownership while continuing to monitor the changes. The empowerment of students is not the aim of business, professionals, or governments, nor does any of these groups base its view of educational reforms on the thinking of students; the Alberta government, for example, has refused to accept the United Nations Convention on the Rights of the Child (Ruttan, 1995, September, p. B1).

Even when it is recognized that students relate people to concepts, just as they also connect art to science, a change in the direction of reform toward thinking by students is being made (Oddleifson, 1995). The integration of thinking between educators and students is often prevented by a very instrumental view of values and visions that is still in vogue. Alternatively, one can focus on individual and expressive thinking by students which will make their visions more meaningful to them. The instrumental visions can produce extreme dejection as revealed by many of the songs that appeal to the young. As was suggested in Chapter 3, by following Freire a shared and affective imagery can provide the poetry, conflicts, and individual revelations that are the ingredients of visions. Reform organizations can provide the opportunities, as in the case of NWP, for students to create their own voluntary activities. Students can become leaders together with parents, community members, and educators to redirect educational reform.

Student leaders are developed by their organizations, which often reflect the adult voluntary groups in the area. Chicago has competing interests that disagree when they cannot fight with the officials. Kentucky's students work with the system, while those in Alberta are controlled by the authorities. For both adults and students, the role of voluntary groups is critical in preventing the dominance of government as is now happening in Alberta. The adult voluntary groups may be chameleons who reflect the current stage of educational change as much as they change it. Voluntary organizations have been discussed as part of a social movement in Chapter 2, alternatives for advocacy in Chapter 3, monitors of governmental changes in Chapter 4, allies of business in Chapters 5 and 6, parties to the coalitions among organizations and professions in Chapter 7, and a stimulus to student movements in this chapter.

REFERENCES

Alberta Education (1995). *Technology integration in education-discussion paper*. Edmonton: Alberta Education.

Appalachia Educational Laboratory (1994, December). Instruction and assessment in accountable and nonaccountable grades. *Notes from the Field*, 4(1), 1–12.

Arnold, M. (1993). Inner city high school newspapers: an obituary? Paper presented at the Association for Education in Journalism and Mass Communication.

Association for Supervision and Curriculum Development (1993, January). When Teachers Become Writers. *Curriculum Update*, 5.

Batiuk, M. (1993). The National Writing Project. Course paper at the University of Calgary.

Berger, M., Hougland, J., & Kifer, E. (n.d.). *The Kentucky Education Reform Act amd the public.* Frankfort: Institute for Education Reform, University of Kentucky.

Bond, S. (1995, October 6). Our turn. *Calgary Herald*, B7.

Bratcher, S. & Stroble, E. (1994, February). Determining the progression from comfort to confidence: A longitudinal evaluation of a National Writing Project site based on multiple data sources. *Research in the Teaching of English*, 28(1), 66–68.

Calgary Writing Project (1986). *The Calgary Writing Project survey of teacher consultants.* Calgary: Calgary Writing Project.

Chicago Area Writing Project (n.d.). *The Chicago area writing project in brief—the 15th year.* Evanston, Illinois: Chicago Area Writing Project.

Click, J. (1990). A few Changes since "Hazelwood." *School-press Review*, 65(2), 12–27.

Consortium on Chicago School Research (1994). *Charting reform: the student speaks, eighth grade survey.* Chicago: Consortium on Chicago School Research.

Consortium on Chicago School Research (1995). *Charting reform in Prairie school.* Chicago: Consortium on Chicago School Research.

Cronk, P.(1977). An interpretive study of EWP. Master's Thesis, The University of Calgary.

Cushman, K. (1994, September). Empowering students: Essential Schools' missing link. *Horace*, 11(1), 1–8.

Daniels, H. & Zemelman, S. (1988). Response to Gomez. *Issue Paper 88-2*. East Lansing: National Center for Research on Teacher Education.

Davis, A. (1994, July-September). Parent involvement projects top committee's agenda. *Perspective*, 5(3), 1, 4.

Dawoud, S. (1991, December). School to become "more relevant." *The Warrior*, 1(3),3.

Dempster, M. (1995, October 6). Newspaper fever. *Calgary Herald*, B7.

Dowling, H. (1989, Fall). NWP Report: A multi-school consortium to promote writing across the curriculum. The BAWAC model. *The Quarterly of the National Writing Project and the Center for Study of Writing*, 11(4), 106–108.

Eastman, A.M. (1981, December 27-30). The foreign mission of the university English department. Paper presented at the Annual Meeting of the Modern Language Association of America.

Forte, L. (1994, November). Schools an oasis from violence, drugs. *Catalyst*, 6(3), 8–9.

Fullan, M. (1982). *The meaning of educational change.* Toronto: Ontario Institute for Studies in Education.

Goldberg, M. (1989, November). Portrait of James Gray. *Educational Leadership*, 47(3), 65–68.

Gomes, M. (1988). The National Writing Project: Creating community, validating experiences, and expanding opportunities. *Issue Paper 88-2*. East Lansing: National Center for Research on Teacher Education.

Gray, J. (1985, December). Joining a national network: The National Writing Project. *New directions for teaching and learning*, 24, 61–68.

Gray, J. (1988). Response to Gomes. *Issue Paper 88-2*. East Lansing: National Center for Research on Teacher Education.

Gray, J. & Sterling, R. (n.d.). *The National Writing Project a university-based, teacher center partnership program*. Berkeley: National Writing Project.

Guskey, T. (1994). *High states performance*. Thousand Oaks, California: Corwin Press.

Hambleton, R., Jaeger, R., Koretz, D. Linn, R., Millman, J., & Phillips, S. (1995). *Review of the measurement quality of the Kentucky instructional results information system, 1991-1994*. Frankfort: Office of Educational Accountability, Kentucky General Assembly.

Hayes, M. (1983). A Paper on "The Ohio Writing Project, Training Professional Teachers of Writing." Oxford, Ohio. (ERIC Document ED 341–078).

Harp, L. (1994, May 18). The plot thickens. *Education Week*, 13(34), 20–25.

Harp, L. (1995, July 12). Ky. student assessments called "seriously flawed." *Education Week*, 14(40), 12–13.

Harvard Graduate School of Education (n. d.). Project Zero Development Group. Cambridge, Massachusetts: Harvard Graduate School of Education.

Hill, R. (1994, April). Stepping into Prom. *New Expression*, 18(3), 7-9.

Holland, H. (1995). Focus: Kentucky's educational reforms show successes & pitfalls. *Perspectives*, 6(1), 4–5.

Holmes, C. & Mielcarek, G (1993, December). *Governor's scholars promote education reform*. Lexington: Partnership for Kentucky School Reform.

Hood, J. (1994, April). Cuts are coming. So, now what? *Herald High*, 1.

Ius, D. (1994, April). Letter from the Editor. *Herald High*, 2.

Jensen, M. (1995, May). Students participate in assessment. *Herald High*, 2.

Jones, B. (1994, January-March). Education reform: The creator of dreams. *Perspectives*, 5(4) Supplement, 8.

Kentucky Department of Education (1993). *Transformations: Kentucky's curriculum framework*. Frankfort: Kentucky Department of Education.

Kentucky Education Association (1994, August). *Teachers to the power of two*. Frankfort: Kentucky Education Association.

Krendl, K. & Dodd, J. (1987, October). Assessing the National Writing Project: A longitudinal study of process-based writing. (Report No. CS 210 848). (Eric Document No. ED 289 167).

Lain, L. (1992). A national study of high school newspaper program: Environmental and adviser characteristics, funding and pressures on free expression. Paper presented at the Annual Meeting of the Association for Education in Journalism and Mass Communication.

Lamers, M. (1995, January). The reasons why... *Scarlett Fever*, 5(4), 3.

Little, J. & McLaughlin, M. (1991). *Urban math collaboratives: As teachers tell it*. Stanford, California: Center for Research on the Context of Secondary School Teaching, Stanford University.

Lundy, J. (1995, June). Stevenson gets just reward. *Scarlett Fever*, 5(8), 1.

MacArthur Foundation (n.d.). Update on the collaboration project. Chicago: MacArthur Foundation.

March, D., Knudsen, D., & Knudsen, G. (1987). Factors influencing the transfer of Bay area writing workshop experiences to the classroom. Paper presented to the Annual Meeting of the American Educational Research Association.

McDiarmid, G. (1994). *Realizing new learning for all students.* East Lansing: National Center for Research on Teacher Learning, Michigan State University.

Mills, E. (1993, December). *Education ambassador creates KERA council.* Lexington: Partnership for Kentucky School Reform.

Mitchell, A. (1995, January 10). Grading of schools planned in Alberta. *Globe and Mail,* 1–2.

Mitchell, S. (1992). *Innovation and reform.* York, Ontario: Captus Press.

Mitchell, S. (1995). *Sociology for education.* York, Ontario: Captus Press.

National-Louis University (1993). *Best practice.* Evanston: National-Louis University.

National Writing Project (1995). *National Writing Project 1995 fact sheet.* Berkeley: National Writing Project.

New Expression (1985, September). Students (from the inside) report on Chicago high schools. *New Expression,* 9(5), Supplement, 1–12.

New Expression (1995, April). Celebrating New Expression's 1995 High School Art Competition. *New Expression,* 19(4), Supplement, 1–4.

North Central Regional Educational Laboratory (1990). *Many roads to fundamental reform* (Videos). Chicago: North Central Regional Educational Laboratory.

Oddleifson, E. (1995). Education reform through community dialogue: An Address to the Texas Education and the Arts Conference: Partnership 2000. Sponsored by the Texas Alliance for Education and the Arts.

Partnership for Kentucky School Reform (1995). *An Investment for the future* (Video). Lexington: Partnership for Kentucky School Reform.

Poole, J. (1995, May). Opportunity knocks...but schools don't answer. *Herald High,* 2.

Pritchard, R. (1989). The impact of American Ideas on New Zealand's education policy, proactive, and thinking. Wellington, New Zealand (Eric Document: ED 338-517).

Purves, A. (1992, February). Reflections on research and assessment in written composition. *Research in the teaching of English,* 26(1), 108–122.

Putka, G. (1992, September 11). 'riting and more 'riting. *Wall Street Journal,* B5.

Raath, D. (1994, December). The charter system. *Scarlett Fever,* 5(3), 25.

Rigden, D.(1991). *Business and the schools.* New York: Council for Aid to Education.

Ruttan, S. (1995, September 13,). Klein cabinet's rejection of kids rights is contemptible. *Calgary Herald,* B1.

Sizer, T. (1992). *Horace's school.* Boston: Houghton Mifflin.

Vasquez, N. (1994, May). Clements tries something different. *New Expression,* 18(4), 9.

Vopat, J. (1993). Thirteen ways of looking at the parent project. *Best Practice,* 4, 10–11.

Walker, L. (1988, June). *Kentucky statewide writing program.* Lexington: Council of State Governments.

Walsh, M. (1995, June 7). Hard news. *Education Week,* 14(3),2–25.

Washburn, W. (1991). Ten years of the Calgary Writing Project. *Alberta English*, 29(2), 5-6.

Watkins, B. (1981). Participating teachers' perceptions of and attitudes towards a National Writing Project workshop. Doctoral dissertation, Georgia State University, College of Education, 1981. *Dissertation Abstracts International*, 42 (Eric Document ED 210-704).

Wells Network (1994, November/December). *Wells Network*. Chicago: Wells Community Academy.

Zasloff, E. & O' Neill, M. (1992, September/October). Reporting reform: Metcalfe School uses the Illinois Writing Project across the curriculum. *Reform Report*, 3(1), 8–10.

Zemelman, S., Daniels, H., & Hyde, A. (1993). *Best Practice*. Portsmouth, New Hampshire: Heinemann.

Selected Bibliography

Bowen, L. & Sellers, S. (1994). *Family support & socially vulnerable communities.* Chicago: Family Resource Coalition.

Dove, R. (1991). *Creative constitutional law: The Kentucky school reform law.* Lexington: Prichard Committee for Academic Excellence.

Immerwahr, J., Johnson, J. & Kerman-Schloss, A. (1991). *Cross talk.* Washington, D.C.: The Business-Higher Education Forum.

Jones, B. & Maloy, R. (1988). *Partnerships for improving schools.* Westport, Connecticut: Greenwood Press.

Kyle, C. L. & Kantowicz, E. R. (1992). *Kids first-primero los ñinos.* Springfield: Illinois Issues.

Levine, M. & Trachtman, R. (Eds.) (1988). *American business and the public school.* New York: Teachers College.

Lisac, M. (1995). *The Klein revolution.* Edmonton: NeWest Press.

Melville, A. & Blank, M. (1993). *Together we can.* Washington, D. C.: U. S. Department of Education.

O'Connell, M. (1992). *School reform: Chicago style.* Chicago: Center for Neighborhood Technology.

Osborne, D. & Gaebler, T. (1992). *Reinventing government.* Reading, Massachusetts: Addison-Wesley.

Schorr, L. (1985). *Within our reach.* New York: Doubleday Anchor.

Zemelman, S., Daniels, H. & Hyde, A. (1993). *Best Practice.* Portsmouth, New Hampshire: Heinemann.

Index

About the Author

SAMUEL MITCHELL is Associate Professor in the Department of Educational Policy and Administrative Studies at the University of Calgary. Professor Mitchell is the author of *Innovation and Reform* (1990) and *Sociology for Educating* (1995).

ISBN 0-275-95644-X

90000>

9 780275 956448

EAN

HARDCOVER BAR CODE